Intellectual Property Rights - Patent

Edited by Sakthivel Lakshmana Prabu, Suriyaprakash TNK, Eduardo Jacob-Lopes and Leila Queiroz Zepka

Published in London, United Kingdom

IntechOpen

Supporting open minds since 2005

Intellectual Property Rights - Patent
http://dx.doi.org/10.5772/intechopen.73458
Edited by Sakthivel Lakshmana Prabu, Suriyaprakash TNK, Eduardo Jacob-Lopes and Leila Queiroz Zepka

Contributors
Cecilia Hasner, Douglas Alves Santos, Araken Alves De Lima, Sakthivel Lakshmana Prabu, Hetal Patel, Sandesh Lodha, Mohamad Taleuzzaman, Iqra Rahat, Fernanda De Carvalho, Érika Silva, Paula Nunes, Karen Ramos, Nayara Santos, Abhishek Kumar, Arkady Trachuk, Natalia Linder, José Martins, António Abreu, João Calado, Eduardo Jacob-Lopes, Aline Meireles Dos Santos, Leila Queiroz Zepka, Sebua Semenya, Kai Zhao, Lixiang Wang

First published in London, United Kingdom, 2020 by IntechOpen
IntechOpen is the global imprint of INTECHOPEN LIMITED, registered in England and Wales, registration number: 11086078, 5 Princes Gate Court, London, SW7 2QJ, United Kingdom
Printed in Croatia

British Library Cataloguing-in-Publication Data
A catalogue record for this book is available from the British Library

Additional hard and PDF copies can be obtained from orders@intechopen.com

Intellectual Property Rights - Patent
Edited by Sakthivel Lakshmana Prabu, Suriyaprakash TNK, Eduardo Jacob-Lopes and Leila Queiroz Zepka
p. cm.
Print ISBN 978-1-78985-713-9
Online ISBN 978-1-78985-714-6
eBook (PDF) ISBN 978-1-83968-788-4

For EU product safety concerns:
IN TECH d.o.o., Prolaz Marije Krucifikse Kozulić 3, 51000 Rijeka, Croatia, info@intechopen.com or visit our website at intechopen.com.

Meet the editors

Dr. Sakthivel Lakshmana Prabu has a Ph.D. from Manipal University, Manipal. He pursued his Post Graduate Diploma in IPR Law from the National Law School of India University, Bangalore. Presently he is working at Anna University Chennai, BIT Campus, Trichy, India since 2009. He has more than 20 years' experience including both in reputed pharmaceutical industries and academic institutions. From his research contribution he has published 98 peer-reviewed publications in reputed international and national journals, authored 19 book chapters, edited 4 books, and written 1 full book as co-author. To his credit he also has 5 international patents to his name. He serves as a reviewer and editorial board member for various reputed journals. Added to his credit, he organized various national and international conferences, hands-on training, workshops and symposiums. He has received funds from various Government funding agencies in India. He has a strong association with Intech Publication, Croatia since 2012. His major achievement is evidenced in his Intech Publication, Croatia book chapters entitled "Extraction of Drug from the Biological Matrix: A Review", which has been downloaded more than 23,500 times and "Biopharmaceutics and Pharmacokinetics", which has been downloaded more than 23,000 times worldwide.

TNK Suriyaprakash is a proud alumnus of Madurai Medical College, Madurai, Tamil Nadu, for BPharm, and Birla Institute of Technology and Science, Pilani, (BITS Pilani), Rajasthan, for MPharm. He was awarded his PhD in Pharmaceutical Technology by the Tamil Nadu Dr. MGR Medical University, Chennai. He has published nearly 50 original research and review papers in reputed journals and authored 2 books, edited 3 books and has written 12 book chapters published in Elsevier, IGI Global, and IntechOpen publishers. Two of his research works have been published by the Indian Patent Office, Chennai. Book chapters entitled "Extraction of Drug from the Biological Matrix: A Review," and "Biopharmaceutics and Pharmacokinetics", of Intech Publication, have been downloaded more than 25,000 times worldwide. To his credit he has received the equivalent of 50,000 USD in research grants from various funding agencies. During his tenure as principal, the Al Shifa College of Pharmacy was recognized as a top-ranked college for the past three years in Kerala State by Ministry of Human Resource Department, New Delhi, under National Institutional Ranking Network (NIRF).

Prof. Dr. Eduardo Jacob-Lopes is currently an Associate Professor at the Department of Food Technology and Science, Federal University of Santa Maria (UFSM). He has more than 15 years of teaching and research experience. He has coordinated/coordinates more than 50 research projects and/or technological developments financed by public funding agencies and private initiatives. He has published more than 550 scientific publications/communications, which include 10 books, 45 book chapters, 100 original research papers, 370 research communications in national and international conferences, and has registered 12 patents. He is a member of the editorial board of 10 journals and acts as a reviewer for several national and international journals. His research interests includes bioprocess engineering with an emphasis on microalgal biotechnology.

Prof. Dr. Leila Queiroz Zepka is currently an Associate Professor at the Department of Food Technology and Science, Federal University of Santa Maria (UFSM). She has more than 15 years of teaching and research experience. She has published more than 450 scientific publications/communications, which includes 10 books, 40 book chapters, 90 original research papers, 350 research communications in national and international conferences, and 12 patents. She is a member of the editorial board of 5 journals and acts as a reviewer for several national and international journals. Her research interest includes microalgal biotechnology with an emphasis on microalgae-based products.

Contents

Preface

The purpose of this book, *Intellectual Property Rights – Patent*, is to discuss the issues pertaining to IPR, more specifically on patents. We have taken into account divergent issues related to patents starting from invention to filing of a patent and issues that come along with it. The authors were selected from different countries with varied backgrounds and this gives the reader an understanding of global issues.

At the outset, a country or a person who possesses intellect will make huge impact upon the world. Today's technological applications are yesterday's intellect of an individual or an organisation. A nation builds on that platform. It is imperative that we build strong intellectual property.

With this idea, we chose authors from different countries who could add the issues and solutions of their country that enable us to understand this topic better.

The diversity of authors helped us to divulge the advances of Intellectual Property Rights worldwide. Their inputs will give the readers an insight into the issues faced by academicians, industry, and research institutes, and directions for future.

This book is recommended for research scholars, students, industrial experts, technologists, and scientists to gather knowledge on worldwide patenting issues. It was a great experience to write and edit this book and particularly the support extended by the publishers and their team had been extremely good.

The Prologue one by **Sakthivel Lakshmana Prabu and Suriyaprakash TNK** discusses the genesis of patenting and discusses in length the drafting of a patent form.

D.Sc. Hasner Cecilia authored a chapter titled 'Technological Trajectories Studies of Sugarcane Ethanol Production Using Patent Citation', where they discussed how the production of ethanol from sugarcane has migrated from the first to the second generation thanks to the biotechnological advancement in the production process.

The chapter titled 'Case Study on Rejected Patents in India' is by **Dr. Patel Hetal.** India is a country that has understood the importance of strong patent systems for the growth of industry and commerce to bring it in line with the modern world. In this chapter, the authors have discussed a few of the cases of rejection under the Indian Patent Act.

Taleuzzaman Mohamad has written a chapter on 'Patent Application Preparation and Filing, which helps the reader to understand the nuances of writing a patent application.

The chapter titled 'The Patenting of Products and Processes Used for the Treatment of Smoke Inhalation' by **M.D. De Carvalho Fernanda** describes how Intellectual Property enables the transformation of knowledge in principle and the link between knowledge and the market.

In Prologue two: Transfer of Technology , Dr. **Jacob-Lopes Eduardo** discusses the technology transfer that holds an important portfolio in the present scenario.

'Patents as a Yardstick for Economic Growth: Case of Indian R&D System' by **Kumar Abhishek** discusses how novel creations by human are well appreciated and acknowledged but there exists several lacunae such as illegal copying.

Kai Zhao and **Lixiang Wang** discuss the 'Internal Relationship and Impact Path between Innovation and Entrepreneurship: Based on China's High-Tech Industry'. Innovation is the source of entrepreneurship, entrepreneurship is the value embodiment of innovation, and the two are inseparable.

Semenya Sebua has written a chapter titled "Activities Pivotal for the Sustainability of Newly Established Technology Transfer Offices: A Case Study of Publicly Financed South African Universities".

The chapter 'Dissemination of Distributed Energy Technologies' by **Trachuk Arkady** analyzes the amplification of distributed power generation technologies among industrial companies, as well as the factors for the adoption of new technologies by industrial companies in Russia.

Martins José titled a chapter 'Business Incubator and Economic Development' and this chapter aims to divulge the details of Technology Business Incubator and its importance for entrepreneurship.

We acknowledge the full support of all the authors and special thanks to IntechOpen for their help and full support on the completion of the book.

Dr. Sakthivel Lakshmana Prabu
Bharathidasan Institute of Technology,
India

Suriyaprakash TNK
Al Shifa College of Pharmacy,
India

Dr. Eduardo Jacob-Lopes and Dr. Leila Queiroz Zepka
Professor,
Universidade Federal de Santa Maria,
Brazil

Section 1

Overview of IPR

Chapter 1

Prologue One: Drafting of Patent Specification

Sakthivel Lakshmana Prabu and Suriyaprakash TNK

1. Introduction

In nineteenth century, the foundation for Intellectual Property Protection (IPP) was created. In the 1883 Paris Convention, the Protection of Industrial Property was created. Intellectual property is the intangible product of the mind's work. Intellectual Property Right (IPR) is rights recognized by the Trade-Related Aspects of Intellectual Property Rights (TRIPS) agreement and governed by the World Trade Organization (WTO), and they are given to persons for a certain period of time over the creations of their minds [1].

TRIPS agreement provides different norms and standards with respect to different categories of IPR. They are as follows:

- Patents
- Trademarks
- Copyrights and related rights
- Industrial designs
- Layout designs of integrated circuits
- Geographical indications
- Plant varieties
- Protection of undisclosed information (trade secrets) [1]

Patent is an exclusive right or a set of specific rights given to an inventor or a person or an organization, who claims to be the first inventor by the Patent and Trademark Office to exploit their invention for a limited period of time to make, use, or sell the invention.

In general patents are issued to protect new product, apparatus, and process provided that the invention is not in the public domain also not disclosed anyplace in the world; it must be nonobvious and should have a practical application [2].

Living organisms including animal species, plants, and biological empowered with biotechnological inventions are categories of patents on bio-patents or life-forms [2].

Patent system can motivate the technical process in different ways:

1. Inspires the research and invention
2. Motivates the inventor to disclose their invention

3. Reward for the expenses of their newly developed inventions

4. Provides an inducement to invest capital in new lines of production which might not appear profitable [1]

IPR has become a knowledge industry [3]; many corporate organizations to get a leadership in the market have designed their project management system with sustained growth and enriched profits. The different approaches in their project management systems are as follows:

- Managing the IPR strategy

- Managing research collaborations with internal expertise member

- Acquiring knowledge and invention inputs from external resources

- Making mutual beneficial licenses

2. Impact and benefits of stronger IPR in developing countries

Granting monopoly rights as patent for their invention, developing countries can have the benefits like the following:

- Motivation of innovative research by private agents

- Creation of new productive activity by utilizing knowledge or utilization of knowledge for creation of new productive activity

- Distribution of knowledge to others [4–6]

3. Reason for the patent search

Different sorts of people like lawyers, historians, educators, students, government agencies, and inventors conduct patent search. The reasons for the patent search are as follows:

- Research and development

- Educational

- Technology

- Patentability

- Financial

- Economic

- Historical

- Legal

- Genealogy
- Marketing (patent search) [7]

3.1 Types of patent system

Patent system is broadly categorized into the following:

1. Design patent—consumer product (ornamental aspects)-related inventions
2. Utility patent—functional attribute-related inventions
3. Plant patents (patent application) [8]

4. Patent application

To get an exclusive IPR rights for their innovation/invention as patent, patentee has to disclose their invention in the specific format into the public domain. Incorporation of invention details in the patent specification needs to be submitted along with the patent application. Consequently the specification should meet the basic requirements such as written description, best mode, and enablement. In order to accomplish this goal, the invention must be disseminated to the public in a manner that will allow its appreciation and exploitation.

Patent application is a complex one. Drafting the patent specification is indisputably difficult; however, it is a very essential part in the patent application. The description of invention should include both technical and nontechnical. Sufficient technical details need to be incorporated to enable the researchers to reproduce the invention, whereas nontechnical description details need to understand the reason for its advance over the art and economic value by jurors, judges, licensees, business people, etc. Also the patent application should have the provision for the incorporation and changes in near future perceptions and in critical circumstances. Hence patent specification in the patent application becomes the heart and soul. Drafting the patent specification and claim has a vital role in getting the invention to get patent. Patent application should be filed as quickly as possible to claim the priority of their invention [9, 10].

5. Drafting of patent specification

Types of patent specification

1. Provisional specification
2. Complete specification

5.1 Provisional specification

Provisional specification in the patent application is a placeholder application, because it is not examined and patent is not issued. This provisional patent application will last irreversibly after completion of 12 months from the date of filing.

Major advantages of provisional applications are as follows:

1. Required information for filling is minimal and inexpensive.

2. Provisional application is not examined but can claim the priority of their invention.

Major drawbacks of provisional applications are

1. Application will last irreversibly after completion of 1 year, hence to mark this dead line and ensure that it is not missed inadvertently.

2. The application is not examined during its pendency and will be examined later during checking the superseding application utility. Provisional application is not a draft; it should be framed cautiously taking claims in an enabling manner. The patent examiner may certify that the application is unpatentable one based on the prior art reference.

Important points for construction of specification

- Complete specification must be read underlining the importance of subsequent infringement.
- Legal expertise may be involved in drafting the claims.
- General statement always leads to misinterpretation of facts.
- The specification should be described as a technical constructive one rather than literal one.

5.2 Parts of the complete specification

Complete specification is constructed with the following:

- Title of the invention
- Opening description of the invention
- Prior art description
- Objectives of the invention
- Statement of invention (optional)
- Detailed description of the invention
- Claims

5.2.1 Title

The tile of the patent specification is a concise description related to their invention including its operation, use, and method by which it is to be performed. The primary concern in choosing a title for a complete specification is to specify the scope of the invention, and the second step is to say clearly what their invention is. Hence, care should be taken to incorporate the entire scenario related to the invention in the title itself.

5.2.2 Opening description of the invention

Opening description of the invention must provide more detail about the invention than the title. Patent draftsman should have a clear understanding about the invention, and then he/she can draft the specification and claims of the patent application. The specification also should describe how the invention is to be carried out.

5.2.3 Prior art references

Consequent to the opening description of the invention, prior art references are described in detail in the specification. In prior art references, brief information about the relevant invention are disclosed in the public domain or anywhere in the world.

5.2.4 Objectives of the invention

The objectives should briefly state the invention in detail. To start with, the invention information should describe the main objective, whereas invention-related information can describe the ancillary objectives of the invention separately.

5.2.5 Statement of invention

If the applicant wanted to include one or more omnibus claims, then the omnibus claim supporting details should be described in detail with the main claims.

5.2.6 Detailed description of the invention

In this section, the applicant or patent draftman should describe the invention in detail. Also the patent-drafting person should remember that the invention details need to be understood by a person having an average skill and average knowledge in the art to work the invention.

5.2.7 How to make

The specification must describe the invention in detail so that a person skilled in the art can be able to make the invention as it is claimed.

5.2.8 How to use

The claimed invention must have an industrial applicability (utility) and should not be obvious to the skilled reader.

5.2.9 Best mode

The applicant should describe and disclose their invention in a best possible method in the patent specification.

They can disclose the invention as follows:

1. Sufficiently and fairly describe the invention

2. Fully and particularly describe the invention

3. Sufficiently and clearly describe the invention

Each and every aspect of invention must have clarity and be specific to the invention.

5.2.10 Claims

Claim or claims are defined as the exclusive rights (monopoly or protection) for their invention.

General rules in the interpretation of claims:

1. The scope of the claim in the application must be clearly defined.

2. If the meaning of the words in the claim is not disputed, the undisputed claims will be interpreted as a matter of law.

5.2.11 Function of claims

Among the different claims in an invention, at least one claim should define the subject matter for which protection is sought. For that reason a patent drafter must draft the claim in such a way that the competitor should not get scope for infringing the invention by interpreting in such a way beneficial to him/her. The claims of a patent have to be supported by the description, and also the claims do not stand alone.

Description must be the precursor for claims which will be drafted on the basis of earlier study on prior art which will be cited during prosecution.

5.2.12 Claim categories

All claims fall into one of two broad categories. The claims are either product (something tangible such as a mechanical device, a machine, an electronic circuit, a chemical compound, or a formulation) or process (a method of making, using, or testing something).

5.2.13 Independent and dependent claims

Claims can either be independent or dependent. Independent claim may refer back to the earlier claim. A dependent claim, however, includes all the limitations of that claim and adds much more limitations.

5.2.14 Form of claims

Claims must be precise, definite, and explicit for the skilled reader. Words like "for example" or "preferably" should not be incorporated in the claims; also avoid the internal codes or trademarks or names.

5.2.15 Length of text

In general, the patent specification in the patent application should be kept as short as possible with sufficient disclosure of the invention in all aspects [11–23].

6. Conclusion

IPR has an important role in the creation of technology and protection of ideas, innovation, and designs. In developing countries this IPR has a potential significance in protecting their investment; also it can help to achieve the desired technological advancement and economical level in the competitive world. IPR can assist the technology transfer of the invention through licensing and encouraging the further development of the invention with joint ventures. The specification in the patent application is a key element and has important role in the granting of patent for a particular invention. In the patent application, the patentee should fully disclose their invention in the section for what they expect for the exclusive rights. Claim or claims in the specification of the patent application are statements describing in a best possible method of the invention. Hence, drafting of patent specification has been considered as the heart and soul of any patent. It has an important role in protecting the invention from any infringement by the competitors. If any argument arises regarding the validity or infringement of patent, the scope of the invention will be verified based on the specification. While drafting the claims in the specification of the patent application, all possible equivalent variations are needed to be considered to safeguard the invention from infringement. Also the claims should be described legally in a defi¬nite, precise, and clear manner so that a competitor should not get scope to infringe upon the invention.

Author details

Sakthivel Lakshmana Prabu[1*] and Suriyaprakash TNK[2]

1 Department of Pharmaceutical Technology, University College of Engineering (BIT Campus), Anna University, Tiruchirappalli, Tamil Nadu, India

2 Department of Pharmaceutics, Al Shifa College of Pharmacy, Poonthavanam, Kizhattoor, Kerala, India

*Address all correspondence to: slaxmanvel@gmail.com

References

[1] Lakshmana Prabu S, Suriyaprakash TNK, Dinesh Kumar C. Intellectual property rights and its development in India. Pharmacy Times. 2010;**44**(3):19-22

[2] Ghai D. Patent protection and Indian pharmaceutical industry. International Journal of Pharmaceutical Sciences Review and Research. 2010;**3**(2):43-48

[3] Ganguli P. Intellectual property rights. Imperatives for the knowledge industry. World Patent Information. 2000;**22**:167

[4] Moschini GC. Intellectual Property Rights and the World Trade Organization: Retrospect and Prospects. Available from: https://www.card.iastate.edu/faculty/profiles/giancarlo_moschini/moschini-trips-preprint-oct-04.pdf [Accessed: 14 May 2019]

[5] Available from: https://www.wto.org/english/tratop_e/trips_e/ta_docs_e/8_bgd_trips_89_e.pdf [Accessed: 14 May 2019]

[6] Intellectual Property Laws. Delhi, India: Universal Law Publishing Co. Pvt. Ltd.; 2006

[7] Jim B. Introduction to Patent Searching. Available from: http://www.integrityip.com/Patent_Library/Community/Other/PatentSearching.pdf [Accessed: 15 March 2019]

[8] Runge J. What Are the Different Types of Patents? Available from: https://www.legalzoom.com/articles/what-are-the-different-types-of-patents [Accessed: 14 May 2019]

[9] Jeffrey IA. Patent Law Principles. Available from: http://euro.ecom.cmu.edu/program/law/08-732/Patents/PatentLawPrinciples.pdf [Accessed: 18 March 2019]

[10] Ramakrishna T. Basic Principles and Acquisition of Intellectual Property Rights. Bangalore: CIPRA, NLSIU; 2005. pp. 45-70

[11] Ganguli P. Patenting innovations new demands in emerging contexts. Current Science. 1998;**75**:433-439

[12] Ganguli P. Intellectual property rights in transition. World Patent Information. 1998;**20**:171-180

[13] Ganguli P. Intellectual property rights: Mothering innovations to markets. World Patent Information. 2000;**22**:43-52

[14] Gupta MS. Sufficiency of disclosure in patent specification. Journal of Intellectual Property Rights. 2009;**13**:307-316

[15] Draft Manual of Patent Practice and Procedure. Mumbai, India: The Office of Controller General of Patents, Designs & Trademarks; 2011. Available from: http://www.ipindia.nic.in/writereaddata/Portal/IPOGuidelinesManuals/1_28_1_manual-of-patent-office-practice_and-procedure.pdf

[16] Manual of Patent Practice and Procedure. 3rd ed. 2008. Available from: http://www.ipindia.nic.in/writereaddata/Portal/IPOGuidelinesManuals/1_59_1_15-wo-ga-34-china.pdf [Accessed: 20 March 2019]

[17] Drafting Patent Specification. Available from: http://www.fpapatents.com/drafting-patent-specifications [Accessed: 20 March 2019]

[18] Guidelines on Writing Patent Specification. Available from: https://www.patentwire.co.in/images/Guidelines.pdf [Accessed: 20 March 2019]

[19] Gene Q. Patent Application Drafting: Using the Specification for more than the Ordinary Plain Meaning. 2017. Available from: https://www.ipwatchdog.com/2017/04/01/patent-application-drafting-specification-ordinary-plain-meaning/id=74047/ [Accessed: 23 March 2019]

[20] Patents: Drafting a Patent Specification. Available from: https://www.bananaip.com/ip-news-center/patents-drafting-patent-specification/ [Accessed: 23 March 2019]

[21] The Importance of a Well-Drafted Patent Specification. Available from: https://www.lexology.com/library/detail.aspx?g=6aafc912-3b7e-47a4-b5ab-51897db93e98 [Accessed: 25 March 2019]

[22] WIPO Patent Drafting Manual. Available from: https://www.wipo.int/edocs/pubdocs/en/patents/867/wipo_pub_867.pdf [Accessed: 25 March 2019]

[23] Masafumi I. Drafting Description, Drawing, and Abstract. Available from: https://www.wipo.int/edocs/mdocs/aspac/en/wipo_ip_bkk_16/wipo_ip_bkk_16_t8.pdf [Accessed: 28 March 2019]

Chapter 2

Technological Trajectories Studies of Sugarcane Ethanol Production Using Patent Citation

Cecilia Häsner, Douglas Alves Santos and Araken Alves de Lima

Abstract

The production of ethanol from sugarcane has migrated from the first to the second-generation thanks to the biotechnological advancement in the production process. From the survey of patent documents in the area, it is possible to highlight the most relevant patents according to the impact index, measured by the number of citations, and to evaluate the technological trajectories involved in the production of ethanol using a patent citation as a methodology. In addition, it is possible to identify the main actors involved in the technological field, as well as the network of international collaborators. In this context, the study of patent citations will help better understand the main technological advances and global geopolitics in an environment of globalization of technological innovations.

Keywords: ethanol, sugarcane, patent, technological trajectories

1. Introduction

The recent growing demand for energy alternatives to fossil fuels has been a reality shared by many countries in the first few decades of the twenty first century. Economic and environmental issues, population growth, industrial consumption, energy insecurity as well as existing conflicts around the use of raw materials for the production of food types used in the making of fuels, are some of the factors driving governments, universities and multinational corporations to broaden the scalability of their biofuels, such as ethanol, using renewable sources such as lignocellulosic types.

Ethanol can be produced from various raw materials, which can be classified into three categories: (a) simple sugar sources; (b) starch sources; and; (c) lignocellulosic material sources.

As to the technological profile of such categories, when presented in a timeline, they form the technology trajectories representing the production of ethanol, each one related to a specific technological paradigm. Therefore, one considers first generation ethanol ethical alcohol whose production requires raw materials that are rich in saccharosis (sugar cane juice, saccharine sorghum, beetroot, etc.) and/or rich in starch (sweet potato, wheat, potato, corn, cassava, etc.). Regarding second generation ethanol, it is made from biomass that is rich in lignocellulosic materials, such as wood, straw, stems and grass leaves. Finally, third generation ethanol comes from the processing of microalgae biomass after the extraction of lipidic materials (this production modality does not have an industrial representativity yet).

Taking into account this theoretical basis and considering the raw materials that are suitable for ethanol production, as well as the three modalities of the technological trajectory of ethanol production, we conclude that ethanol produced from sugarcane is currently the bioenergy production with the highest yield per unit and higher total energy balance, when we consider the proportion of energy in the final product (ethanol and mechanical energy, thermal and electric) and the fossil energy needed for its production. Besides, sugarcane ethanol offers the possibility of two technology trajectories that are almost consecutive (first- and second-generation productions with the use of sugar cane juice and bagasse).

In this context and in the light of the current technological scenario, this chapter develops an innovative approach to the production of ethanol that comes from sugarcane, combining concepts of patent heuristics with studies of technology trajectories, dependence and paradigms [1]. The study uses technology prospection techniques with analyses of "Breakthrough Inventions," also applying "Forward citations" for an analysis of future technology affinity. Finally, it seeks to obtain a consolidated profile to forward the technology trajectory of sugarcane-based ethanol production.

The piece is divided into three sections: methodology, results and final conclusions. Results and discussions are, in their turn, subdivided into five subsections: general panorama, breakthrough inventions—geographic and current owner distribution analysis, breakthrough inventions—technology analysis, breakthrough inventions—forward citation analysis and recent innovations and technological advances in ethanol production.

2. Material and method

The methodology is based on the study of patent citation and is divided into two stages. In the first stage, patent documents were retrieved with bibliometric analysis carried out through the PatSeer® commercial patent database. It uses keywords such as: alcohol, bioalcohol, ethanol, bioethanol, saccharum, sugarcane, "sugar cane," bagasse, cellulose, biomass, lignocellulose and molasses. In the title and summary fields, it used the extend family filter. The study made use of Boolean operators "OR," "AND" and words truncated with asterisk (*). We covered the period between 2000 and 2018, according to the priority date. All the retrieved documents were classified according to the keywords in the title, summary and claim fields, which resulted in the following categories: (i) pretreatment with acid and enzymatic hydrolysis, (ii) fermentation with yeast, bacteria or non-yeast fungus, (iii) distillation and (iv) sugarcane.

The second step was the data analysis per se, composed by:

(1) Evolution over time of patent documents according to priority year, highlighting quoted documents (>5);

(2) Analysis of patent documents (heavily cited > 5) in different types of citations: patent literature—PL (backward and forward), non-patent literature—NPL (references), family size and documents made available. Calculation of self-citations (difference between forward citations (individual and non-self-citation));

(3) Calculation of the patent index citation of "breakthrough inventions" (CPR: citation patent ratio) [2, 3] according to the priority origin country:

$$CPR = \frac{\text{\%of a variable"s patents forward citation in the breakthrough inventions}}{\text{\%of all patents in the breakthrough inventions}} \quad (1)$$

A ratio of >1 is good, a ratio of <1 is relatively low.

(4) Analysis of the profile of main authors of "breakthrough inventions";

(5) Analysis of the interrelation of the technologies in the most cited "breakthrough documents" and the calculation of the technical impact index (TII) of the breakthrough inventions—the percent of patents in a period analyzed, which are in the most highly cited of all the breakthrough inventions. The expected value of the TII has been normalized to equal 1. "A TII below 1 indicates that patents are not especially highly cited" ([3], p. 272).

(6) Analysis of citations of the downstream of breakthrough inventions.

3. Results and discussion

3.1 Overview

As highlighted in the methodology section, the technology focus of the study is the production of ethanol from sugarcane in its various first-generation (ethanol) and second-generation (bioethanol) modalities. The search strategy used retrieved 223 patent documents in the 2000–2018 period according to the year of priority. Out of those 301 have more than five forward citations by patent family. An expressive range of data on first-generation (ethanol) and second-generation (bioethanol) production were observed positively that when stimulated and directed, there is a growing interest in the patent protection of the intellectual assets (in the form of patent depositories) coming from research and industrial developments (**Figure 1**).

It is worth highlighting again that, on industrial levels, ethanol is considered to be a very relevant biofuel for producer countries, and which can be obtained from various primary and secondary (lignocellulosic biomass types) sources, such as:

i. through the hydrolysis of starch of cereal grains (corn, sorghum, wheat, triticale, rye, malted barley, rice);

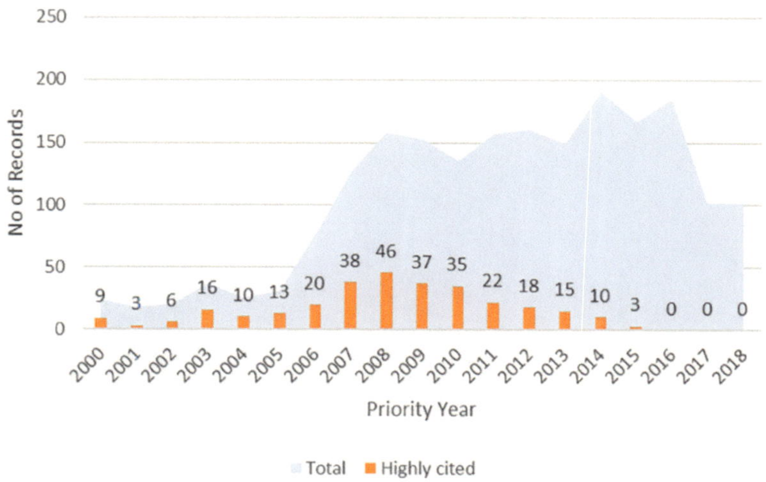

Figure 1.
Distribution over time of patent documents related to the production of sugarcane ethanol, highlighting 301 highly cited documents. Period: 2000–2018. N = 2023. Source: Compiled by the authors, PatSeer® database.

ii. tubers (potatoes);

iii. through direct use of molasses sugar and juice from: (a) sugarcane; (b) saccharin sorghum; (c) saccharin beetroot;

iv. through the breakdown and decomposing of the lignocellulosic structure of biomass materials, followed by processes of saccharification and fermentation, which can happen through intervention with: (I) yeast; (II) bacteria and (III) non-yeast fungus; finally;

v. by implementation of algae crops, with the potential of a co-production of biodiesel and bioethanol.

The global ethanol production from various raw materials has grown year on year, mainly because of its usability as a fuel (or supplementary fuel), and also thanks to its availability from renewable sources as a result of incentives and social and environmentally friendly credentials. This growth in the global ethanol production noticeable from **Figure 2** takes place independently from the struggle between the use of its primary raw materials (grains and sugarcane juices/extracts, sorghum and saccharin beetroot) and food production for the global population.

From an economic point of view, when we compare **Figures 1** and **2**, we perceive a noticeable alignment of evolutions over time given that the patent system, as it reflects the advances of investments in R&D, reveals the bias that paired the economic development of a nation to its technological development thus highlighting the strong maintenance of interests in the technologies in question. It also important to emphasize that patent data analysis aids significantly to understand technology tendencies as well as forecast future technology perspectives.

This way, with a focus on studies of future technology perspectives, we applied here the analysis of "patent citation" (PC). The methodological effort made here is in line with what many researchers across the globe have been doing for decades, using methodologies based on "patent citation analysis." This methodology has gained traction and has been developed and adapted to increase access to valuable information among companies, researchers, research centers, universities and countries. The information contained in patent documents reveals the extent and conduction of applied technical research. Therefore, the use of this tool (patents) makes it possible to show that information available in those patent documents overcomes all barriers and can be used for the expansion

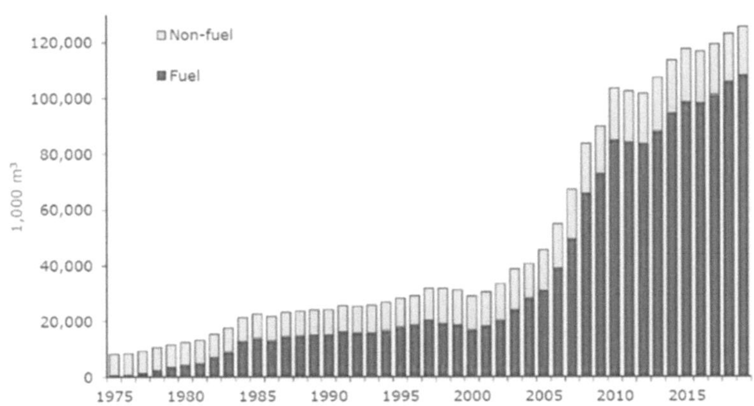

Figure 2.
World ethanol production. Source: KNect365 Energy, 2019.

Document quality indicators retrieved	Total	Most highly cited (>5) (Percentage of total)
No documents	2023	301 (14.9%)
No. of extended family members	5128	811 (15.8%)
NPL—non patent literature:		
No. of references	1612	642 (39.8%)
PL—patent literature:		
No. of backward citation	5585	1780 (31.9%)
No. of forward citations (individual)	6807	5280 (77.7%)
No. of non self citations (forward citation)	5054	3954 (78.2%)
Auto-citation	1753	1326 (21.8%)
Granted	685	137 (20%)
Average year	2011.4	2008.1

Source: Compiled by the authors, PatSeer® database.

Table 1.
Main quality indicators of retrieved documents.

of the technique and technology development. Therefore, "patent citation analysis" reveals the creation and propagation of information, as well as promotes its applicability in various technical fields which will be able to originate/spawn new technologies [4–6].

Figure 1 also shows the evolution of highly cited patent documents based on retrieved data (orange bars), whose extraction can be observed in **Table 1**, which shows a summary of the main quality indicators of the retrieved documents, comparing the total number of retrieved documents in comparison with the most cited ones.

We can see that around 78% of the individual forward citations concentrate in 15% of retrieved documents, denoting a high concentration around specific technology nuclei, while 25.1% of individual forward citations also refer to self-citations of patent documents.

Another very relevant information from **Table 1** refers to the relation between the values of "patent literature" (PL) and "non-patent literature" (NPL). According to Demet et al. [7], this relation (PL/NPL) infers a state of industrial maturity hoped to be reached. In other words, values below the first inferior quarter (>25%) suggest a favorable state for innovation and the commercialization of products/processes of a given technology sector. Therefore, it is possible to conclude there are well-established maturity nuclei in detriment of the possibility of the existence of nuclei that are not mature yet. A better definition of these maturity nuclei was set out by "breakthrough inventions" study of "patent citations" [8].

3.2 Breakthrough inventions: geographic and current owner distribution analysis

According to Yan et al. [9], "breakthrough inventions" can be understood as inventions that aspire to or serve as technology bases for the creation of subsequent inventions. They are inventions that are a relevant source of competitive edge and can be part of a viable strategy to boost a company" capacity to generate innovative inventions. They can help meeting the challenge to create radical/disruptive inventions through the recombination of non-redundant knowledge, mainly by using patent publications of industrial competitors' patent publications. In this case, the technology sector of first- and second-generation ethanol production.

Kerr [10] used "breakthrough inventions" to identify important areas for future research in the area. Similarly, Egli et al. [11] used "breakthrough inventions" to identify and induce applied technologies to climate change mitigation. This way, in this paper we used such studies as reference in the investigation of the efforts and technology maturity, patenting growth and the influence of patents in the technology development of first- and second-generation ethanol production. This way, this work presents "breakthrough inventions" through "patent citations" with an analysis of the main technology clusters within the ethanol production sector and its temporal and spatial migrations.

Before we continue with the present analysis, it important to understand the relevance of the study on geographic distribution and the owners of technologies in "breakthrough inventions." Therefore, the analysis of components of geographical distribution and the ownership of inventions is key as it provides information on the flow of knowledge of the analyzed technology [4]. For that matter, we drew from Kaki's study on citations performances ratio (CPR). CPR comes from a comparative study based on the presence of highly cited patents in a given patent database, a specific timeline and category. The values whose ratio are bigger than the unit (CPR > 1) indicate a good performance. According to Narin and Olivastro" study [12], any patent document cited 06 (six) or more times can be considered as very relevant for the "patent citation analysis." They can also be considered "breakthrough inventions."

In this sense, **Table 2** sums up the main indicators of patent quality according to the country of origin of the priority request. The importance of analyzing this parameter is to understand which countries dominate the technology. Only the USA, China and Japan have CPR numbers above 1, which are considered good. Other countries did not obtain a good performance during analysis.

When we analyze **Table 2**, we can see a strong performance by the United States as the conductor of technology within the analyzed setting. Therefore, even if it does not have its ethanol matrix focused on sugarcane crops, the United States present a relevant patent achievement in terms of "breakthrough inventions". This suggests technology leadership in related areas when a sugarcane matrix is used. Also relevant is the fact that the United States are the biggest ethanol producers in the world, followed by Brazil, EU, China and Canada (**Figure 3**) while the largest sugarcane producer are Brazil, India, China, Thailand and Pakistan [13].

Priority country	No. of records	CPR	% granted of the priority country	% of extended family members
United States	61	8.35	42.6	61.7
China	172	6.21	50.6	23.7
Japan	52	2.53	32.7	8.6
Germany	5	0.18	0.0	2.2
Korea	4	0.11	50.0	1.5
Czech Republic	2	0.06	50.0	0.9
Russian Federation	2	0.04	0.0	0.6
Brazil	1	0.02	100	0.5
France	1	0.02	100	0.2
United Kingdom	1	0.02	100	0.1
Total	301		45.2%	100%

Source: compiled by the authors, PatSeer database.

Table 2.
Country of origin profile analysis of "breakthrough inventions."

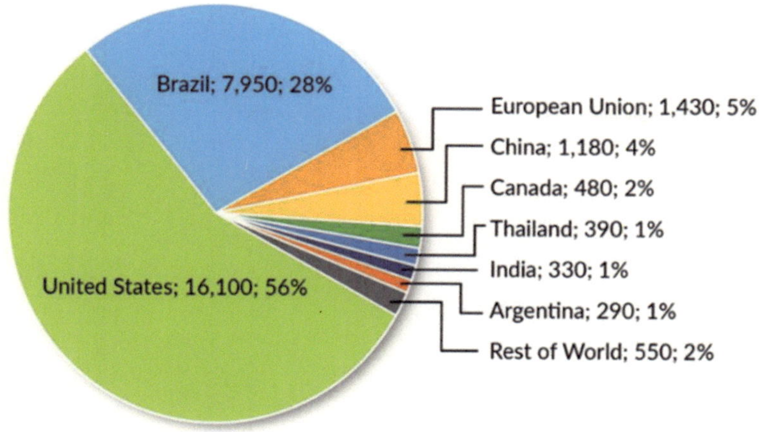

Figure 3.
Global ethanol production by country of 2018 (country; million gallons; share of global production). Source: RFA analysis of public and private data source.

Following the same logic, we can see that China plays an important role in the "breakthrough inventions" analyzed scenario, that is, it appears as one of the five global ethanol powers, as well as one of the five countries with the highest number of innovative inventions. We should highlight here that the Chinese government is planning the implementation of a policy of an E10 ethanol addition to gasoline across its territory by 2020. This will be very important for countries like the United States and Brazil, whose CPR of the latter is only 0.02. Such piece of information about Brazil (CPR = 0.02) may suggest a strong dependence and even propensity to the technology "colonization" in specific sub-sectors and the existence of "Patent Pools" [14, 15] and "Patent Trolls" [16, 17].

Regarding the profile of the main holders of "breakthrough inventions" retrieved during the CPR analysis, **Table 3** shows the importance of Chinese companies. This is a very important piece of information for this analysis of technology trajectory because it enables a clear visualization of the steps taken by companies and Chinese university research centers toward control and technology independence of methods of first- and second-generation ethanol production.

Although the companies listed in **Table 3** show low CPR (<0.5), an indicator they produce little impact with the dissemination of their technologies, their respective values often surpass by several times the CPR of countries like Germany (2.8×); Russia (12.5×); Brazil (25×); and France (25×).

Also relevant is the fact that the number of "breakthrough inventions" documents retrieved from these companies and Chinese universities present low statistical dispersion (average standard deviation = 1.88). This, however, suggests something positive. These figures can indicate a cohesive movement of technology ascension for the sector, cluster or grouping formation. We must also call attention to the high number of documents made available by these actors, except for Toshiba Corp, Institute of Process Engineering, and the Chinese Academy of Sciences, who until the time when the analysis was made did not have patents issued for the technologies herein studied.

The analysis of **Table 3** also reveals the absence of actors from other countries. For example, the presence of actors such as the United States and Japan merely indicates them to be countries with a considerable number of "breakthrough inventions" documents. However, it can be concluded there is great dispersion of patent document ownership, which in its turn suggests an open and competitive market, without business clusters. Regarding the technology aspect of ethanol production,

Current owner	No. records	CPR	No. granted	Sugarcane	Biomass	Pretreatment		Fermentation		
					Acid hydrolysis	Enzymatic hydrolysis	Yeast	Bacterium	Fungus without yeast	Distillation
China petroleum & chem-sinopec	9	0.27	9	1	3	3	4	5	0	4
Univ tsinghua	8	0.32	8	4	3	3	4	3	1	4
Tsukishima kikai Co Ltd	7	0.32	2	0	2	2	1	0	0	0
Univ tianjin	7	0.29	5	2	0	1	4	1	1	5
Toshiba corp	5	0.12	0	0	0	1	2	0	0	0
Oji holding corp	5	0.20	4	0	0	0	1	0	0	2
Inst process Eng Cas	4	0.13	0	0	0	1	2	0	0	3
Hitachi group	3	0.10	1	0	0	0	0	0	0	1
Cofco Ltd	3	0.10	3	0	2	3	3	3	0	0
Dalian chem physics inst	3	0.08	3	0	0	0	0	0	0	0

N = 301. Source: Compiled by the authors, PatSeer® database.

Table 3.
Analysis of the profile of the main patent holders of "breakthrough inventions".

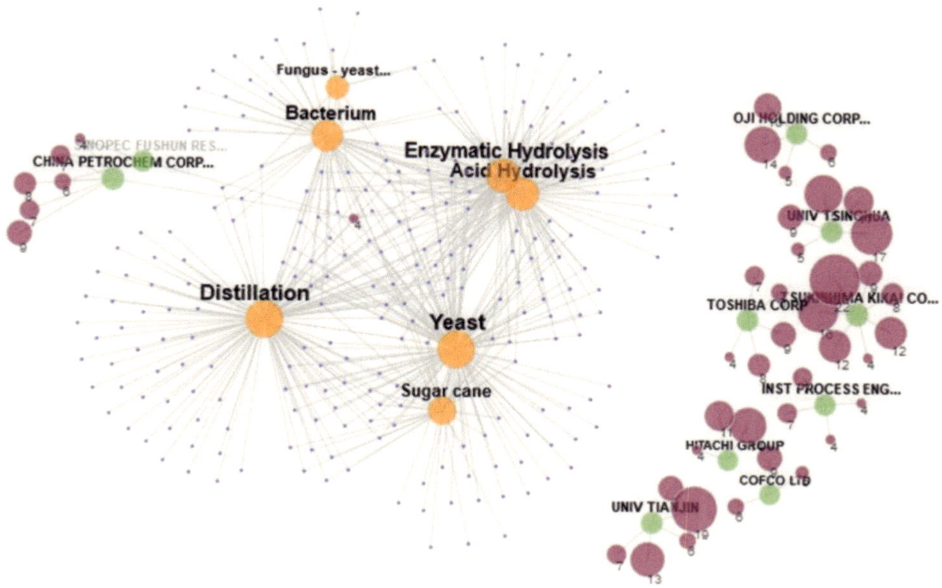

Figure 4.
Relationship network among the 10 main holders of technologies associated to the production of ethanol, "breakthrough inventions" and biomass categories (sugarcane), pretreatment (acid hydrolysis and enzymatic hydrolysis), fermentation (yeast, bacterium and yeast-free fungus) and distillation. N = 301. Source: Elaborated by the authors, PatSeer® database.

Table 3 reveals to readers that the great intellectual effort by Chinese companies is in areas such as: (i) pretreatment of raw materials (hydrolysis); (ii) fermentation; and, (iii) post-treatment (distillation); in that order.

From that point of view, **Figure 4**, created from 301 "breakthrough inventions" documents-corroborates previous understandings of **Table 3** analysis, showing a relationship between actors and technology areas in each category. Therefore, it is possible to verify a certain level of non-binding cohesion among the analyzed actors, there being no sharing of technology in those supposed partnerships.

China Petrochem Corp (Sinopec) appears as an exception to the block composed by all the other actors. The data suggests low adhesion by that company to the cluster formed by other companies and universities. There seems to be no apparent link between them and no effort of interaction among them.

In the case of technology associated to the production of ethanol, the "breakthrough inventions" and the analysis of biomass (sugarcane) analysis, pretreatment (acid hydrolysis and enzymatic hydrolysis), fermentation (yeast, bacterium and yeast-free fungus), post-treatment (distillation) indicates possible dispersion.

3.3 Breakthrough inventions: technology analysis

In 2016, the United Nations Conference on Trade and Development (UNCTAD) [18] launched a report where they laid out the main distinctions between first and second generation renewable fuels, based on their raw materials' features (**Table 4**). Therefore, **Table 4** shows that first generation biofuels are made from seeds, cereals and sugar types (from extracts and juices) while second generation biofuels are produced from the pretreatment of cellulosic and lignocellulosic biomass, such as: carbonaceous materials of renewable vegetable sources (wood, bagasse, straw, barks, grass, etc.).

In order to comply with the time-based interval adopted in this paper, it is necessary to highlight that the conversion of lignocellulosic biomass materials into

First-generation biofuels (from seeds, grain and sugar)	Second-generation biofuels (from lignocellulosic biomass, such as crop residues, woody crops or energy grasses)
Petroleum-gasoline substitutes • Ethanol or butanol by fermentation of starches of sugars	**Biochemically produced Petroleum-gasoline substitutes** • Ethanol or butanol by enzymatic hydrolysis
Petroleum-diesel substitutes • Biodiesel by transesterification of plant oils (FAME and FAEE) • Can be produced from various crops such as rapeseed (RME), soybeans (SME), sunflowers, coconut oil, palm oil, jatropha, recycled cooking oil and animal fats. • Pure plant oils (straight vegetable oil)	**Thermochemically produced Petroleum-gasoline substitutes** • Methanol • Fischer-Tropsch gasoline • Mixed alcohols **Thermochemically produced Petroleum-diesel substitutes** • Fischer-Tropsch diesel • Dimethyl ether (substitutes propane as well) • Green diesel

Source: UNCTAD [18].

Table 4.
Differences between the production of first- and second-generation biofuel according to raw materials.

biofuel was already viable in the mid-2000s and, on an industrial level, biofuels derived from this process involving enzymatic stages were not a common practice nor were they produced in great volumes for the market before the year 2005 [19]. Besides, it is possible to notice a significant change in the alcohol (ethanol) production from 2005 onwards (see **Figure 2**), the year when the Kyoto protocol was signed by most ethanol-producing countries and regions. At first, China and the United States did not agree to sign the protocol. However, after discussions that lasted more than half a decade, those countries ratified the protocol and started a global pact aimed at mitigating the production of greenhouse gases, in 2011 [20].

This global agreement directed, once and for all global efforts and interests in ethanol-producing technologies from lignocellulosic materials (biomass route: **Figure 5**). This way, it boosted their sustainability footprint and benefits for the

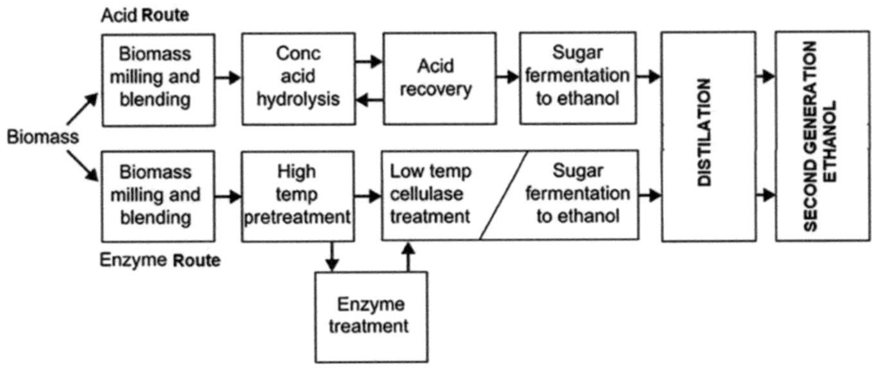

Figure 5.
Schematic representation of the stages of second-generation ethanol production. Source: Elaborated by authors.

Biofuel type and production capacity (millions of liters per year)								
Fuel	2009	2010	2011	2012	2013	2014	2015	2016
Advanced Ethanol	27.71	42.36	46.52	922.62	2.522.22	4.770.26	8.538.41	8.848.82
Cellulosic Sugars Ethanol	0.00	0.04	0.08	0.08	3.82	3.82	102.21	102.21

Source: Biofuels digest, 2011. Note: 2012–2016 data represents 2011 estimates.

Table 5.
Biofuel type and production capacity.

environment and also appeased disputing parts regarding sources of raw materials to be used to produce energy in detriment of food for people, as is the case of sugarcane in Brazil and China [21].

In this sense, after 2013 the whole political debate about the implementation of second-generation fuels became a new reality of technological-industrial trajectory, while for example, ethanol coming from lignocellulosic materials (vegetable biomass and cellulosic residue) began to be produced at industrial/commercial scale (**Table 5**), representing an opportunity for a number of countries to be inserted technologically and take part of the emerging industry of second generation biofuels [18].

As we can see from **Table 5**, the advanced route of ethanol production, similarly to biomass route (cellulose), gains momentum from 2013, when several new technologies started to be implemented in the industrial field. This way, using studies on clusters of the topic-based documents of "breakthrough inventions" as a departing point, a series of more detailed analysis was carried out about the technology profile of the main routes of ethanol production (**Figure 6**).

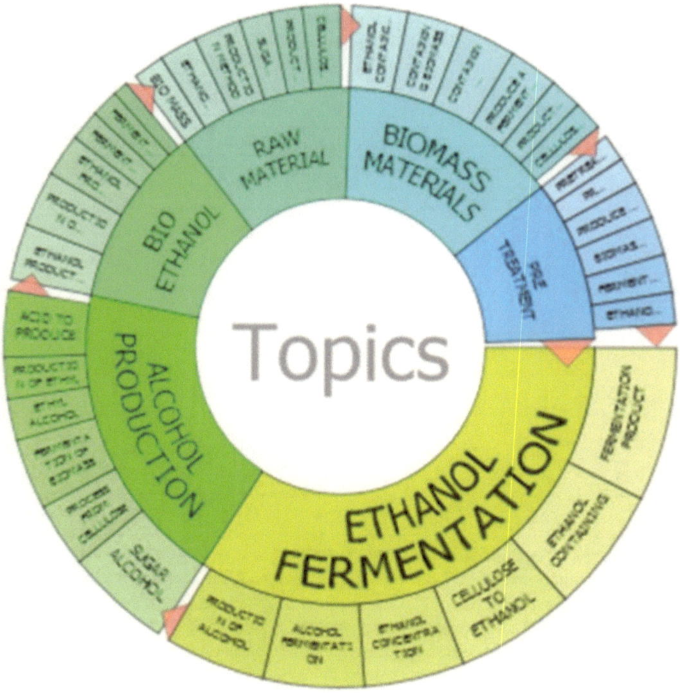

Figure 6.
Graphic representation of the topics in documents of patents of "breakthrough inventions". Source: Compiled by the authors, PatSeer® database.

By reading **Figure 6**, we can see that technology linked to the Ethanol Fermentation phase and pre-treatment (Alcohol Production) are the base of new technology trajectories in the production of ethanol. The image allows us to see subsections related to the conversion of cellulose into ethanol, as well as the treatments with the use of acids and enzymes for the preparation of sugars that will be consumed by microorganisms during fermentation. Regarding the raw materials the analysis in **Figure 6** comprises, it is possible to see the technological inclination toward the use of biomass material (lignocellulosic) as a pillar for the technology trajectory in the production of fuel alcohol that will continue into coming years. The greater emphasis is on the biomass material that is not consumable by humans and animals, especially the waste from the lignocellulosic base.

As a way to corroborate this timely analysis, **Table 6** shows the relation of the 10 main international classifications of patents with the biomass categories (sugarcane), pre-treatment (acid and enzymatic hydrolysis), fermentation (yeast, bacterium, yeast-free fungus) and post-treatment (distillation). We noticed the main classification is C12P (fermentation or enzyme-using processes to synthesize a desired chemical compound or composition or to separate optical isomers from a racemic mixture), with a TII higher than one (3.67), proving to be a relevant technology field for the production of ethanol. The most representative categories were related to yeast and distillation, because during the ethanol production process, both first and second generation, fermentation and distillation are crucial. However, TII for both was low (0.37).

Based on the data in **Table 6**, it must be highlighted that the classification code C12P, (Fermentation or enzyme-using processes to synthesize a desired chemical compound or composition or to separate optical isomers from a racemic mixture) was the main classification for the analysis, using a TII above one (3.67), a technology field

IPC	No. records	TII	Biomass	Pretreatment		Fermentation			Posttreatment
			Sugarcane	Acid hydrolysis	Enzymatic hydrolysis	Yeast	Bacterium	Fungus (without yeast)	Distillation
C12P	1105	**3.67**	130	322	363	562	264	35	379
C12R	370	**1.23**	50	139	151	261	135	15	125
C12N	260	**0.86**	23	47	56	151	80	17	54
C07C	200	**0.66**	17	20	14	18	4	1	71
C02F	126	**0.42**	7	2	2	11	16	4	25
C12M	110	**0.37**	13	16	19	35	16	3	47
C10L	107	**0.36**	10	17	19	20	16	2	42
C08L	99	**0.33**	1	8	1	2	12	0	18
B01J	78	**0.26**	0	7	2	0	0	0	8
B01D	63	**0.21**	6	4	5	3	1	0	32
TII			**0.11**	**0.23**	**0.25**	**0.37**	**0.18**	**0.03**	**0.37**

N = 301. C12P: Fermentation or enzyme-using processes to synthesize a desired chemical compound or composition or to separate optical isomers from a racemic mixture; C12R: Indexing scheme associated with subclasses; C12N: Micro-organisms or enzymes; compositions thereof; C07C: Acyclic or carbocyclic compounds; C02F: Treatment of water, waste water, sewage or sludge; C12M: Apparatus for enzymology or microbiology; C10L: Fuels not otherwise provided for; natural gas; synthetic natural gas obtained by processes; C08L: Compositions of macromolecular compounds; B01J: Chemical or physical processes; B01D: Separation. Source: Compiled by the authors, PatSeer® database.

Table 6.
List of the top 10 IPC main class with document classification according to "breakthrough inventions" patent technology process, and technical impact index–TII.

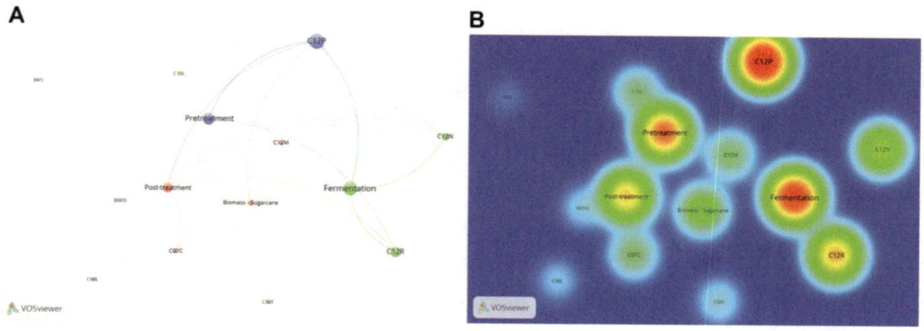

Figure 7.
Networking of the top 10 IPC Main class and the categories (pre-treatment = acid hydrolysis, enzymatic hydrolysis; fermentation = yeast, bacterium, fungus without yeast; distillation), (A) and density graph of the same networking (B). Source: Compiled by the authors, PatSeer® database and VOS viewer visualization [22].

that is essential for ethanol production. Meanwhile, the other technology categories (IPCs) involved in the ethanol process have proven to be statistically with TII impacts but without major discrepancies or significant dispersion (average TII = 0.434; Average deviation = 0.163). They are hierarchically ranked in the relevance sequence that follows: (1st): Fermentation technologies (Yeast, Bacterium and Yeast-free Fungus), because both in first and second generation, fermentation is a crucial stage to obtain ethanol. (2nd) pre-treatment technologies (Acid and enzymatic hydrolysis- slight tendency toward the latter); finally (3rd) Post-treatment technologies (Distillation). This hierarchical configuration can be confirmed in **Figure 7**, which shows the relation between all networks of relationship between technology clusters.

Still looking at **Figure 7A** and **B** it is possible to see strong and direct relations between the stages of the ethanol production process, especially between the pre-treatment and fermentation stages, which are interrelated and form a network of weak knots. But when isolated, they are intense. We can observe that, together, such stages make up the central technology focus of ethanol production.

In the sequence, we present some of the most highly cited patent documents of "breakthrough inventions" within the context of previous analysis.

WO2003078644-A2 (25 September 2003): Conversion of cellulose to glucose involves treating a pre-treated lignocellulosic substrate with cellulase.

WO2006007691-A1 (26 January 2006): Obtaining a product sugar stream from cellulosic biomass, involves hydrolyzing a neutralized cellulosic biomass with cellulase enzymes.

WO2006110900-A2 (19 October 2006): Production (P1) of ethanol comprising biomass with aqueous solution containing ammonia, a saccharification enzyme consortium to produce fermentable sugars, and a fermentation conditions with a suitable biocatalyst to produce ethanol.

JP4522797-B2 (11 August 2010): Pre-processing of lignocellulose-containing raw material for use in ethanol production.

JP5233452-B2 (10 July 2013): System for saccharification and fermentation of woody biomass raw material, by adding cellulose degrading enzyme, hemicellulolytic enzyme and alcohol fermentation microorganism.

BR200100762-A (06 November 2001): The method involves grinding lignocellulosic biomass (LB) followed by steam-explosion pre-treatment.

3.4 Breakthrough inventions: forward citation analysis

Currently, the analysis of "Forward Citation" is often used by authors of non-patent literature when the objective is a better understanding of patterns, for example, of formation of a portfolio of patent documents for a systematic analysis of the international codes of patent classification. Carpenter, Narin and Woolf [23] and Trajtenberg [8], in their respective works, managed to measure the relationship between "Forward Citation" and the future value of an invention, therefore the "Forward Citation" number that a given patent document receives, and which accumulates over time, is related to the significant technology impact of the technical content of those documents (that is, "breakthrough inventions"). That suggests that patents with a high number of citations have a relevant technology impact and contribute significantly to the advance of technology [24].

Keeping that in mind, it was necessary for the present analysis of investigation of the technology trajectory for the field of first and second generation ethanol production sector to use "Forward Citation" analysis as a "proxy" for the measurement of intangible added value that those "breakthrough inventions" documents really have. This way, under the prism adopted by this study, it was noted that: the more valuable a patented technology, the newer the incentives are created from past learnings; this way, looking at it from an economic point o view, "Forward Citation" results in the measurement of the valuing of those documents of "breakthrough inventions".

This way, the "Forward Citation" analysis of the 301 documents of "breakthrough inventions" was carried out by taking into account the codes of international classification of patents retrieved in previous analyses (**Figure 8**). From that analysis it was possible to identify: (i) 3506 patent documents in "forward citation"; and, (ii) 1524 patent documents in "backward citation"; the main classifications in the documents in (i) were: (a) C12P7 (count-1337); (b) C12P19 (count-532); (c) C07C29 (count-434); and, (d) C12M1 (count-359).

Still looking at **Figure 8**, it is possible to note that the ratio between the quantity of retrieved documents to (i) "forward citation" and (ii) "backward citation" outnumbers the unit by 2.3 times, thus indicating that the 301 "breakthrough inventions" documents analyzed in this study presented a strong impact on subsequent technology generations [25].

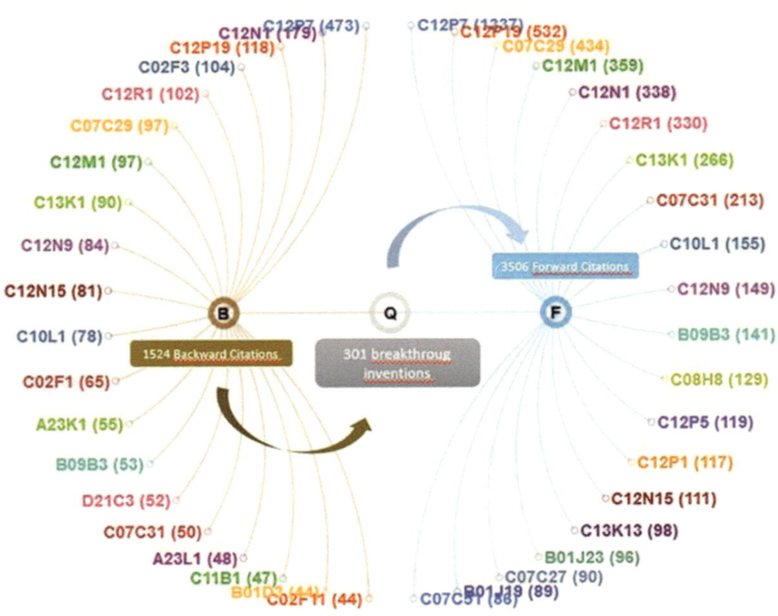

Figure 8.
Analysis of citations of breakthrough inventions. Source: Compiled by the authors, PatSeer® data.

Moving on, the 3506 patent documents in "forward citation" were treated and filtered through extended family, resulting in 2406 original documents of patent family (no document doubling). These were equally stratified and analyzed according to technology categories and international codes of patent classification (IPC), which resulted in **Table 7**.

Analyzing **Table 7** in relation to **Figure 7A** and **B**, it is possible to see there is a prevalence of subclass C12P in detriments to other classification codes (IPC). This highlights that the technology trajectory in analysis is clearly directed to the production of second generation ethanol, through the use of cellulosic waste (biomass).

IPC full class	No. records	Biomass	Pretreatment		Fermentation			Post-treatment
		Sugarcane	Acid hydrolysis	Enzymatic hydrolysis	Yeast	Bacterium	Fungus (without yeast)	Distillation
C12P7/10: Substrate containing cellulosic material	460	56	165	192	179	59	0	95
C12P7/06: Ethanol	362	50	61	75	147	57	0	75
C12P19/14: Produced by the action of a carbohydrase	262	38	95	133	64	29	0	41
C12M1/00: Apparatus for enzymology or microbiology	167	24	29	33	32	12	0	45
C12P19/02: Monosaccharides	161	21	61	72	22	11	0	10
C12R1/865: *Saccharomyces cerevisiae*	149	22	47	63	112	47	0	31
C13K1/02: By saccharification of cellulosic materials	148	18	50	33	10	6	0	10
C12P7/16: Butanol	114	23	39	32	25	17	0	27
B09B3/00: Destroying solid waste or transforming solid waste into something useful or harmless	113	8	14	19	16	6	0	23
C12P7/08: Produced as by-product or from waste or cellulosic material substrate	113	11	26	29	42	12	0	39

N = 2406. Source: Compiled by the authors, PatSeer® database.

Table 7.
List of top 10 IPC full class with document classification according to the technology process of forward citation of "breakthrough inventions" patents.

This information can be inferred by the sequenced information of the main classifications, as follows: (i) C12P7/10: Substrate containing cellulosic material; (ii) C12P7/06: Ethanol; (iii) C12P19/14: Produced by the action of a carbohydrase (set of enzymes that catalyzes 5 types of breakdown during carbohydrates into simple sugars); (iv) C12M1/00: Apparatus for enzymology or microbiology; (v) C12P19/02: Monosaccharides; (vi) C12R1/865: Saccharomyces cerevisiae; (vii) C13K1/02: By saccharification of cellulosic materials; (viii) C12P7/08: Produced as by-product or from waste or cellulosic material substrate. Besides, there is emphasis on the use of enzymes during the initial stage of pre-treatment of raw materials through enzymatic hydrolysis.

This way, it is clear that the stages of pre-treatment and fermentation are the strongest and most relevant technology nuclei for the sector in the near future.

3.5 Recent innovations and technological advances in ethanol production

The theory of trajectory and technology paradigm that we use these days were laid out and drafted by Dosi [1]. In his study, the researcher adopted similarities in the process of innovation to incremental innovation and disruptive innovation, to the assessment of process of diffusion between science and technology, taking into account heuristics methodology, well-structured in the form of a strategy of search that directed toward the solution of problems under the existing paradigms. The heuristics sustained by the author, in thesis, boosts incremental innovation in the context of a given technology trajectory, like a driving force that unleashes changes for new trajectories or technology paradigms through the disruptive or radical innovation [1, 26]. Therefore, the heuristics seems to be essential for a better comprehension of the dynamics of the technology involved in ethanol production.

In this analytical context, a new heuristic context was created for the final part of this study, which enable the making of data profiling, on various levels: (i) geographical; (ii) temporal; and, (iii) technological; employing the same data on the family documents of the "forward citation" in a scenario of recent deposits—between 2017 and 2018. This led to **Figure 9** and **Table 8** as shown in sequence.

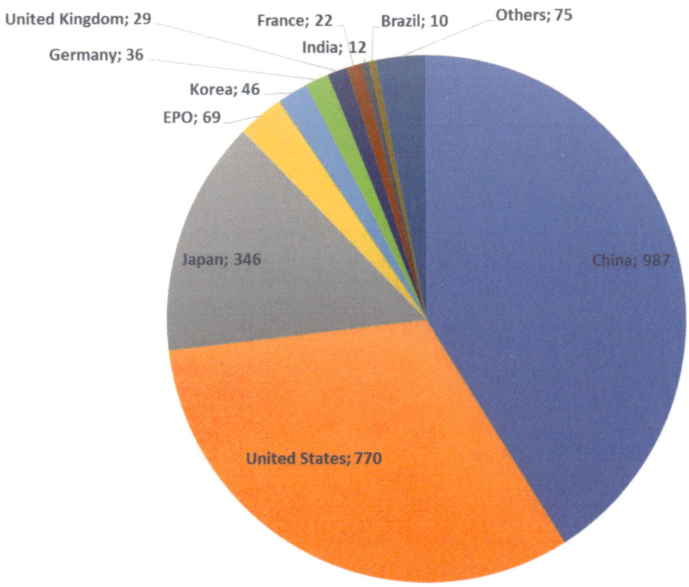

Figure 9.
Country of origin of "forward citations" for 2017 and 2018. Source: Compiled by the authors, PatSeer®.

IPC main	Sugarcane	Pretreatment	Fermentation	Post-treatment
C08L		2		
C10L			1	
C12N		1	4	
C12P	1	2	3	
C11C				1
D21B	1	1		
D21C		1	1	
Total Geral	2	7	9	1

Source: Compiled by the authors, PatSeer®.

Table 8.
Main IPC related to categories.

By analyzing the data set in **Figure 8** and **Table 8**, it is possible to infer that the technology trajectory from the data mined points to China as the country with the biggest technology power to rise in the future and replace the United States as the leader of ethanol-producing technologies, mainly in technologies related to the enzymatic pre-treatment and the fermentation stage. It is worth highlighting the presence of patent documents on the technologies that use modified bacteria and/or yeast-free fungus, which process the raw cellulosic material, and alternately absorb the stages of pre-treatment and fermentation of sugars resulting from the saccharification of lignocellulosic matter in one stage only (see: CN105154416-B, 2018; CN108603186-A, 2018; CN106755011-A, 2017; IN201741014528-A, 2018; IN201831041905-A, 2018; US2018230420-A1, 2018; BR102016030305-A2, 2018).

4. Final remarks

The study highlights some considerations to be taken up in a broader research agenda in sugarcane ethanol's production chain.

The first point is that the strategy of patent data retrieval used by the authors in this and other works and for a smaller spatial dimension proved totally valid to characterize technological advances in the aforementioned production chain at the global level. This reveals that the methodology experimented by the authors involving the use of the technological information contained in the patent documents consorted to the specific study of patent citations are very adequate to identify and understand the technology trajectories resulting from investment decisions, research and public policies related to the study of industrial sectors.

A second point to be considered concerns the dynamism of research on second generation technologies for ethanol production from sugarcane in the early years of the twenty-first century. However, what stands out is the prominence of the Chinese research system and its articulation with companies in areas of extremely high complexity, such as biotechnology, especially in the areas of fermentation and enzymatic processes.

Finally, looking at the Brazilian ethanol research and production system, the study indicates routes to be followed and bridges to be built in case the country should want to retake the leading role it has played in this sector in the twentieth century. And this is an important feature of the methodology used in this study that, in prospecting and extracting data and information from the patent system, stripped relevant sources of technological knowledge and research and development networks with which it will be essential to establish partnerships for the development of a collaborative work.

Author details

Cecilia Häsner[1*], Douglas Alves Santos[2] and Araken Alves de Lima[3]

1 Prospective Inovação Tecnológica e Ambiental Ltda., Vila Velha, Brazil

2 INPI's Representative in Paraná State, National Institute of Industrial Property—INPI, Curitiba, Brazil

3 INPI's Representative in Santa Catarina State, National Institute of Industrial Property—INPI, Florianópolis, Brazil

*Address all correspondence to: cecilia.hasner@gmail.com

References

[1] Dosi G. Technological paradigms and technological trajectories: A suggested interpretation of the determinants and directions of technical change. Research Policy. 1982;**11**:147-162

[2] Ahuja G, Lampert CM. Entrepreneurship in the large corporation: A longitudinal study of how established firms create breakthrough inventions. Strategic Management Journal. 2001;**22**(6-7 Special Issue on Strategic Entrepreneurship: Entrepreneurial Strategies for Wealth Creation):521-543

[3] Karki MMS, Krishnam KS. Patent citation analysis: A policy analysis tool. World Patent Information. 1997;**19**(4):269-272

[4] Sharma P, Tripathi RC. Patent citation: A technique for measuring the knowledge flow of information and innovation. World Patent Information. 2017;**51**:31-42

[5] Lee M, Kim Y, Woncheol J. Patent citation network analysis. Korean Journal of Applied Statistics. 2016;**29**:613-625

[6] Hasner C, de Lima AA, Winter E. Technology advances in sugarcane propagation: A patent citation study. World Patent Information. 2019;**56**:9-16

[7] Demet AE, Tanchoux N, Centi G, De Luca R, Di Renzo F, Vermeiren W. Chapter 8: On the R&D landscape evolution in catalytic upgrading of biomass. In: Studies in Surface Science and Catalysis. Elsevier; Vol. 178. 2019. pp. 149-171

[8] Trajtenberg M. A penny for your quotes: Patent citations and the value of innovations. The Rand Journal of Economics. 1990;**21**(1):172-187

[9] Yan Y, Dong JQ, Faems D. Not every coopetitor is the same: The impact of technological, market and geographical overlap with coopetitors on firms' breakthrough inventions. Long Range Planning. In Press. 2019. Available from: https://www.sciencedirect.com/science/article/abs/pii/S0024630118301031 [cited: 02 June 2019]

[10] Kerr WR. Breakthrough inventions and migrating clusters of innovation. Journal of Urban Economics. 2010;**67**(1):46-60

[11] Egli F, Johnstone N, Menon C. Identifying and inducing breakthrough inventions: An application related to climate change mitigation. OECD Science, Technology and Industry Working Papers. Paris: OECD Publishing; 2015. http://dx.doi.org/10.1787/5js03zd40n37-en

[12] Narin F, Olivastro D. Technology indicators based on patents and patent citations. In: Handbook of Quantitative Studies of Science and Technology. Elsevier; 1988. pp. 465-507. Available from: https://linkinghub.elsevier.com/retrieve/pii/B9780444705372500209 [cited: 02 June 2019]

[13] Food and Agriculture Organization of the United Nations—FAO. FAOSTAT—Statistics of Sugarcane Crop [Internet]. 2019. Available from: http://www.fao.org/faostat/en/#data/QC [cited: 02 June 2019]

[14] Ishihara A, Yanagawa N. Dark sides of patent pools with compulsory independent licensing. SSRN Electronic Journal. 2016. pp. 1-59. Available from: http://www.ssrn.com/abstract=2885620 [cited: 02 June 2019]

[15] Dequiedt V, Versaevel B. Patent pools and dynamic R&D incentives. International Review of Law and Economics. 2013;**36**:59-69

[16] Appel I, Farre-Mensa J, Simintzi E. Patent trolls and small

business employment. SSRN Electronic Journal. 2016. pp.1-68. Available from: http://www.ssrn.com/abstract=2887104 [cited: 02 June 2019]

[17] Turner JL. Patent thickets, trolls and unproductive entrepreneurship. SSRN Electronic Journal. 2011. Available from: http://www.ssrn.com/abstract=1916798 [cited: 02 June 2019]

[18] UNCTAD. Second generation biofuel markets: Satet of play, trade and developing country perspectives. In: United Nations Conf Trade Dev [Internet]. 2016. p. 69. Available from: http://unctad.org/en/PublicationsLibrary/ditcted2015d8_en.pdf

[19] Hamelinck CN, Faaij APC. Outlook for advanced biofuels. Energy Policy. 2006;**34**(17):3268-3283

[20] Ferreira L. Em decisão histórica, EUA e China comprometem-se a cortar gases estufa em pacto global: 11/12/2011-UOL Notícias. UOL Ciência e Saúde, em Durban [Internet]. 2011. Available from: https://noticias.uol.com.br/ciencia/ultimas-noticias/redacao/2011/12/11/em-decisao-historica-eua-e-china-comprometem-se-a-cortar-gases-estufa-em-pacto-global.htm [cited: 02 June 2019]

[21] Tomei J, Helliwell R. Food versus fuel? Going beyond biofuels. Land use policy [Internet]. 1 Nov 2016;**56**: 320-326. Available from: https://www.sciencedirect.com/science/article/abs/pii/S0264837715003579 [cited: 02 June 2019]

[22] Van Eck NJ, Waltman L. VOS viewer: Visualizing scientific landscapes [Internet]. 2016. Available from: http://www.vosviewer.com/ [cited: 12 April 2017]

[23] World Intellectual Property Organization. MP, Commission of the European Communities. F, Woolf P, Carpenter MP, Narin F, Woolf P. World patent information [Internet]. WIPO jointly with the Commission of European Communities, Vol. 3; 1979. pp. 160-163. Available from: https://econpapers.repec.org/article/eeeworpat/v_3a3_3ay_3a1981_3ai_3a4_3ap_3a160-163.htm [cited: 02 June 2019]

[24] Wagner RP, Parchomovsky G. Patent portfolios. SSRN Electronic Journal. 2004. Available from: http://www.ssrn.com/abstract=582201 [cited: 02 June 2019]

[25] Aristodemou L, Tietze F. Citations as a measure of technological impact: A review of forward citation-based measures. World Patent Information. 2018;**53**:39-44

[26] Martinelli A. An emerging paradigm or just another trajectory? Understanding the nature of technological changes using engineering heuristics in the telecommunications switching industry. Research Policy. 2012;**41**(2):414-429

Chapter 3

Case Study on Rejected Patents in India

Hetal Patel and Sandesh Lodha

Abstract

India is a country that has understood the importance of strong patent systems for the growth of industry and commerce to bring it at par with the modern world. As per WIPO statistical database September 2018, 45,379 patent applications were filed in India. Out of which, 12,387 applications were granted and 29,789 applications were withdrawn or abandoned by the applicants. About 3203 patents were rejected on the ground of non-fulfillment of patentability criteria by the invention, that is, Novelty, non-obviousness and Industrial applicability or non-patentability criteria mentioned under Sections 3 and 4 of Indian Patent Act. In this chapter, the authors have discussed few of the cases of rejection under the Indian Patent Act.

Keywords: Indian Patent Act, refused U/S 15, novelty, non-patentable, inventions

1. Introduction

The three patentability criteria for any inventions are novelty, non-obviousness and industrial applicability. Few inventions fulfilled all three patentable criteria but still not patentable based on morality, public order or human rights considerations of each country. The Indian patent rights provide mutual benefits to the patent holder and user of patented medicine by considering socio economical welfare of the society [1–5].

As per the Indian Patent Act, Section 2 describes patentability criteria, whereas Sections 3 and 4 describe non-patentable inventions [6, 7].

2. Statistical database of patent filling in India

India has stringent patenting system, policies and enforcement system to protect IPR laws. Due to the TRIPs Agreement and amendments in the Indian Patent Act, technological innovations are encouraged and protected in India [8, 9]. As per Indian Patent Act, Section 15 deals with the power of the controller to refuse applications for grant of patent [10, 11].

As per WIPO statistical database September 2018, 45,379 patent applications were filed in India. Out of which 12,387 applications were granted and 29,789 applications were withdrawn or abandoned by the applicants. About 3203 patents were rejected on the ground of non-fulfillment of patentability criteria by the invention i.e. novelty, non – obviousness and industrial applicability or non-patentability criteria mentioned under Sections 3 and 4 of Indian Patent Act [12]. Indian Patent office rejected 1723 pharmaceutical patent applications between January 2009 and January 2017. Among them, 945, 466 and 1113 patents were rejected based on Sections 2(1)(j), 2(1)(ja) and Section 3, respectively. Ground for patents rejection may be one or more for one case [13]. As per Annual report of IPR 2017–2018 in India, number of patent applications examined, number of grant of patents and disposal of applications increased by 108.2, 32.5 and 57.6%, respectively as compared to 2016–2017 [14].

Sections 2 and 3 were the major reasons for the rejection of patents filled in India hence some case studies related to rejected patents are discussed in this chapter.

3. Case studies of rejected patents as per Section 2 of the Indian patent act

Section 2 describes the patentability criteria of inventions.

Section 2(j) Inventions means a new product or process which involves an inventing step and having industrial applicability;

Section 2(ja) Inventive step means invention should show technical advancement in comparison with the existing knowledge or having economic significance or both and invention must not be obvious to a person skilled in the art;

Section 2(1)(ac) "capable of industrial application", in relation to an invention, means that the invention is capable of being made or used in an industry [15, 16].

Case 1: Patent application entitled "Powder Formulation for Valganciclovir"

Patent application detail of case 1 is given in **Table 1**. The solid-state of valganciclovir hydrochloride exhibits acceptable physical, chemical, and light stability when stored under ambient conditions. The applicant prepared a liquid dosage form of valganciclovir hydrochloride for the pediatric patient as well as for patients who require flexibility. However, short-term stability data indicated that a liquid dosage form would be unstable for the anticipated shelf life of the product.

The applicants, therefore, focused on powder dosage forms, for later constitution with water, to provide reasonable shelf life for valganciclovir hydrochloride and the resulting (constituted) liquid dosage form. The formulation procedure was changed from a dry mix granulation to a wet mix granulation. Because valganciclovir hydrochloride is readily soluble under acidic conditions, a solid pharmaceutical dosage form must contain an organic acid present in an amount sufficient to solubilize and stabilize the valganciclovir hydrochloride in a predetermined amount of water for the proposed shelf life of the resulting (constituted) liquid dosage form. Hygroscopic organic acids were found to degrade the solid valganciclovir hydrochloride pharmaceutical dosage forms. Therefore, the applicant's claimed for a solid pharmaceutical dosage form which needs to be reconstituted in water before giving by the oral route. The product contained a therapeutically effective amount of drug (valganciclovir hydrochloride) and non-hygroscopic organic acid present in an amount sufficient to stabilize the drug in a predetermined amount of water. They claimed non-hygroscopic organic acid from the group consisting of fumaric acid, succinic acid, and adipic acid and amount of that acid was selected such to lower the pH of the constituted solution of valganciclovir hydrochloride to 3.8 or below.

The patent examiner argued that stability of valganciclovir below pH 3.8, using organic acid i.e. citric acid, is already reported in the prior art. Thus, there is no technical advancement achieved from the present invention. As the patent did not involve any inventive step, it was refused as per Section 15 on the ground of Section 2(1)(ja) of the Patent Act [17]. Examination report of the case can be studied in detail from Dynamic Patent Utilities: The Controller's Decision mentioned on website of Indian patent.

Application number	3350/CHENP/2009
Application status	Application Refused U/S 15
Application type	PCT NATIONAL PHASE APPLICATION
Date of filing	12/06/2009
Applicant name	F.HOFFMANN -LA ROCHE AG
Title of invention	POWDER FORMULATION FOR VALAGANCICLOVIR
Field of invention	PHARMACEUTICALS
PCT international application number	PCT/EP07/63151
PCT international filing date	03/12/2007
Priority date	13/12/2006
Request for examination date	12/06/2009
Publication date (u/s 11a)	21/08/2009
Reply to fer date	31/01/2015

Table 1.
Patent application detail for case 1 entitled powder formulation for valganciclovir.

4. Case studies of rejected patents as per Section 3 of the Indian patent act

Section 3 of Indian Patent Act describes non-patentable inventions.

Section 3(a). An invention which is frivolous or which claims anything obviously contrary to well established natural laws [16];

Example: Machine that gives more than 100% performance, A perpetual motion machine of the first generation which claimed to produce work without energy input which is contrary to law of thermodynamics (law of conservation of energy - energy can be neither created nor destroyed. It simply changes from one form to another).

Case 2: Patent application entitled "Gravity wheel–a perpetual motion machine"

This invention claimed to produce a powder delivery wheel, which is a perpetual motion machine working by gravitational force. This machine was claimed to be never stopped except human means. The claimed machine was a stationary engine of the unlimited size which was capable of continuous power output from gravity force and the gravity force can be universally available in any planet. The patent was abandoned under Section 21(1)on the ground of **Section 3(a)**as its performance was contrary to the law of thermodynamics. The patent application detail of case 2 is given in **Table 2** [17–19].

Section 3(b). An invention the primary or intended use or commercial exploitation of which could be contrary to public order or morality or which causes serious prejudice to human, animal or plant life or health or to the environment [16];

Application number	771/MAS/2002
Application type	Ordinary application
Date of filing	18/10/2002
Applicant name Title of invention	ShanmugasundramVnkatesan Gravity wheel -a perpetual motion machine
Field of invention	Mechanical engineering
Request for examination date	08/03/2004
Publication date (u/s 11a)	20/02/2009

Table 2.
Patent application detail for case 2 entitled "Gravy wheel – a perpetual motion machine."

Example: The Oncomouse, genetically modified to develop cancer for the purposes of medical research is not patentable because cancer can be transmitted to the public [20, 21].

Companies developing animal models are arguing for patenting of animal models as 1. Microorganisms are now patentable, 2. Animal models are very close to human disease and hence contribute significantly to the process of drug discovery, and 3. The patents provide a means of compensation for investment of millions of dollars in research which in turn stimulates further research and eventually better treatments. However, based on ground of morality and reproducibility the patent applications on animal models are not granted [22–24].

Case 3: Patent application entitled "Electro-Mechanical Sexual Stimulation Device"

Patent application detail of case 3 is listed in **Table 3**.

This patent deals with sexual stimulating vibrator and its intended use or commercial exploitation which is contrary to public order or morality hence the patent was rejected based on ground Section **3(b)**.

Claims 1 and 17 have been drafted as separate independent claims although they belong to the same category of claims. Said claims, therefore, lack clarity and conciseness under Section **10(5)** of the Act.

Claims lack Novelty and/or Inventive step of **u/s 2(1)(j)**of the Patent Act. The problem with the present invention is the fact that its distinguishing features depend on relative dimensions, i.e. they depend on the anatomy of the users.

Patent drafting errors in abstract and drawing were also mentioned in the report.

Applicant or applicant's agent neither appeared for the hearing on the scheduled date nor filed any written submission in response to the hearing notice [17].

Section 3(c). The mere discovery of a scientific principle or the formulation of an abstract theory or discovery of any living thing or non-living substance occurring in nature [16];

Example: Newton's Laws, Discovery of micro-organism, Raman effect and Theory of Relativity [25].

Application status	Application Refused U/S 15
Application number	4668/DELNP/2007
Application type	PCT NATIONAL PHASE APPLICATION
Date of filing	18/06/2007
Applicant name	STANDARD INOVATION CORPORATION
Title of invention	"ELECTRO-MECHANICAL SEXUAL STIMULATION DEVICE"
Field of invention	MECHANICAL ENGINEERING
PCT international application number	PCT/CA2005/001916
PCT international filing date	19/12/2005
Priority date	17/12/2004
Request for examination date	12/12/2008
Publication date (u/s 11a)	17/08/2007
Reply to fer date	18/03/2015

Table 3.
Patent application detail for case 3 for electro-mechanical sexual stimulation device.

Application status	Application Refused U/S 15
Application number	6541/CHENP/2008
Application type	PCT NATIONAL PHASE APPLICATION
Date of filing	02/12/2008
Applicant name	LG LIFE SCIENCES LTD.
Title of invention	"GENE FAMILY (LBFL313) ASSOCIATED WITH PANCREATIC CANCER"
Field of invention	BIOTECHNOLOGY
PCT international application number	PCT/KR2007/002848

Table 4.
Patent application details for case 4—gene family (LBLF313) associated with pancreatic cancer.

Case 4: Patent application entitled "Gene Family (LBFL313) Associated with Pancreatic Cancer"

Patent application detail of case 4 is given in **Table 4**.

The invention relates generally to the changes in gene expression in human pancreatic adenocarcinoma. The invention relates specifically to a human gene family which is differentially expressed in cancerous pancreatic tissues compared to corresponding non-cancerous pancreatic tissues.

The hearing was offered on 10th April, 2014 intimating the following outstanding objections:

1. The applicant used 777 base pairs and in prior art it was 764 base pairs. The claimed sequence ID having extra 13 base pairs but the applicant does not show any advantages due to these extra 13 nucleotide base pairs. Further, it is very much possible that the 764 base pairs may retain the natural property.

2. Objection 2 of FER is not met as amended claim 6(Production of Polyclonal Anti-LBFL313 Antibody) is directed to a host cell, which is not allowable u/s 3 (j) of the Act.

3. Objection 3 of FER is not met as the amended claims 1–4 & 7–8 are not patentable as the subject matter of claim 1–4 are directed to isolated nucleic acid/PP sequence from human genomic DNA, which is considered to be an isolated non-living substance occurring in nature, is not allowable to be patented under the provision of Section 3(c) of the Act in the absence of any clear cut recombination in these molecules. The same observation applies to the subject-matter of claim 7–8, which encodes polypeptides from the isolated nucleic acid of claims 1 i.e. sequence ID No-2.It already stated that said nucleotide sequence is isolated from nature, the polypeptide, which encodes by them, would be available in the source from which the said nucleic acid is isolated. Consequently, the subject-matter of claims 7–8 also falls within the scope of Section 3 (c) of the Act. 3.

4. Amended claims 7 and 8 does not sufficiently define the invention, Claims should contain all the essential feature of the polypeptide which refers by its amino acid sequence ID, not by its nucleotide sequence ID. As stated above the said claim should be defined by its essential technical features, if any, otherwise it is not acceptable in the present form.

5. While filing amended claims the applicant should at the same time bring the description into conformity with the amended claims. Care should be taken during revision, not to add subject matter, which extends beyond the content of the application as originally filed.

6. In reply to the hearing notice, the Applicant's agent submitted a faxed letter dated 9th April, 2014 with the following statement: "We have been informed by our client that they are not interested in pursuing this application further and accordingly we will not be attending the hearing scheduled for April 10, 2014". Considering the Applicant's interest of not to pursue the instant application, it is hereby decided that the requirements communicated in the hearing notice are still outstanding and hence, the application was refused for grant of a patent [17].

Section 3(d). Section 3(d) of the Patents Act 1970 was as follows: The simple discovery of any new attributes or new utility for a known substance or of the mere utilization of a known method, machine or apparatus except if such known method results in a new product or employs at least one new reactant;

Section 3(d) of the Patents Act 1970 was amended in 2005 as follows: the simple discovery of a new form of a known substance which fails to result in the improvement of the known efficacy of that substance or the simple discovery of any new attribute or new utility for a known substance or of the mere application of a known method, machine or apparatus unless such known method results in a new product or employs at least one new reactant. Explanation—For the purposes of this clause, salts, esters, ethers, polymorphs, metabolites, pure form, particle size, isomers, mixtures of isomers, complexes, combinations and other derivatives of known substance shall be anticipated to be the same substance, unless they vary significantly in properties with consideration to efficacy [26, 27].

Case 5: Patent application for the "beta crystallineform of the imatinib mesylate salt" by Novartis

As per Trade-Related Aspects of Intellectual Property Rights (TRIPS) agreement, India has started providing product patent After 1 January 1995 [28, 29]. Novartis filed patent applications of pharmaceutically acceptable salts of a drug - "imatinib" and the patents were granted in the USA. After this Novartis filled patents application which claimed for "beta crystalline" form of imatinib mesylate and a patent was granted in the USA and other countries. The Indian Patent Office rejected the patent based on the ground of failure to promise novelty and non-obviousness. They said it is a modified version of an existing drug hence on the ground of Section 3(d) the patent cannot be granted. Novartis argued that beta crystalline form is a polymorph of imatinib mesylate and it showed better flow property, improvement in thermodynamic stability, reduced hygroscopicity and augmented bioavailability. At last, the Supreme Court declared that although the beta crystalline form of imatinib mesylate enhanced the bioavailability of the drug, it did not prove enhancement of efficacy hence it was found to be non-patentable under **Section 3(d)** in India [30, 31]. The same product patent was granted in USA but rejected in India as patentability criteria have been provided in TRIPS but their interpretation may vary from country to country [32]. In India, the many aspects of intellectual property rights are dealt with in particular legislations enacted by the Parliament [33].

In 2015, the patent of BoehringerIngelheim Pharma GmbH & Co for drug "Spiriva®" was granted even after pre-grant opposition by one domestic firm. Cipla proceeded for post grant approval and the patent was revoked [34].

Section 3(d) has created a significant impact in determining the patentability of pharmaceutical derivatives in India [35]. Indian Patent Office opposes the concept of "evergreening" which is a practice of inventors of patented products for extending their monopoly period by various strategies (for example over associated delivery systems, or new pharmaceutical mixtures, etc.) [36, 37].

Section 3(e). A product obtained by a mere admixture resulting only in the aggregation of the properties of the components thereof or a process for producing such substance [16];

Case 6: Patent application entitled "Sterile Pharmaceutical Composition"

Patent application detail of case 6 is given in **Table 5**.

The applicant's claim 1 includes a sterile pharmaceutical composition including a water-insoluble anticancer agent and a pharmaceutically acceptable carrier, albumin. The ratio (w/w) of albumin to the anticancer agent was 1:1 to 9:1. The applicant claimed that the size of particles was less than 200 nm. Claims 2 to 12 were dependent claims which depend on claim 1.

The opposition was filed by M/s Natco Pharma Ltd., Hyderabad. Based on submitted documents and hearing from both the parties, the patent application was refused under Section 15 based on ground section u/s 2(1)(j), u/s 3(e) and u/s 10 of the Patents Act, 1970 on 24/07/2009.

The applicant filed an appeal in 'Intellectual Property Appellate Board' (IPAB) against the said decision. The Hon'ble IPAB again reconsiders the case on dated 20/01/2014.

Aplication status	**Application Refused U/S 15**
Application number	2899/DELNP/2005
Application type	PCT NATIONAL PHASE APPLICATION
Date of filing	29/06/2005
Applicant name	AMERICAN BIOSCIENCES, INC.
Title of invention	STERILE PHARMACEUTICAL COMPOSITION
Field of invention	BIO-CHEMISTRY
PCT international application number	PCT/US2003/038941
PCT international filing date	09/12/2003
Priority date	09/12/2002
Request for examination date	30/11/2005
Publication date (u/s 11a)	13/04/2007
Reply to fer date	05/01/2009

Table 5.
Patent application details for case entitled Sterile Pharmaceutical Composition.

Second representation was considered by Assistant Controller as revised fresh representation and not the continuous hearing as the applicants have amended the claims 1 day before the hearing and opponent came to know it on the day of hearing (09/04/2009).

After hearings, the patent was refused on the ground of u/s **2(1)(j)**, **3(d)** and **3(e)** of the Patents Act, 1970. The specifications were also insufficient so rejection was also on the ground of u/s **10** of the Patents Act, 1970 [17].

Case 7: Patent application entitled "Gel Useful for The Delivery of Ophthalmic Drugs"

Patent application detail of case 7 is reported in **Table 6**. The application was rejected by Indian Patent Office of Sigma-Tau Industrie Farmaceutiche Riunite S.P.A of Italy as it does not mate the requirements of Section 2(1)(j), Section 3(d), Section 3(e) and Section 3(n) of the Patents Act, 1970. The claims were aimed at a solid powder comprising a mixture of (a) a carboxy vinyl polymer as a gelling agent; (b) a buffer; (c) a saccharide, (d) one or more drugs used for the treatment of diseases of the eye. However, the Controller was dissatisfied by applicant's reply to the FER and sustained objection therein and gave the applicant's a chance to be heard.

The Controller sustained the objections that the amendments to claim 1 did not hold as per Section 59 (1) read with Section 57(2) of the Patent Act; revised claims were not novel, obvious and did not comprise an inventive step w.r.t. cited prior art documents; the revised claims were unacceptable under Section 3(d), Section 3(e) and Section 3(n) of the Patents Act, 1970 and last of all a few of the claims were ambiguous.

After conducting trial, the Controller accepted the agent's submissions that the amended claim 1 contained by the scope of the firstly filed PCT claims and hence was in consonance with the provisions of Section 59(1) and 57(2) of the Indian Patents Act. Further, claims remonstrated under Section 3(n) were also deleted.

With reference to Section 2(1)(j), the Controller in his verdict stated that the composition of the ophthalmic preparation (solid powder) of the claimed invention was not novel since all the ingredients were unveiled in the prior art, hence, the product did not meet the criteria as a "new" product. Further, the inventive step is missing in the drug delivery system claimed as no therapeutic efficacy

Application status	Application Refused U/S 15
Application number	1314/KOLNP/2009
Application type	PCT NATIONAL PHASE APPLICATION
Date of filing	08/04/2009
Applicant name	SIGMA-TAU INDUSTRIE FARMACEUTICHE RIUNITE S.P.A.
Title of invention	GEL USEFUL FOR THE DELIVERY OF OPHTHALMIC DRUGS
Field of invention	PHARMACEUTICALS
PCT international application number	PCT/EP2007/062929
PCT international filing date	28/11/2007
Priority date	22/12/2006
Request for examination date	19/11/2010
Publication date (u/s 11a)	29/05/2009
Reply to fer date	13/05/2015

Table 6.
Patent application details for case 7 – gel useful for the delivery of ophthalmic drugs.

was exhibited. Creating a drug delivery system (powder or gel) of different well known components and verifying release rate of drug (amount of drug released after 30 min to 6 h) are regular experimentation carried out by medicinal chemist or trained artisan. The rejection was on the basis of Section 2(1)(j). Merely showing enhancement in bioavailability and retention time of the drug system was not adequate to evade the requirements of Section 3(d) and data indicative of the therapeutic efficacy was needed for the product. In absence of such data, the drug delivery system as claimed was precluded under **Section 3(d)** [17–38].

Section 3(f). The mere arrangement or re-arrangement or duplication of known devices each functioning independently of one another in a known way [39];

Section 3(g). Omitted by the Patents (Amendment) Act, 2002.

Section 3(g) was as follows: 'a method or process of testing applicable during the process of manufacture for rendering the machine, apparatus, or other equipment more efficient or for the improvement or restoration of the existing machine, apparatus or other equipment or for the improvement or control of manufacture'. Omission of this section widens the scope of patentability [40].

Section 3(h). A method of agriculture or horticulture(Note: But Agricultural Equipment are patentable) [16].

Case 8: Patent application entitled "Process for the Production of Recombinant Proteins Using Carnivorous Plants"

Patent application detail of the case is given in **Table 7**. The applicant claimed that carnivorous plant can be used as a medium for the production of the protein of interest. The applicant claimed a process in which plant was genetically modified by transformation and protein was expressed in the digestive secretion of the genetically modified plant. Hence, this patent application was refused under Section

Application number	2245/DELNP/2009
Application status	Application Refused U/S 15
Application type Date of filing	PCT national phase application 06/04/2009
Applicant name	Plant advanced technologies PAT SAS
Title of invention	"Process for the production of recombinant proteins using carnivorous plants"
Field of invention	Biotechnology
PCT international application number	PCT/EP2007/058950
PCT international filing date Priority date	29/08/2007 04/10/2006
Request for examination date	07/09/2010
Publication date (u/s 11a)	12/06/2009
Reply to FER date	01/10/2014

Table 7.
Patent application detail for case 8 entitled "Process for the production of recombinant proteins using carnivorous plants."

15 based on ground of **Section 3(j)**. Cultivation of plant, growing of the plant, harvesting of fluid from the trap was considered as a method of agriculture hence it was also not a patentable invention as per **Section 3(h)** [17].

Section 3(i). Any process for the medicinal, surgical, curative, prophylactic, diagnostic, therapeutic or other treatment of human beings or any process for a similar treatment of animals to render them free of disease or to increase their economic value or that of their products [16];

Case 9: Patent application entitled "Method for Hybrid Gastro-Jejunostomy"

Table 8 enlists patent application detail of case 9.

The invention is related to methods for joining one piece to the tissue to another piece of tissue. In one embodiment, the method can include inserting an applier device having an actuation portion into a first body lumen through a natural body orifice, forming a first opening in a first piece of tissue within the first lumen and a second opening in a second piece of tissue defining a portion of a second lumen adjacent to the first piece of tissue, and inserting the applier device through the first and second openings such that the actuation portion is between the first and second piece of tissue. The method can further include deploying a fastener into the first and second pieces of tissue through the actuation portion of the applier device, thereby joining the first and second pieces of tissue to form an anastomosis between the first and second lumens.

The patent controller said that as claims 1–10 recite "A method for joining tissue", which is a surgical method. The subject matter is excluded from patentability according to **Section 3(i)** of the prevailing Act [17, 41].

Section 3(j). Plants and animals in whole or any part thereof other than micro-organisms but including seeds, varieties, and species and essentially biological processes for production or propagation of plants and animals [16];

Application status	**Application Refused U/S 15**
Application number	**447/KOL/2007**
Application type	**CONVENTIONAL APPLICATION**
Date of filing	**22/03/2007**
Applicant name	**ETHICON ENDO-SURGERY, INC**
Title of invention	**METHOD FOR HYBRID GASTRO-JEJUNOSTOMY**
Field of invention	**BIO-MEDICAL ENGINEERING**
Priority date	**23/03/2006**
Request for examination date	**23/03/2010**
Publication date (u/s 11a)	**12/10/2007**
Reply to fer date	**04/12/2015**

Table 8.
Patent application details for case 9 – method for hybrid gastro-jejunostomy.

Example: Clones and new varieties of plants, a process for the production of plants or animals, if it consists entirely of natural phenomena such as crossing or selection i.e., essentially biological process are not patentable. However, processes or methods of preparing genetically modified organisms are patentable [42, 43].

Case 8 has covered the case study of rejection of patent as per Section 3(j).

Section 3(k). A mathematical or business method or a computer program per se or algorithms [16];

Example: Computer program by itself or as a record on a carrier (Note: Combination of hardware and software is patentable).

In India, the Patent Amendment Act 2005 sought to introduce software patents. The amendment proposed in the Patent Amendment Act 2005 for Clause 3(k) was, "a computer program per se other than its technical application to industry or a combination with hardware; a mathematical method or a business method or algorithms." However, this amendment was rejected by the Indian Parliament, which chose to retain Clause 3(k) as it is [44–46].

Case 10: Patent application entitled "Chaos Theoretical Exponent Value Calculation System"

Patent application detail of case 10 is provided in **Table 9**.

The Appellant's invention is about the system which can analyze a time series signal using a method based on Chaos Theory and calculation of a chaos theoretical exponent value (CTEV). The conventional CTEV system was not calculating the temporarily changing dynamics as a significant value. In the present invention, the inventor proposed a system which can process at a high speed and on a real-time basis to calculate a CTEV even from a time series signal which includes noises. The average CTEV can also be calculated in a shorter time of two decimal orders or more.

As per First Examination Report (FER) of the Patent Office, the invention was not found to be patentable on the ground of clause (k) of Section 3 and Section 2(1)(j) of the Indian Patent Act, 1970. A response to the first examination report (FER) was filed by the applicant on 9th April 2008. The Deputy Controller rejected a patent under Section 15 by declaring that the invention still falls under **Section 3(k)** of the Patents Act.

APPLICATION STATUS	Application Refused U/S 15
Invention Title	"A CHAOS THEORETICAL EXPONENT VALUE CALCULATION SYSTEM"
Publication Number	16/2007
Publication Date	20/04/2007
Publication Type	INA
Application Number	3624/DELNP/2005
Application Filing Date	17/08/2005
Priority Number	Japan2003-045386
Priority Country	Japan
Priority Date	24/02/2003
Field Of Invention	ELECTRONICS
Classification (IPC)	G06F 17/10
Inventors	SHIOMI KAKUICHI and KOBAYASHI SUSUMU

Table 9.
Patent application details for case 10 on A Chaos Theoretical Exponent Value Calculation System.

The Manual of Patent Office Practice and Procedure provides a reason as to why mathematical or business methods are not considered patentable.

"Mathematical methods" includes mental skill as they are not patentable. Mathematical methods are used for writing algorithms and computer programs for different applications are also not patentable although the applicants may argue that the said invention is of technical advancement, not the mathematical model [17, 47, 48]."

Section 3(l). A literary, dramatic, musical or artistic work or any other esthetic creation whatsoever including cinematographic works and television productions [16] (Note: These subject matters fall under the copyright and related right protection);

Example: Prepare a drama from a book.

The patents protect ideas, not just expressions of them.

Section 3(m). A mere scheme or rule or method of performing mental act or method of playing a game;

Example: Method for solving a crossword puzzle, Method of learning a language

Section 3(n). A presentation of information;

Example: Spoken words, symbols, diagrams [49].

Section 3(o). The topography of integrated circuits [50];

Three-dimensional configuration of the electronic circuits used in microchips and semiconductor chips is not patentable because protection of Layout Designs of Integrated Circuits is governed separately under the Semiconductor Integrated Circuit Lay-out Designs Act, 2000 [51].

Section 3(p). An invention which in effect, is traditional knowledge or which is an aggregation or duplication of known properties of a traditionally known component or components.

Use of turmeric, neem, tulsi, etc. is not patentable as it is traditionally known. Although, if someone develops a medicine from tradition plant, for example. Ointment having an active ingredient that is an extract from leaf of the plant, is patentable [52].

Case 11: Patent application entitled "device used for manually hauling agricultural produce"

One device to collect agricultural produce was patented by DhanpatSheth. He made this device so flexible that it can fit to persons of varying height and size. Initially this patent was granted but afterward it was revoked as Nil Kamal Plastic Crates Ltd. sui him in Himachal Pradesh High Court. The patent was revoked on the ground of lack of novelty (Section 2(1)(ja)), mere duplication of traditionally known component known as "Kilta" **(Section 3(p))** and mere replacement of raw material as plastic has been used in the patented product whereas bamboo was used in kilta [Section 3(d)] [53].

5. Non-patentable inventions as per Section 4 of Indian Patent Act

No patent shall be granted in respect of an invention relating to atomic energy falling within sub-section (1) of Section 20 of the Atomic Energy Act, 1962 (33 of 1962) [54–57].

6. Conclusions

The patent is granted to the inventor to encourage innovations by providing exclusive rights to the owner for the limited period of time and to reveal his invention for propagation of knowledge and welfare of the society. Intellectual property protection is of larger importance to the researcher and research industries as the research and development process is expensive and time-consuming. In the present chapter, the authors have used a case study approach to explain patentability criteria and non-patentable inventions as per the Indian Patent Act. By disseminating the knowledge on patentability and non-patentability criteria, the author will guide the researchers for answering the question of whether the research which they are doing is patentable or not? It will save time, money and manpower for the patent drafting, application, and examination process as well as promote researchers for doing patentable research.

Conflict of interest

The authors declare no conflict of interest.

Author details

Hetal Patel*† and Sandesh Lodha†
Maliba Pharmacy College, Uka Tarsadia University, Surat, India

*Address all correspondence to: hetalppatel1986@gmail.com

†These authors contributed equally.

References

[1] Fialho AM, Chakrabarty AM. Patent controversies and court cases: Cancer diagnosis, therapy and prevention. Cancer Biology & Therapy. 2012;**13**(13): 1229-1234. DOI: 10.4161/cbt.21958

[2] Jauhar A, Narnaulia S. Patenting life the American, European and Indian way. Journal of Intellectual Property Rights. 2010;**15**:55-65

[3] The Patent Office, India. Manual of Patent Practice and Procedure. 2008. Available from: http://www.ipindia.nic.in/writereaddata/Portal/IPOGuidelinesManuals/1_59_1_15-wo-ga-34-china.pdf [Accessed: 05 May 2019]

[4] Prifti V. The limits of "ordre public" and "morality" for the patentability of human embryonic stem cell inventions. Journal of World Intellectual Property. 2018;**22**(1-2):2-15. DOI: 10.1111/jwip.12109

[5] The Office of Controller General of Patents, Designs and Trademarks. Manual of Patent Practice and Procedure. 2011. Available from: http://www.ipindia.nic.in/writereaddata/Portal/IPOGuidelinesManuals/1_28_1_manual-of-patent-office-practice_and-procedure.pdf [Accessed: 02 June 2019]

[6] Tiwari R, Tiwari G, Rai AK, Srivastawa B. Management of intellectual property rights in India: An updated review. Journal of Natural Science, Biology and Medicine. 2011;**2**(1):2. DOI: 10.4103/0976-9668.82307

[7] Tulasi GK, Rao BS. A detailed study of patent system for protection of inventions. Indian Journal of Pharmaceutical Sciences. 2008;**70**(5):547. DOI: 10.4103/0250-474X.45390

[8] Srinivasa RY. Intellectual property rights in India: Significance of patents. SCIPR-2014. pp. 121-134. Available from: http://eprints.rclis.org/24966/ [Accessed: 10 June 2019]

[9] Chaudhry S. Product v. Process Patent in India. SSRN. 2011. Available from: https://ssrn.com/abstract=1758064 [Accessed: 10 July 2019]

[10] Khurana & Khurana IP advocates and Attorneys. Various Options after Patent Application Being Rejected In India. Available from: https://www.khuranaandkhurana.com/2019/12/17/various-options-after-patent-application-being-rejected-in-india/ [Accessed: 19 December 2019]

[11] Jain S, Jain RK. Patents: Procedures and Practices. New Delhi: Universal Law Publishing Co. Pvt. Ltd.; 2011. p. 113

[12] World Intellectual Property Indicators. 2018. Available from: https://www.wipo.int/edocs/pubdocs/en/wipo_pub_941_2018.pdf [Accessed: 03 March 2019]

[13] Ali F, Rajagopal S, Mustafa M, Prabhu C. Rejected in India: What the Indian Patent Office Got Right on Pharmaceuticals Patent Applications. 2016. Bengaluru: AzimPremji University; 2017. pp. 19-24

[14] The Office of Controller General of Patents, Designs, Trademarks and Geographical Indications. Annual Report of IPR. 2017-2018. Available from: http://www.ipindia.nic.in/writereaddata/Portal/IPOAnnualReport/1_110_1_Annual_Report_2017-18_English.pdf [Accessed: 03 April 2019]

[15] The Office of the controller General of Patents, Designs and Trademarks. Guidelines for Examination of Patent Applications in the Field of Pharmaceuticals. 2014. Available from: http://www.ipindia.nic.in/writereaddata/Portal/IPOGuidelinesManuals/1_37_1_3-

guidelines-for-examination-of-patent-applications-pharmaceutical.pdf. [Accessed: 03 January 2019]

[16] Intellectual Property India. The Patents Act, 1970. 2017. Available from: http://ipindia.nic.in/writereaddata/Portal/IPOAct/1_113_1_The_Patents_Act_1970_-_Updated_till_23_June_2017.pdf [Accessed: 06 April 2019]

[17] Indian Patent Advanced Search System. Available from: http://ipindiaservices.gov.in/publicsearch [Accessed: 10 April 2019]

[18] Official Journal of the Patent Office. 2009. Available from: http://ipindia.nic.in/ipr/patent/journal_archieve/journal_2009/pat_arch_022009/official_journal_20022009_part_i.pdf [Accessed: 12 December 2018]

[19] Wadlow C. Patents for perpetual motion machines. Journal of Intellectual Property Law and Practice. 2007;**2**(3): 136-144. DOI: 10.1093/jiplp/jpl242

[20] World Intellectual Property Organization. Bioethics and Patent Law: The Case of the Oncomouse. 2006. Available from: https://www.wipo.int/wipo_magazine/en/2006/03/article_0006.html [Accessed: 02 February 2018]

[21] Vogt TF. OncoMouse®. 2001. Available from: https://www.sciencedirect.com/topics/biochemistry-genetics-and-molecular-biology/oncomouse [Accessed: 09 July 2018]

[22] Kandhare AD, Raygude KS, Ghosh P, Gosavi TP, Bodhankar SL. Patentability of animal models: India and the globe. International Journal of Pharmaceutical and Biological Archive. 2011;**2**(4):1024-1032

[23] Porter D. Ethical scores for animal experiments. Nature. 1992;**356**:101-102. DOI: 10.1038/356101a0

[24] Macer D. Shaping Genes: Ethics, Law and Science of Using New Genetic Technology in Medicine and Agriculture. New Zealand: Eubios Ethics Institute; 1990. pp. 127-143

[25] Gupta S, Bansal R, Pal S, Sodhi S, Brar G, Bansal R. Patent: A journey from idea to patent. Innoriginal: International Journal of Science. 2018;**5**(6):5-11

[26] Mani VS, Srivastava D, Chakrapani M, Erstling J. The India patent system: A decade in review. Cybaris. 2017;**8**(1):1-61

[27] Basheer S, Reddy TP. The efficacy of Indian patent law: Ironing out the creases in Section 3 (d). SCRIPTed. 2008;**5**:232

[28] Sampat BN, Shadlen KC. Indian pharmaceutical patent prosecution: The changing role of Section 3 (d). PLoS One. 2018;**13**(4):e0194714

[29] Koshy S. The effect of TRIPS on Indian patent law: A pharmaceutical industry perspective. Journal of Science & Technology Law. 1995;**1**:123

[30] Adams & Adams. Novartis A.G. V Union of India - The Gleevec Case and Evergreening. 2013. Available from: https://www.lexology.com/library/detail.aspx?g=97441a81-b27b-43aa-a8ee-bf2522339cf0 [Accessed: 15 April 2019]

[31] Gabble R, Kohler JC. To patent or not to patent? The case of Novartis cancer drug Glivec in India. Globalization and Health. 2014;**10**(3): 1-6. DOI: 10.1186/1744-8603-10-3

[32] Roderick P, Pollock AM. India's patent laws under pressure. Lancet. 2012;**380**(9846):2-4. DOI: 10.1016/S0140-6736(12)61513-X

[33] Bhat SR. Innovation and intellectual property rights law—An overview of the Indian law. IIMB Management Review.

2018;**30**(1):51-61. DOI: 10.1016/j.iimb.2017.12.003

[34] Horner R. The impact of patents on innovation, technology transfer and health: A pre-and post-TRIPs analysis of India's pharmaceutical industry. New Political Economy. 2014;**19**(3):384-406. DOI: 10.1080/13563467.2013.796446

[35] Arora S, Chaturvedi R. Section 3 (d): Implications and key concerns for pharmaceutical sector. Journal of Intellectual Property Rights. 2016;**21**(1):16-26

[36] Dwivedi G, Hallihosur S, Rangan L. Evergreening: A deceptive device in patent rights. Technology in Society. 2010;**32**(4):324-330. DOI: 10.1016/j.techsoc.2010.10.009

[37] Basant R, Srinivasan S. Intellectual property protection in India and implications for health innovation: Emerging perspectives. Innovation and Entrepreneurship in Health. 2016;**3**:57-68. DOI: 10.2147/IEH.S56236

[38] Kapoor A. Patent Office Decision on Certain Provisions of Indian Patents Act, 1970. 2016. Available from: https://www.lexorbis.com/patent-office-decision-on-certain-provisions-of-indian-patents-act-1970/ [Accessed: 13 April 2019]

[39] Azmi IM, Alavi R. TRIPS, patents, technology transfer, foreign direct investment and the pharmaceutical industry in Malaysia. Journal of World Intellectual Property. 2005;**4**(6):947-997. DOI: 10.1111/j.1747-1796.2001.tb00144.x

[40] Nair GG. Impact of TRIPS on Indian pharmaceutical industry. Journal of Intellectual Property Rights. 2008;**13**(5):432-441

[41] Malhotra D, Lakshmikumaran M. Scope of Section 3(i): An Analysis on Diagnostic Methods of Treatment. Available from: https://www.lakshmisri.com/News-and-Publications/Publications/Articles/IPR/scope-of-section-3i-an-analysis-on-diagnostic-methods-of-treatment [Accessed: 14 April 2019]

[42] Non patentable invention, Section 3(j). https://www.slideshare.net/pedprasad/non-patentable-inventions-10168269 [Accessed: 03 December 2019]

[43] Radhakrishnan R, Balasubramanian S. Intellectual Property Rights: Text and Cases. New Delhi: Excell Books; 2008. p. 75

[44] Chingale R, Rao SD. Software patent in India: A comparative judicial and empirical overview. Journal of Intellectual Property Rights. 2015;**20**:210-222

[45] The United States Patent and Trademark Office. 2018. Available from: https://www.uspto.gov/web/offices/pac/mpep/s2106.html [Accessed: 09 August 2019]

[46] The Center for Internet and Society. Guidelines for Examination of Computer Related Inventions: Mapping the Stakeholders Response. Available from: https://cis-india.org/a2k/blogs/guidelines-for-examination-of-computer-related-inventions [Accessed: 14 June 2019]

[47] Bananal P. Section 3(Ka): A Decision on a Patent Application Related to Mathematical Method. 2013. Available from: https://www.bananaip.com/ip-news-center/section-3ka-a-decision-on-a-patent-application-related-to-mathematical-methods/[Accessed: 11 April 2019]

[48] Inventree. Patenting Mathematical Methods. 2013. Available from: https://www.invntree.com/blogs/patenting-mathematical-methods#more-526 [Accessed: 12 April 2019]

[49] Sigh R, Sinha S, Kumar S. Unfolding Intellectual Property Rights: A Practical Patent Guide for Researchers, Academicians and Start-Ups. Chennai: Notion Press; 2019

[50] The Office of Controller General of the Patents, Designs and Trademarks. Guidelines for Examination of Computer Related Inventions. 2017. Available from: http://www.ipindia.nic.in/writereaddata/Portal/IPOGuidelinesManuals/1_86_1_Revised__Guidelines_for_Examination_of_Computer-related_Inventions_CRI__.pdf [Accessed: 03 January 2019]

[51] Heera NS, Prabhavathi N. Non patentability inventions under the Patent Act 1970 – An analysis. IJSRP. 2016;**6**(12):124-129

[52] Chopra S. Indian Patenting System and Patent Agent Examination. Chennai: Notion Press

[53] Patnaik P. The Himachal Pradesh High Court Revokes Patent Grant Invoking Section 3(p). Available from: https://spicyip.com/2018/07/the-himachal-pradesh-high-court-revokes-patent-grant-invoking-section-3p.html [Accessed: 25 February 2019]

[54] Goel D, Parashar S. IPR, Biosafety and Bioethics. Noida: Dorling Kindersley Publishing Pvt Ltd; 2013. pp. 66-68

[55] Topic 3 - Chapter II.B Legal Requirements for Patentability. WIPO. 2017. Available from: https://www.wipo.int/edocs/mdocs/africa/en/wipo_pat_hre_15/wipo_pat_hre_15_t_3.pdf [Accessed: 06 April 2019]

[56] Verma M. Inventions Not Patentable in India – Non Patentable Inventions under the Indian Patent Act 2019. Available from: https://blog.ipleaders.in/non-patentable-inventions/ [Accessed: 28 March 2019]

[57] Kumaran NV. Non Patentable Inventions in India. 2014. Available from: https://www.slideshare.net/altacitglobal/non-patentable-inventions-39085199 [Accessed: 08 March 2019]

Chapter 4

Patent Application Preparation and Filing

Mohamad Taleuzzaman and Iqra Rahat

Abstract

The issuance of a patent by the government office is basically done by a patent application record that is an agreement between the inventor and the government office. Correspondingly, a patent application is in many ways like a contract. Preparation of a standard patent application is curious because it sets out in a transparent way, the terms and condition by which the patent owner and others will be bound. These criteria of the patent application make it different from writing a scientific paper. The technical subject matter that is available in the patent application have bear some similarities to a scientific or technical paper, although it does not usually need to rise to the level of a blueprint for making the invention protected by the patent. Public officials of government take a long time to review the patent as examiners and judges and business partners. Therefore it is necessary that a patent application should be drafted with these important audiences in mind. The parts of the patent application typically include the Background, Summary, Detailed Description and Drawings, Claims, and Abstract. The patent agent is unlikely to draft the patent application in this order and should ordinarily draft the claims first.

Keywords: application, patent, filing, government official

1. Introduction

From last many decades, national and international organizations have made to try with best efforts to homogenize the laws governing intellectual property. To attempt the standardization, the little bit restriction always comes it is either infrastructure or capital, especially in pharmaceutical industries. That is the reason a continuous tension exists in multinational pharmaceutical companies (MNCs) in developing nations. Intellectual always give their maximum efforts to overcome these problems which the easier business environment worldwide. In the World Trade Organization (WTO) earlier, India does not recognize product patents in pharmaceutical. Without product patents, Indian pharmaceutical companies were able to agitate countless generic drugs. In the world, India contributes to leading manufactures in generic drugs. Results of these are that the relative moderate of these generic drugs as compared to patented drugs not only provide chief drugs but also made India the de facto pharmacy for many developing countries [1].

The basic object of the Intellectual Property Right (IPR) to deliver unquestionable absolute right over the fabrication of the mind and to finite exploit it for a fixed duration of time, in order to enable them to gather commercial benefits from their creative efforts.

The application and filing is the first step to patent the drugs for trade world-wide, which provide a platform for the exclusively business without a doubt or question regarding the quality of drugs and its efficacy. The evolution of innovation can explain by the diagram [1, 2] (**Figure 1**).

The Intellectual property known as IP, gives the right to the people to own their innovation, invention, and creativity in the same way as they own their physical property. In can cover the different forms like **Figure 2**.

In a general way, IPR plays an important role in two principal areas which impact in the Pharmaceutical Industry. First, the pricing and access where the focus on securing competitive marketing which creates the problems in the pricing of drugs. Second, is an issue related research and development incentive, which is the marketing of the new medicines and its price? The consequence of IPRs on R&D expenditure and its grant across the different disease, countries, and organization.

The IPRs patent application preparation and filing, the right of legal work it might be sold, uses, offers for sale and/or imports any technology can be protected by the IPR documents, that gives the power to trade in an authentic way. The inventors are completely satisfy if he/she has legal documents of IPR. For this, there is a process which is followed by the regulatory bodies in every country.

Before, the patent approved a step that is called the provisional application in some country like the United State of America. The provisional patent application duration is 1 year and it provides smoothly, rapidly and affordably got the pending status. The patent is ownership for creativity or innovation product protected by the patent's claims. Before revealing the innovative idea the patent application filing is necessary. The patent should persuade all legal requirements it covers like time limits related to how long the invention was disclosed to the public. Before filing a patent application if the inventions communicate in public it will be denied without any grace period [2–4].

A detailed audit is a must before filing the application itself. From this consequence the broader concept or the principle which are important for the public and it will be drafted in very well manner. The application prepares on the facts of the principle or new idea that is highlighted in the drafts, its importance, and scope in that respective field.

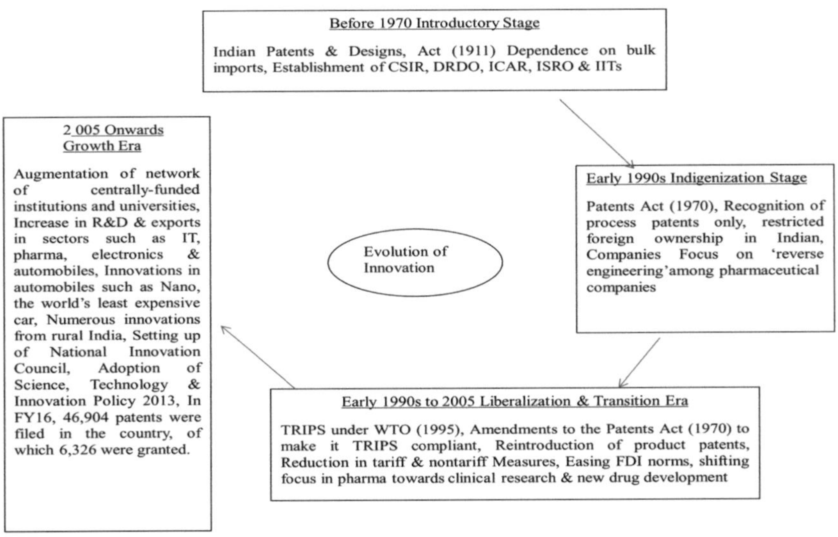

Figure 1.
Evaluation of IPR.

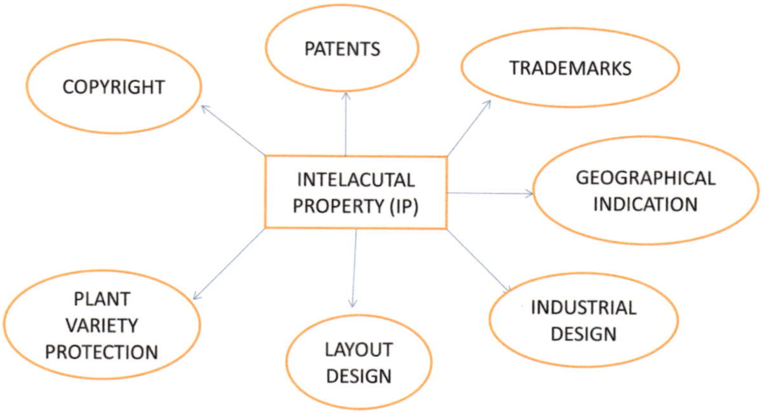

Figure 2.
Different types of IPR.

In facts, patents are "regional" its consideration only on those countries where they have been applied for and granted. Every country has its own legal office where it documented that the patent applicability is worldwide or it is only to its own country. Patent acceptability and its innovative idea can be challenged and if it's finding any demerits should be rejected. To maintain the discipline and hierarchy in the legal office the team must examine the whole content of the application properly, so further it is no possibility of challenge.

After World War II, The international pharmaceutical Industry grows rapidly. The demands of antibiotics create a challenge for the company in the research and development division. As the year gone following the wars saw the rapid growth in number industry and establish as MNCs by infiltration in many countries. The headquarters of such MNCs established in developed countries from where business manage. Due to the lack of trained skill human source in developing countries as well as a necessary technology for which big capitals are required to developed a new molecule make not a possibility such corporation.

After independence India was faced many challenges like as one of the poorest countries in the world, with also increase problems in the health sector to overcome this government takes any initiative for the amendment in patent law which make the business easy. For this government of India appoint two committees one is the Patent Enquire Committee (1948–1950) and the Patents Revision Committee (1957–1959). The object was to review the patent law and ensure that the patent system was more conducive and interest for the nation.

India by 2020 reached as a global leader in the field of the pharmaceutical industry. This country established as a leader of generic drugs manufacturers. India passed its first patent law in 1856 under the British colonial rule and it is based on the British Patent Law of 1852, here inventors have right for 14 years duration privileged. In 1911, the British government introduces the Indian Patents and Design Act with removing the Inventions and Designs Act of 1888 which is effective till 1972.

Worldwide the developing countries as a consumer for the many products its importance partly increase, in 1994 all members of the World Trade Organization were required to adopt the Trade Related Intellectual Property Standards (TRIPS).

By growing the Pharmaceutical MNCs worldwide, The World Trade Organization came into existence on 1 January 1995, and along with it came the Trade-Related Aspects of Intellectual Property Rights TRIPS Agreement. Covering the international instruments for strengthens the IPR. India initially not in favor of TRIPS as other developing countries. As a member of WTO India modifies its domestic intellectual property laws in order to comply with the agreement.

In the world, the most difficult aspect of the World Trade Organization's Agreement on Trade-related Aspects of International Property Rights (TRIPS) is over the issue of patents for pharmaceutical drugs. From 1 January 1995, The TRIPS agreement come into effect, this agreement stretches the scope of intellectual property rights. Patents shall be available for any invention it declared in article 27, whether the products or process in all fields of technology. In India Parliament granted by act 1970 that patent rights only to manufacturing processes, rather than to the end products themselves,"

In the world, India is the country which not only a chief exporter of drugs but also the primary producer of drugs for its own population. Generic drug share market is large portion covered by this country [1–3].

2. Patent basic

The basic aspects of the patent system must know very well and it is outlined before to practical aspects. The primary logic behind the generation of a patent system was to honor an inventor by a full right to the invention of duration for a number of years it depends upon the country legal authority. The new inventions which support to stimulate and promote the further technological process and innovation, it is fruitful when the patent has public access. The countries or group of countries have legal authority that patent is the exclusive rights for the innovations. In a trade or commercial business, a patent provides their owners which stop from the making, using, offering for sale, selling or importing a product or a process without their permission (a license). By the patent system, it is clear that how the inventor can protect their patent and also it is necessary that how to respect other innovation by participating in it. Keep in mind that the patent itself is a regional right, it workable in limited either in a country or a group of countries. Patent never is "world patent" as it only territorial. Therefore the filing of a patent is a choice of the territory and the region where the patent protected. The desire of territory is based on the country market potential, manufacture's competitor place, research center place, and various other places. It is a fundamental part of the patent application filing. The basic criteria of patentability—Must be patentable subject matter in US geography, Unity of invention, capable of industrial applicability. In most of the countries, the primary object is the novelty, in some countries also seen the double standard of novelty depending on the place of the invention it is inside the territory or outside the territory. The comparison of novelty and art of skill in the invention should be superior to the existing patent in the same field. In a patent, the non-obviousness is one of the most difficult things to define. Its contribution to defining the level of technology. The examiner of the patent has the ability to disclose in the prior art but also identifies the art of the skill in the innovative person. In the Pharmaceutical world, patent protection is very important which uplift the development of the new medicine for disease those consequences these countries. The patent protection boosts the pharmaceutical industry for the investment of the billion to develop the new molecules, making sure that the product sale [3, 4].

The pharmaceutical product takes a very long time to develop and enter the market for human use. A new dosage form an average takes around 10–15 years during this period medicine efficacy and safety must be proved by a different phase of a clinical trial. A significant period lost the new drug before entering the market that is a disadvantage in the pharmaceutical field. On innovation

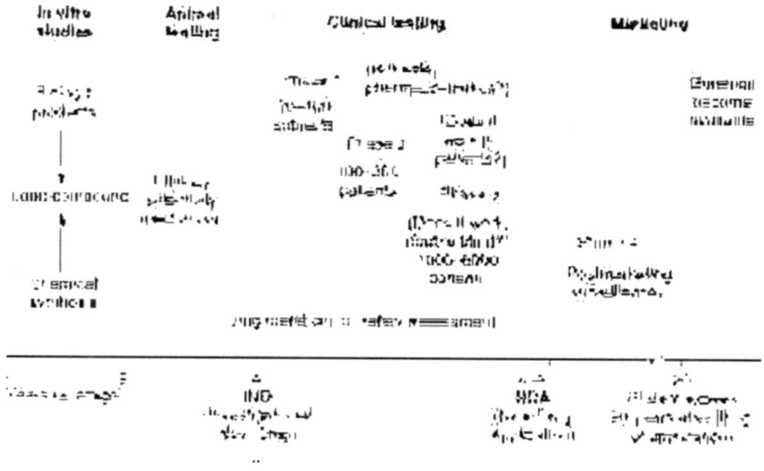

Figure 3.
New drug development.

patent role is that it protect the innovation it either territorial or global, but in case of pharmaceutical product, there must be some extent of flexibility by which the monopoly right decrease so that it does not affect the cost of medicine. The world moving towards the differential pricing of medicines, making the cost of medicine cheaper in developing countries. From the developing countries, the revenue generated is very less and around 1% as compared developed countries. Developing countries contribute the minimum incentive to the research, it comes maximums from the developed countries. To provide the health patent is not only the obstacle along with it has other factors like poor infrastructure lack of sanitation and shortage of funding for even generic drugs **Figure 3** (New drug development).

The concept behind the patent for innovation is a contract on a temporary basis, where society agrees to the monopoly that allowing a high level amounts that doing so provide will provide a strong incentive for innovation. Creating revenue from manufacturers and production give the strong back up to research and development also encourage in the interest in development for the new molecule in pharmaceutical. A balance is necessary between the research and development in aspect to economic, because from research and development there is no scope to generate direct revenue from the customer. Indirectly it gives very strong revenue to the market [4, 6].

3. Structure of application

For filling of application, the ideal requirements of the patentability and also the application must be filed by the competent authority for a certain country or a group of countries. A quick focus must be given when filing the application and try to cover the application with the following parts.

a. Claims

b. Detailed description (or specification)

c. Drawings

d. Background

e. Abstract

f. Summary

Who that file the application; the title must be itself descriptive and creative. The title properly indicates the subject matter of the application. The patent application itself should also include all priority information, such as the identification of related applications. The audience for the application basically is the judges and patent examiner. Also, apart from these the patent agent's client and the inventor are also audiences.

3.1 Claims

In the patent filing, the claims for the inventor prepared by the agent that is first it must be easy in language and plan should be in at least three. The patent agent outlines a diagram in the first disclosure meeting and discusses with the inventor. The language or the terminology used for the filing the might be difficult to understand by the inventor. So, the agent explains it in pictures or another diagram by which it is easy to understand.

In practice, the agent prepares the several drafts for the communication and select the best one for further proceeding. The clam is the legal part of the application. For the preparation of quality contents draft, the agent must give the time and during writing focus on that, it is concise and explanatory. In any case, it is seen that due to short of time the ideal paper not prepare and such situation the technical paper of the inventor consider a claim. For convenient the claim may present in a picture that is easy to understand. By pictures language the novelty of the paper is high.

As the claims completed the patent agent require to check the specification to verify and confirm that the claim terms appropriately explain in the paper.

The detailed description section, sometimes known as the "preferred embodiment of invention" section or the "disclosed embodiment of the invention" section breathes life into the claims and provides a sufficient explanation of the invention for an ordinary person skilled in the art to make and understand the invention. In some jurisdictions, the term "specification" is also used to refer to the description in addition to the summary and background sections of the application; suffice to say that "detailed description" and "specification" are generally the same for purposes of patent drafting.

The detailed description section must be closely tied to the drawings. This section cannot be substantively amended once the application has been filed. Consequently, the patent agent must make sure that the detailed description section provides an appropriate degree of technical disclosure on the day that the application is filed as he won't have a second chance to alter this part of the application. The patent agent cannot amend his application to include new technical disclosure during prosecution.

If the patent agent uses a highly abstract term in the claims he should consider using the term in the detailed description section, but in a manner that ties the abstract term to a specific embodiment of the invention. For example, if the claims use the term "warning device" for automobile horn, the specification could either say: "One example of warning device 10212 is an automobile horn. Other warning devices may be used, consistent with the spirit of the invention," or, "Automobile horn 102 constitutes a warning device. Many other such warning devices may be used consistent with the spirit of the invention."

As mentioned above, the detailed description section cannot be substantively amended once the application is filed. Thus, a patent agent should take care that the patent application (1) reflects the disclosure material provided by the inventors, (2) provides sufficient information to enable an ordinary artisan to reproduce the invention and (3) provides sufficient depth so that the claims can be narrowed during patent prosecution to avoid close prior art. Further considerations about the scope and importance of the detailed description section will be discussed below and are also illustrated by the following example [2, 5, 6].

3.2 Detailed description (or specification)

For the preparation of filing, the specification should be full filling the basic requirements. The condition as per the country rule regulation. For example, Canadian practices are more or less different from those of American practice. But worldwide the American practice is more considering that the Canadian practice regarding the specification.

The specification discusses in three parts:

I. Describing the Invention: The first object is to give a hint of what to be claimed. Explain the patent by the inventor through the electronic circuit compromising a combination of a logic gate. In such a way if the inventor wants to file another one application need to only change the logic gate where the microprocessor change. Therefore, all claimed elements must be shown in the specification. In specification there is no limit, it must be broad and require covering most of the points in a general way, where it full fill all terms that cover the patent application.

II. Professional Person enables to explain Invention: It is in the concern to update software have full knowledge to a patent agent. For convenient, the agent explains all the content of the application in drawing with the help of updated version of the software. By block diagrams, is easy to understand the whole contents of the patent.

III. The Best Mode by the Inventor: The inventor discloses his best knowledge at the time of filing of the application. Two ways by which it explains. First, the invention carries out as claimed, not disclose invention for commercial in the market. The second is subjective here; the inventors may be not disclosing the proper knowledge in such case some aspects of the invention in dilemma.

3.3 Drawings

In this part, the presentation of the invention is the best way of drawing which makes easy to understand the facts of the invention. The patent agent describes the innovative idea with good visual supporting materials. It is found that the drawings are the most important of the patent after the claims. The preparation of the picture itself an innovative idea, the patent agent first read all the contents of the application and thick on the designing of the picture. Some time it is very difficult to explain the principle or innovative idea by drawing a picture. During the explanation of innovation by drawing the agent focus on the using of minimum words and that itself explanatory, use in some way a reference in the picture.

3.4 Background

This part is very less important for the filing of the application, the patent agent focus on that very least al last. If the background of the application prepares first the value of the draft it finishes. The patent agent trying to explain the background in brief. If the background of the patent application describes in detail it is not good for the inventor, so some practitioners intentionally not saying too much about the innovation in the background section, in the way patent can be protected in public space.

3.5 Abstract

This section is not necessary here, generally it is described in first or some time not requires in a patent application. The innovation idea expresses in very few words where it is smartly explained. In some countries, the court demand first abstract, by study the abstract the patent application can be understood very easily if it is discussed in properly. The preparation of abstract after completing the draft of the patent application, if it is prepared earlier, there is a chance of mistake my it is poorly written or not completely explanatory. But the drawback of this section is that here, some time the innovation specification explains.

3.6 Summary

In most of the country National Law did not ask the legal authority to submit the summary, but it comes in practice by the patent agent. Patent agent prepares the summary parts with the help of the expert, so it is helpful for the jurisdiction to understand what the inventor wants to say. In this section avoid putting the picture or explaining the contents thoroughly. The patent agent focuses to write the summary that it does not explain the parts of the whole claim. The words used in this section are not very turning to mean and try to complete in one paragraph [4–6].

4. Patent filling strategy and tools

As it discussed that patents are territorial rights, the designing of the application explains itself how the patent protection would be preferable. The filing of the patent application is a basic requirement for each country. The grant of a patent and thus patent protection is necessary. The filings of application in many countries are a financial resource for legal bodies, some it is the uncertainty of the potential success of the invention.

During filing the patent agent has the responsibility and accountability to present all the information in the given specification that the inventor ownership uses their best mode of mechanism to develop for easy access. The chronicle must not contain incorrect or confusing statement calculated to cheat the person to whom the specification is addressed and make it hard for them, by not considering proper tests and experiments, to understand and construct the invention. From the filing of the patent, it must be clear that it is useful, certain points relating to its utility must be in the specification. The Chronicle may be invalid if it is not properly completed.

It is the duty of the inventor that he or she provides the all information very properly to the patent agent of its invention and not hide any information which it may be lead to the lawsuit later, which should be legal during the duration of the patent. The inventor whatever the content submits to the patent agent either it's in drawing from or in the very good language, the patent agent drafts his or her application based on that. The patent agent when preparing the application should demand the artwork or the facts from the inventor prior to his work, it may be helpful for the agent to draft the application properly. The patent agent put the proper address, correct affiliation and place of work in the application. Which must appear in the application? The right of the invention may be individual or its transfer to the company or another one, for such things the patent agent must be written with very effectively in the application latter it is not questionable [7, 8].

5. Development and importance in pharmaceutical industry

India's modern pharmaceutical industry was primarily shaped by Patents act 1970. Before that Indian market dominated western Multinational Corporation that controlled over third fourth market basically through imported drugs. At that time most of the pharmaceutical product was held by foreign companies and domestic drug price was among the highest in the world. An important point of the 1970 patents act was the special delivery connects to the pharmaceutical that allowed patent protection only for a new method or process of manufactures in the synthesis of a molecule in the Indian market. This patent protection was provided for only 7 years for pharmaceuticals.

This robust domestic manufacturing industry for pharmaceuticals stems, in part from the 1970 Patents Act effectively encouraging the reverse engineering of internationally patented products. If the large price increases that some predicted following the adoption of TRIPS were realized, they should be evident in the aggregate data. Our primary identifying assumption is that the timing of patents being granted was orthogonal to other events that might also have affected the market outcomes of newly patented products. To further address concerns regarding heterogeneity in the strength of patents or the importance of the patented molecules in the Indian market, we next examine the subset of patent applications identified. Perhaps the most direct is a decrease in the number of producers due to the increased exit rate of incumbent firms or a lower entry rate of new firms. The change in prices can occur without any actual difference in the observed market structure. As evidence of the existence of this phenomenon, we note that some of the firms receiving patents for molecules never appear in the retail sales data. India has granted hundreds of patents to both domestic and multinational firms. This represents one of the first attempts to apply an entirely new patent system to an existing market of this size and scope. Prior to the new patent system, there were many products being sold containing molecules that were patented outside of India but were domestically manufactured and sold by a large number of firms [9, 10].

Author details

Mohamad Taleuzzaman[1*] and Iqra Rahat[2]

1 Department of Pharmaceutical Chemistry, Faculty of Pharmacy, Maulana Azad University, Jodhpur, Rajasthan, India

2 Department of Pharmaceutics, Glocal School of Pharmacy, Glocal University, Saharanpur, India

*Address all correspondence to: zzaman007@gmail.com

References

[1] Provost A, Morin L. The Preparation of a Patent Application LEGER ROBIC RICHARD, Lawyers, ROBIC, Patent & Trademark Agents Centre CDP Capital. Available from: www.robic.ca-info@robic.com

[2] Bessoth F. Practical aspects of the preparation and filing of patent applications. Methods in Molecular Biology. 2013;**949**:85-102

[3] Bennett WJ. Indian pharmaceutical patent law and the effects of Novartis Ag v. Union of India. Legal Challenges of Globalization: A View from the Heartland (Symposium Edition). 2014;**13**(3):1-24

[4] Zacharias N, Farias S. Patents and the Indian Pharmaceutical Industry. Pharmatech: IP Rights and Patents, Business Briefing; 2002

[5] Preparation and Filing of a Provisional Patent Application. Available from: https://www.uspto.gov/patents-getting-started/patent-basics/types-patent-applications/provisional-application-patent

[6] Tuominen N. Patenting Strategies of the EU Pharmaceutical Industry–Crossroad between Patent Law and Competition Policy. 2011. pp. 1-30. Available from: www.coleurope.eu

[7] Siddiqi A. Patents and Pharmaceutical Drugs the Need for Change. Intellectual Property Law: Spring; 2005. pp. 1-9

[8] Dissolving Films. Particle Science. Drug Development Services. Technical Brief. 2010. 3p

[9] Duggan M, Garthwaite C, Goyal A. The market impacts of pharmaceutical product patents in developing countries: Evidence from India. NBER Working Paper Series; 2014. pp. 1-56

[10] Goldberg PK. Intellectual property rights protection in developing countries: The case of pharmaceuticals. NBER and BREAD; 2010. pp. 1-35

Chapter 5

The Patenting of Products and Processes Used for the Treatment of Smoke Inhalation

Fernanda Oliveira de Carvalho, Érika Ramos Silva, Paula Santos Nunes, Karen Perez Pereira Ramos and Nayara Gomes Lima Santos

Abstract

Intellectual property enables the transformation of knowledge in principle and the link between knowledge and the market. The right of exclusivity guaranteed by the patent refers to the right to interfere with other products and use and sell a patented invention. On the other hand, access to the public is made available on the knowledge of the essential points and as those that characterize a novelty does not exist. Patent registries, because they are available in open access databases, are great bases of technological knowledge, which can be used in research in several areas, among them smoke inhalation treatments. Inhalation injury is the leading cause of death in burn patients and is usually caused by the uninhibited absorption of smoke, which has an extremely toxic effect on the respiratory system. The physiopathology of inhalation injury covers multiple factors, and the injured respiratory system may present deterioration in a few hours. Respiratory distress is one of the major causes of morbidity and mortality in patients affected by fire incidents. The search for suitable treatments for inhalation injury is continuing, and the treatments used for smoke inhalation are discussed.

Keywords: patents, smoke inhalation, pulmonary injury, natural products, synthetic products

1. Introduction

A patent is a public concession, granted by the State, which grants the holder the exclusive right to commercially exploit his creation. The exclusivity right secured by the patent refers to the right to prevent others from manufacturing, using, selling, offering, or importing such invention. In compensation, access is available to the public on the knowledge of key points and the claims that characterize the novelty in the invention [1].

Patent registrations, because they are available in open access databases, are a great base of technological knowledge, which can be used in researches across several areas, among them smoke inhalation treatments [1].

The pulmonary injury from smoke inhalation or combustion chemical products is the leading cause of death in burn patients, can be present in 2/3 of the population

IntechOpen

with skin burns exceeding 70% of body surface area, and is mainly caused by inhibited smoke inhalation, which has an extremely toxic effect in the respiratory system [2].

The physiopathology of an inhalation injury encompasses multiple factors, and the injured respiratory system can present deterioration in a few hours. If combined with cutaneous burns, the inhalation injury increases even more the incidence of pulmonary complications and the mortality. On average, the mortality from burns is less than 10%, but in the presence of an inhalation injury, this increases up to 25–43%. When complications develop, such as pneumonia and multiple organ dysfunction, this can increase up to 60–80% [2].

The prevalence of burns is significantly higher in developing countries than in developed. In the USA, nearly 2 million people are burned every year. Of these, about 100,000 have moderate to severe burns, requiring hospitalization, and 70% of fire victims who die within 12 h have an inhalation injury [3, 4]. In an epidemiological study conducted by Iqbal et al. [5], which evaluated 13,295 patients, it was found that men were the majority of the victims (56.43%); the mean age of adults was 33.63 ± 10.76 years and the children's age was 6.71 ± 3.47 years, the domestic environment being the most common (68%). The mean body surface area burned was 10.64 ± 11.45% in total. Smoke inhalation injury occurred in 149 of these patients (1.12%).

Although many products and techniques have been developed to control cutaneous thermal injury, few specific therapeutical options for diagnosis were found for patients with inhalation injury. Several factors explain the slower improvement progress in the treatment of patients with inhalation injury. Inhalation injury is a more complex clinical problem. The burned cutaneous tissue can be removed and replaced by skin grafts. The injured pulmonary tissue must be protected from a secondary injury due to resuscitation, mechanical ventilation, and infection, while the host's repair mechanisms receive proper support [2].

Many consequences of smoke inhalation result from an inflammatory response involving mediators whose number and functions still remain without a complete understanding, despite enhanced tools to process clinical material. Improvements in mortality by inhalation injury are mainly due widespread improvements in intensive care, instead of interventions focused in smoke inhalation. The search for proper inhalation treatments remains, and the treatments used for smoke inhalation are discussed in this chapter.

2. Intellectual property aimed at the treatment of pulmonary injury by smoke inhalation

Intellectual property enables a transformation of knowledge to principle and a link between knowledge and market. It is also said that a patent is the legal document that represents the set of exclusivity rights granted by the State to an inventor. By receiving the patent rights over his product, the inventor also receives several rights and guarantees, however, with these rights also come obligations that, necessarily, must be fulfilled so the inventor can retain his rights [1].

In case of him not meeting his obligations, he is subject to a mandatory licensing of his invention or utility model. If a patent is requested and granted for technology, of a novelty product or to enhance an invention, there are several proceedings, regulations, and laws to register and grant these patents, which vary for each country, also varying the concession period. The delay in patent granting is pointed as a barrier to innovation in a country. According to the World Intellectual Property Organization (WIPO), the period for an international patent registration varies from 16 to 30 months [1].

On patents deposited with the objective of treating injuries caused by smoke inhalation, the inventors that most developed e patented products were Enkhbaatar P. et al. (6), Keith JC Jr. (5), Schmalstieg F. et al. (1), Brands (5), and Saifer et al. (1).

3. Pulmonary injury and its therapeutical challenges

The constitution and toxicity of smoke and of products generated by combustion compromise the environmental condition and health of exposed individuals, generating local or systemic affections, which may leave sequelae and even progress to death [2].

Inhalation injury by smoke can happen as a consequence of the high temperature of vapor inhaled, decrease of breathed fraction of oxygen, and presence of toxic gases such as carbon monoxide, sulfur dioxide, nitrogen, and ammonia, absorbed or not by the inhaled particulate matter [6, 7].

There are different damages to the different structures of the respiratory system [8]. In the airways, there is scaling of ciliated pseudostratified epithelium, mucosal edema, bronchorrhea, and tracheobronchial obstruction, increasing resistance and limiting air flow [9]. Sometimes, from the histological point of view, depending on the inhalation injury model, such changes can be reversible.

Regarding pulmonary parenchyma, the injuries are characterized by lung emphysema with expressive thinning of intra-alveolar septa, which burst and increase alveolar spaces. This tissue involvement can have progressive character, caused by the arrival of neutrophils in the pulmonary interstice, generating a superoxide radical, which directly harms the membrane of interstitial cells and the endothelium [10–12]. According to Ferreira and Matsubara [13], production and release of reactive oxygen species contribute to the emphysema.

About 6–7 h after initial exposure, there is an increase of IL-1β and IL-8 concentrations [14]. Besides those, other inflammatory process mediators are tumor necrosis factor-alpha (TNFα), IL-6, and nuclear factor-kappa β [2]. The actions of IL-1β, IL-6, and IL-8 stimulate adherence of leucocytes and disseminated intravascular coagulation, with IL-6 highlighted in eosinophil attraction to the injured area [15]. TNF-α is known for being a powerful inflammatory mediator in thermal lesions, inhalation injuries, and generalized infections [16].

Clinical treatment of an inhalation injury is a challenge based on the control of consequences of smoke exposure, there being no gold standard. Some immediate care assures the integrity of organs and systems of victims. It is necessary to start oxygen therapy with hyperoxia (FiO_2 = 100%) for a limited time, to discern the indication of artificial airway and invasive or noninvasive ventilatory support, patient pronation, and extracorporeal membrane oxygenation [17].

It is important to maintain airway perversity as well as alveolar stability. The administration of β2-agonist, heparin and N-acetylcysteine nebulization have a role in the management, as well as the more specific treatment of carbon monoxide or cyanide poisoning, have contributed to good therapeutic results [18, 19].

Acknowledging the systemic effects of the condition, the hydration and monitoring of micro and macro hemodynamics are extremely relevant to prevent further complications. Pharmacological treatment is based on the consequences and additional complications. Corticosteroids, antibiotics, anticoagulants, sedatives, and analgesics and, in cases of intoxication by cyanide, hydroxocobalamin, sodium nitrite, sodium thiosulfate, or sodium nitrite, by intravenous route, can be administered [3, 20].

At the experimental level, the use of mesenchymal stem cells derived from human amnion (hAMSCs) alleviated white smoke-induced lung injury [21]. It is likely that in the future this resource will contribute to the best clinical outcome for victims of this type of injury.

It is known, however, that the best clinical outcome for the victim of inhalation injury depends on other factors. According to Bedri et al. [22], socioeconomic and ethnic factors and the sex of the victims influence the clinical outcome. They found that Afro-descendent Americans, female and uninsured, had more complications, more surgical interventions, longer hospital stay, and higher mortality rates, even though lower body surface area burned and there is a lower proportion of inhaled lesion. These disparities further emphasize the need for further research on the underlying racial and socioeconomic factors that this review of the database could not discern.

In turn, natural products present great therapeutic potential and are the subject of study in several experimental, in vitro, and/or in vivo research. The low cost, the good availability, and the habitual use by the population, considering the regional popular knowledge, are some of the factors that contribute to this reality.

The terpene group deserves special mention, both for being part of traditional medicine for centuries and for having a low toxicity [23]. In addition to being used in the food and cosmetic industries, its effects, anti-inflammatories, antioxidants, analgesics, anticonvulsants, antidepressants, anxiolytics, anticancer, antitumor, neuroprotective, antimutagenic, antiallergic, antibiotics, and antidiabetics, are widely known.

Examples are carvacrol, linalool, borneol, limonene, myrene, and pinene. It is known, for example, that D-limonene has important immunomodulatory properties, ameliorating attacks of atopy and asthma, besides inhibiting the action of cytokines and release of substances reactive to oxygen and containing migration of eosinophils [2, 8].

4. Historical background of patents aimed to control pulmonary injury by smoke inhalation

Two years ago, our research group performed a patent review [24] in three different databases, and only 18 patents, containing the keywords "smoke inhalation" in the title, abstract, or full text, fit in the inclusion criteria for this research. There was a language bias, making it possible for many other patents to exist, regarding the use of natural and synthetic products developed for the treatment of smoke inhalation, but we believe that the results presented provide the reader a perspective on current therapeutic options and new approaches and treatments for smoke inhalation.

The oldest patent was deposited in 1977 and was on "orgotein," which is the generic name of the enzyme superoxide dismutase (SOD), which belongs to the metalloprotein group, contains copper and zinc, and was first described in 1969 by McCord and Fridovich. Those researchers found that a bovine protein (orgotein) was an enzyme that could catalyze the destruction of superoxide radicals through a disproportion in molecular oxygen and hydrogen peroxide. By destructing free superoxide radical, SOD contributes to the physiological balance between pro-oxidants and antioxidants, being known for being a potent anti-inflammatory agent [24].

Dominguéz [25] reported that orgotein is a naturally occurring protein inside a human cell and, when topically and systematically administered, produces physiological effects that do not manifest or manifest in a lower degree by the natural SOD of a patient. This exogenous manifestation decreases the amount of acute inflammatory events and influences late effects.

The most recent patent, according to the patent review mentioned previously [24], was deposited in 2013 and was about ectophosphatases. The ectophosphatases and, especially, the alkaline phosphatases are a subclass of phosphatases (hydrolases that act on ester connections). The role of ectophosphatases is not well established yet; however, it has been suggested that these enzymes perform important tasks in nutrition, proliferation, differentiation, adhesion, virulence, and infection [26]. Furthermore, it is possible to assure that there is a consistent relation between the of an organism to decay extracellular ATP by ectophosphatases activities and its capacity to acquire resistance to toxins.

Brands [27] developed a drug using ectophosphatases for prophylaxis in mammals, preferably humans, at risk of inflammatory diseases or immunocompromised conditions. Intravenous administration of alkaline phosphatase in patients subjected to myocardial revascularization resulted in a subsequent increase in plasma levels of alkaline phosphatase 4–6 h after the onset of the surgery. This endogenous alkaline phosphatase can perform an important role in the immune system, because it acts as an acute phase protein; in addition, high levels of alkaline phosphatase generate an anti-inflammatory effect in the organism.

The two patented products mentioned previously, both the oldest and the newest, were applied and studied at the clinical level, in other words, with humans. The first product was given by inhalation (nebulization) and with a therapeutic purpose of treatment and the second, through intravenous infusion but with a preventive aspect [24].

The oldest patent found was deposited in a US-based patent database, yet the latest was located in Mexico. The year with most patent deposits related to the treatment of inhalation injuries was 2009, followed by 2005 and 2008. Probably, that year had many researches and patent requests due to some disasters involving fires, such as the one in a club in Thailand, that resulted in many deceases [24].

5. Patenting of processes and products aimed at pulmonary injury by smoke inhalation: any evidences?

Besides the two products mentioned and highlighted in the previous topic, since they were the first and the last to be patented, we had three other products studied and patented, e.g., "antithrombin III (ATIII) and heparin," which refers to the exogenous administration of ATIII—a direct inhibitor of thrombin, and heparin, that inhibits coagulation proteases, decreasing fibrotic conditions and improving gas exchange in animal models of acute pulmonary injury. Since there were six patents deposited aimed at the use of this product, it was found that the inhaled administration (using a compressor nebulizer, an ultrasonic nebulizer, or a dry powder inhaler) is more efficient than intravenous injection [28]. The dose used was also mentioned in the patent, stressing that the inhalation of combined products can also be performed according to the need or symptom occurrence [29].

In five other patents, "estrogen receptor-β (ERβ)-selective ligands or compositions," with the objective of treating or preventing acute pulmonary injuries due to local inflammatory processes (smoke inhalation, prematurity with surfactant deficiency, oxygen toxicity, barotrauma by mechanical ventilation with positive pressure) or peritonitis or intravenous bacteremia, both during sepsis, were studied. Furthermore, many preclinical trials proved the anti-inflammatory properties of estrogen [29–31].

Finally, the patent on "anti-IL-8 and anti-L-selectin," which we found only one patent deposited. L-selectin's role in immunity control is as a receptor in T cells. The smoke inhalation model in sheep of Murakami and Traber [32] showed that the anti-L-selectin antibody significantly alleviated airway obstruction. The neutrophil treatment with anti-L-selectin antibody reduces neutrophil capacity of adherence to the endothelium. It is also probable that chemokines such as IL-8 and others direct the neutrophil movement from the vasculature [33]. According to this patent, the effects on vascular permeability may point that both anti-IL-8 and anti-L-selectin decrease the lesions of endothelial cells.

These data help highlight the different means of treatment of injuries caused by smoke inhalation and the drugs being studied to control such injury. We presented the significant progress achieved in the field, demonstrating the growing interest of scholars and pharmaceutical companies in the development of products with the potential to be successful in treatment of smoke inhalation.

6. The challenges of processes and patents aimed at pulmonary injury by smoke inhalation

Intellectual property, one of the subdivisions of business law, is nothing more than the legislative norm that regulates innovations and is now gaining considerable space in the most varied academic discussions. Patent, one of the intellectual property entities, is the guarantee of ownership of the creation offered to its inventors, a fact that has been discussed since it ends up limiting its application and effectiveness [34].

The expression of intellectual property is criticized because of its ambiguity. Richard Stallman wrote an essay on this subject to enlighten this problem and fight, among other things, against other things, against the meaning of the expression, because it is a reminiscence of physical property, whose laws are very different. For him, the term unites a set of heterogeneous concepts with objectives and operation too diverging (or even opposed) to be considered as a whole, such as copyrights, related to patents and trademarks. He advocates a separate consideration of each of these areas and the abandonment of the term intellectual property (especially in the name of the World Intellectual Property Organization) [1, 34]. Actually, part of the free software community rejects this expression and follows Stallman's point of view.

As previously explained, patenting a product guarantees its inventor time to explore its invention safely, but there are a number of limitations in this action [35, 36]. One of the biggest challenges in the patent process in some countries is the delay in the patenting process and the low investment in this area, which does not generate incentives for research, studies, and creations of new products. The cost of a patent goes beyond the process to deposit it into a database; there is still a high investment to keep it active, which discourages some inventors who have low investment in their research.

Once a patent is deposited in a database, the entire population has access to the methodology of the invention as well as its advantages and disadvantages. Analyzing database patents, besides the analysis in the literature, is an important tool in the strategic planning of a research, because approximately 70% of the technological information is described in the patents, according to WIPO. Therefore, a thorough evaluation of patents is essential for a good development of projects and avoids potential wasted resources, in case any other researcher has already reached the expected goal.

Currently, there are several databases for patent deposits. These banks are extremely affordable and consistent, but they have some limitations. A great difficulty encountered is the duplication of patents during a search, which occurs because the same inventor ends up depositing his patent in several databases. In the reviews of patents carried out by our group, we find a considerable number of patents in duplicity, which makes the research more laborious and time-consuming. In addition, some inventors are rather short, brief, and unspecific when carrying out the explanation of their patent. At other times, they are prolix and not objective, which end up generating difficulties in the process of searching and analyzing the most desired patents.

Another limitation is the difficulty of finding a specific patent. Due to various encodings and numberings given to patents, the search for something specific ends up taking more time. The lack of research in clinical trials is, also, another limiting factor. Most inventors carry out the patent filing process with an experimental trial, which can be justified by the interest of patenting their invention more quickly and not running the risk of another inventor developing their research. In the patent review conducted by our research group on inhalation injury 2 years ago, only three patents were found in clinical trials.

Regarding patents aimed at treatment for lung injury induced by smoke inhalation, specifically, we can observe an increasing amount of deposits in the last years. However, morbidity and mortality remain high, probably due to its extremely complicated pathophysiology. Besides the damages of the toxic and harmful gas, the oxidative stress, the interaction between cytokines and inflammatory mediators, and the activation of the NF-κB signaling pathway contribute to a greater difficulty in the treatment and control of this condition, making it difficult to standardize the research of new patents for strategies of treatment [9].

In the patent review conducted by our research group, which aimed to evaluate the development and patenting of natural and synthetic products for the treatment of smoke inhalation, a low number of patents deposited (18 in total) can be observed for this purpose. In addition, a great variety of both the mechanisms of action of the formulations and the form of administration of the formulations were observed [24]. Most new therapies are still at the stage of animal experimentation.

Early treatment remains the key to reducing mortality and improving prognosis. The inconsistent effects of certain therapies may be due to the diverse dose, mechanism of action, therapeutic duration, severity of the patients, and complementary interventions [37].

7. Conclusion

Developing better treatment strategies for this intractable disease still requires research, and the intellectual property enables the transformation of knowledge in principle and the link between knowledge and the market. However, currently, there is no particularly effective treatment for acute lung injury induced by inhalation of smoke; therefore, the search for suitable treatments for inhalation injury is continuing, and the treatments used for smoke inhalation are discussed.

Author details

Fernanda Oliveira de Carvalho*, Érika Ramos Silva, Paula Santos Nunes, Karen Perez Pereira Ramos and Nayara Gomes Lima Santos
Post-Graduation in Health Sciences, Federal University of Sergipe, Aracaju, SE, Brazil

*Address all correspondence to: fsoliveira.fisio@gmail.com

References

[1] Barbieri JC. Uma avaliação do acordo sobre aspectos dos direitos de propriedade intelectual relacionados com o com: Cinco anos depois. RAP Rio de Janeiro. 2001;**35**(3):107-129

[2] Carvalho FO, Felipe FA, Costa ACSM, Teixeira LGB, Silva ER, Nunes PS, et al. Inflammatory mediators and oxidative stress in animals subjected to smoke inhalation: A systematic review. Lung. 2016;**194**(4):487-499

[3] Bassi E, Miranda LC, Tiermo PFGMM, Ferreira CB, Cadarmuro FM, Figueiredo VR, et al. Assistance of inhalation injury victims caused by fire in confined spaces: What we learned from the tragedy at Santa Maria. The Revista Brasileira de Terapia Intensiva. 2014;**26**(4):421-429

[4] Li H, Yao Z, Tan J, Zhou J, Li Y, Wu J, et al. Epidemiology and outcome analysis of 6325 burn patients: A five-year retrospective study in a major burn center in Southwest China. Scientific Reports. 2017;**7**:46066

[5] Iqbal T, Saaiq M, Ali Z. Epidemiology and outcome of burns: Early experience at the country's first National Burns Centre. Burns. 2013;**39**(2):358-362

[6] Peters W. Inhalation injury caused by the products of combustion. Canadian Medical Association Journal. 1981;**125**(3):249-252

[7] Souza R, Jardim C, Salge J, Carvalho C. Lesão por inalação de fumaça. Jornal Brasileiro de Pneumologia. 2004;**30**(6):557-565

[8] Zhi-Hai H, Yi J, Yun-You D, Xiao-Yang W, Yan H, Ting-Zheng F. Oxidative stress in a rat model of cotton smoke inhalation-induced pulmonary injury. African Journal of Traditional, Complementary, and Alternative Medicines. 2016;**13**(5):132-138

[9] Enkhbaatar P, Pruitt JRBA, Suman O, Mlcak R, Wolf SE, Sakurai H, et al. Pathophysiology, research challenges, and clinical management of smoke inhalation injury. Lancet. 2016;**388**:1437-1446

[10] Cox RA, Burke AS, Oliveiras G. Acute bronchial obstruction in sheep: Histopathology and gland cytokine expression. Experimental Lung Research. 2005;**31**:819-837

[11] Cox RA, Burke AS, Jacob S. Activated nuclear factor kappa B and airway inflammation after smoke inhalation and burn injury in sheep. Journal of Burn Care & Research. 2009;**30**:489-498

[12] Yamamoto Y, Sousse LE, Enkhbaatar P, Kraft ER, Deyo DJ, Wright CL, et al. γ-Tocopherol nebulization decreases oxidative stress, arginase activity and collagen deposition after burn and smoke inhalation in the ovine model. Shock. 2012;**38**:671-676

[13] Ferreira ALA, Matsubara LS. Radicais livres: Conceitos, doenças relacionadas, sistema de defesa e estresse oxidativo. Departamento de Clínica Médica da Faculdade de Medicina de Botucatu, Botucatu, SP.43. Revista da Associação Médica Brasileira. 1997;**43**(1):61-68

[14] Kurzius-Spencer M, Foster K, Littau S, Richey KJ, Clark BM, Sherrill D, et al. Tracheobronchial markers of lung injury in smoke inhalation victims. Journal of Burn Care & Research. 2008;**29**:311-318

[15] Heinrich PC, Castell JV, Andus T. Interleukin-6 and the acute phase response. The Biochemical Journal. 1990;**265**(3):621-636

[16] Tartaglia LA, Ayres TM, Wong GH. A novel domain within the 55 kd

TNF receptor signals cell death. Cell. 1993;**74**:845-853

[17] Walker PF, Buehner MF, Wood LA, Boyer NL, Driscoll IR, Lundy JB, et al. Diagnosis and management of inhalation injury: An updated review. Critical Care. 2015;**19**:351

[18] Toon MH, Maybauer MO, Greenwood JE, Maybauer DM, Fraser JF. Management of acute smoke inhalation injury. Critical Care and Resuscitation. 2010;**12**(1):53-61

[19] Sadowska AM. N-Acetylcysteine mucolysis in the management of chronic obstructive pulmonary disease. Therapeutic Advances in Respiratory Disease. 2012;**6**(3):127-135

[20] Gupta K, Mehrotra M, Kumar P, Gogia AR, Prasad A, Fisher JA. Smoke inhalation injury: Etiopathogenesis, diagnosis, and management. Indian Journal of Critical Care Medicine. 2018;**22**(3):180-188

[21] Cui P, Xin H, Yao Y. Human amnion-derived mesenchymal stem cells alleviate lung injury induced by white smoke inhalation in rats. Stem Cell Research & Therapy. 2018;**9**:101

[22] Bedri H, Romanowski KS, Liao J, Al-Ramahi G, Heard J, Granchi T, et al. A National Study of the effect of race, socioeconomic status, and gender on burn outcomes. Journal of Burn Care & Research. 2017;**38**:161-168

[23] Nuutinen T. Medicinal properties of terpenes found in *Cannabis sativa* and *Humulus lupulus*. European Journal of Medicinal Chemistry. 2018;**157**:198-228

[24] De Carvalho FO, Silva ÉR, Felipe FA, Teixeira LGB, Zago LBS, Nunes PS, et al. Natural and synthetic products used for the treatment of smoke inhalation: A patent review. Expert Opinion on Therapeutic Patents. 2017;**27**(8):877-886

[25] Domínguez A. Modificación de la superóxido dismutasa para mejorar sus propriedades biofarmacéuticas. Biotecnologia Aplicada. 2006;**23**:11-16

[26] Freitas-Mesquita AL, Meyer-Fernandes JR. Biochemical properties and possible roles of ectophosphatase activities in fungi. International Journal of Molecular Sciences. 2014;**15**(2):2289-2304

[27] Brands R. Method for increasing the activity of the immune system of a mammal at risk of inflammatory diseases. WO2009106368. 2009

[28] Murakami K, Bjertnaes LJ, Schmalstieg FC, McGuire R, Cox RA, Hawkins HK, et al. A novel animal model of sepsis after acute lung injury in sheep. Critical Care Medicine. 2002;**30**(9):2083-2090

[29] Enkhbaatar P, Murakami K, Traber DL. Method of preventing fibrin clots in pulmonar tissue through the use of aerosolized anticoagulants. EP2322189. 2011

[30] Enkhbaatar P, Murakami K, Traber DL. Method of preventing fibrin clots in pulmonary tissue through the use of aerosolized anticoagulants. EP1725244. 2006

[31] Enkhbaatar P, Esechie A, Wang J, Cox RA, Nakano Y, Hamahata A, et al. Combined anticoagulants ameliorate acute lung injury in sheep after burn and smoke inhalation. Clinical Science. 2008;**114**:321-329

[32] Murakami K, Traber D. Pathophysiological basis of smoke inhalation injury. News in Physiological Sciences. 2003;**18**:125-129

[33] Smith WB, Gamble JR, Clark-Lewis I, Vadas MA. Chemotactic desensitization of neutrophils demonstrates interleukin-8 (IL-8)-dependent and IL-8-independent

mechanisms of transmigration through cytokine-activated endothelium. Immunology. 1993;**78**(3):491-497

[34] Barbosa DB. Tratado da propriedade intelectual. In: Dois Estudos sobre os Aspectos Jurídicos do Patenteamento da Tecnologia Round up Ready no Brasil—A Questão da Soja Transgênica. Rio de Janeiro: Lumen Juris; 2013

[35] Cockburn I, Long G. The importance of patents to innovation: Updated crossindustry comparisons with biopharmaceuticals. Expert Opinion on Therapeutic Patents. 2015;**25**(7):739-742

[36] Jones BW. Broadening the scope of inherent anticipation and its impact on the patentability of chemical structures, comment, Smith Kline v. Apotex. 5. The John Marshall Review of Intellectual Property Law. 2006;**456**:455-476

[37] Guo B, Bai Y, Ma Y, Liu C, Wang S, Zhao R, et al. Preclinical and clinical studies of smoke-inhalation-induced acute lung injury: Update on both pathogenesis and innovative therapy. Therapeutic Advances in Respiratory Disease. 2019;**13**:1-11

Section 2

Industrial Application

Chapter 6

Prologue Two: Transfer of Technology

Aline Meireles dos Santos, Leila Queiroz Zepka and Eduardo Jacob-Lopes

1. A contextual approach of transfer of technology

Economic growth is directly attached to the extension of research and development (R&D) investments once that worldwide changes and progress are attributed to the translation of scientific and technological knowledge into actual innovative products and processes. In this sense, it is major to maintaining a healthy system of knowledge diffusion and application of innovative R&D results to encourage the advent of innovations leading to economic ripple effects [1].

The rise of the knowledge-based economy has increased the notoriety of institutions that create and disseminate knowledge, policymakers, and companies once the effective management of technology as a source of competitive advantage is of vital importance for many organizations [2]. In this sense, the transfer of technology is a managerial process that causes a wide range of positive impacts across society, such as improved human capital, knowledge capital, and entrepreneurship [3].

Widely accepted as essential for enhancing the economy and wealth in changing the competitive landscape, technology is the basic theme of the transfer process. Technology refers to the different types of knowledge, which may be embodied in the form of machinery, equipment, information, know-how, software, as well as their associated management systems [4].

Transfer of technology is defined as the broad set of processes which aims to achieve the equitable sharing of the technological know-how from one organizational setting to another, such as governments, private-sector entities, financial institutions, non-governmental organizations, and research-teaching institutions [1]. The basic obligation among the transferors to the recipient is to identify and implement administrative, institutional, and government structures that enable private and public sector transfer of technology and cooperation, bearing also into account existing work of international organizations [5].

Technologies have been the driver of economic and social development worldwide, but many organizations in developing countries, with technological infrastructure and R&D resources reduced, require assistance with developing human capital, developing appropriate institutions and networks, and acquiring and adapting specific technological know-how. Therefore, developed countries must operate on a broad front to facilitate the transfer of technology into developing countries, finding new paths for economic growth as a whole [6, 7].

Transfer of technology among stakeholders can be realized by a large number of pathways. They vary depending on the type of technology, sectors, and country condition. Pathways may be different for more developed technologies and for technology innovations still in the development phase. Common pathways include licensing, joint ventures, foreign direct investment (FDI), government assistance programs, exchange of scientific and technical personnel, franchising, sale of tum-key plants, contract research, further development, internal start-ups, meetings, mobility scheme, monitoring of activities of the science base, publications, regional technology centers, reverse engineering, science parks, and spin-offs [8, 9].

While the technology transfer process can be complex and interconnected, five general phases for effective actions can be identified (**Figure 1**) [8, 10]. Transfer of technology process starts at new technology development through research, development, and international cooperative partnership initiatives. This phase considers the current state of the art of technology development, the major barriers, and possible mechanisms for overcoming them through public and private actions, including partnerships [11].

The identification of transfer opportunities regarding technological improvements developed through R&D investments stands at the actual beginning of the transfer of technology. At this phase, the research results will be regularized and protected. In addition, the verification of the potential of technology transfer and search for industrial partners are realized [10, 11].

Arrangements for undertaking the actual transfer are taken in the next phase. For proprietary technology, the existence of an enabling legal environment is a key issue during this stage. The identification of transfer needs and opportunities, through appropriate access to and exchange of information with regard to the existence of technologies and their potential for application, is an important initial step in the transfer process [10].

Considering the market differences, input prices, and supplier vendor infrastructure, the adaptation and diffusion of the transferred technology to local cultural, social, and economic conditions are a determining phase for an effective transfer of technology. Insight into the technology adaptation process, its inhibitors, and stimulators help transferor to diffuse their new products and processes more effectively [12].

A number of social, economic, management, and policy implications influence the flow and quality of the transfer of technology. The key elements of successful transfers include the exchange of information, contracting parties' awareness, sound regulatory frameworks and economic policy for capacity building and the

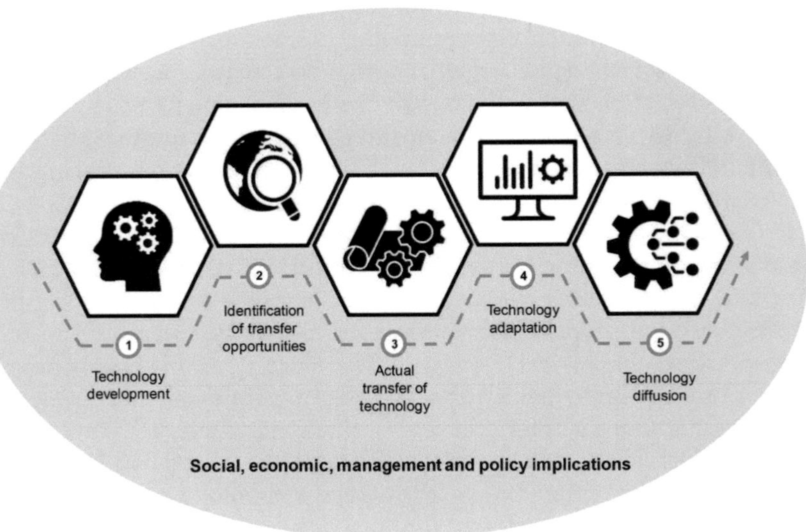

Figure 1.
Phases of transfer of technology.

diffusion of these technologies, and availability of a wide range of technical, business, management, and regulatory skills locally. Transfers of technology that satisfy local demands and priorities have more probability to be successful. But there is no preset answer to improve this process. Interactions and barriers vary according to the sector, type of technology, and country, and recent trends in international financial flows that drive the transfer of technology are altering the relative capacities and roles of different stakeholders. Policy actions, therefore, must be linked to the specific context and interests.

This book provides global trends that enhance the practice of transfer of technology to developing countries and policy, legal and regulatory implications that affect this process. The book is addressed to research scientist of innovation from a variety of disciplines, including management, economics, and human resources whose work has commercial applications.

Author details

Aline Meireles dos Santos, Leila Queiroz Zepka and Eduardo Jacob-Lopes*
Bioprocess Intensification Group, Federal University of Santa Maria, UFSM, Santa Maria, RS, Brazil

*Address all correspondence to: ejacoblopes@gmail.com

References

[1] Min JW, Vonortas NS, Kim Y. Commercialization of transferred public technologies. Technological Forecasting and Social Change. 2019;**138**:10-20. DOI: 10.1016/j.techfore.2018.10.003

[2] Phaal R, Farrukh CJP, Probert DR. Technology management process assessment: A case study. International Journal of Operations & Production Management. 2001;**21**:1116-1132. DOI: 10.1108/EUM0000000005588

[3] Guerrero M, Urbano D, Fayolle A, Klofsten M, Mian S. Entrepreneurial universities: Emerging models in the new social and economic landscape. Small Business Economics. 2016;**47**:551-563. DOI: 10.1007/s11187-016-9755-4

[4] Günsel A. Research on effectiveness of technology transfer from a knowledge based perspective. Procedia - Social and Behavioral Sciences. 2015;**207**:777-785. DOI: 10.1016/j.sbspro.2015.10.165

[5] Viñuales JE, editor. The Rio Declaration on Environment and Development: A Commentary. New York: Oxford University Press; 2015. Available from: 10.1093/law/9780199686773.001.0001

[6] Roffe P. Transfer of Technology: UNCTAD's Draft International Code of Conduct. The International Lawyer, Spring. 1985;**19**:689-707. Available from: https://www.jstor.org/stable/40705630

[7] United Nations Department of Economic and Social Affairs (UN DESA). Climate change: Technology development and technology transfer. New York NY: UN. Available from: https://sustainabledevelopment.un.org/content/documents/1465back_paper.pdf [Acessed: 25 August 2019]

[8] IPCC, Intergovernmental Panel on Climate Change. Methodological and technological issues in technology transfer. Metz B, Davidson OR, Martens J-W, van Rooijen SNM, McGrory VWL, Editors. Special Report prepared by IPCC Working Group III. Cambridge, UK: Cambridge University Press; 2000

[9] Lavoie JR, Daim T. Technology transfer: A literature review. In: R&D Management in the Knowledge Era. Cham: Springer; 2019. pp. 421-438. DOI: 10.1007/978-3-030-15409-7

[10] Djoghlaf A, Freeman J. Third review of the effectiveness of the financial mechanism of the convention on biological diversity. Available from: http://citeseerx.ist.psu.edu/viewdoc/download?doi=10.1.1.178.2408&rep=rep1&type=pdf [Acessed: 25 August 2019]

[11] Fernandes CR, Machado AGC. Technology transfer capability: Development dynamics in higher education institutions. Brazilian Business Review. 2019;**16**:1-15. DOI: 10.15728/bbr.2019.16.1.1

[12] Robertson TS, Gatignon H. Competitive effects on technology diffusion. Journal of Marketing. 1986;**50**:1-12. DOI: 10.2307/1251581

Chapter 7

Patents as a Yardstick for Economic Growth: Case of Indian R&D System

Abhishek Kumar

Abstract

The novel creations by humans were well appreciated and acknowledged, but there exist several lacunae such as illegal copying. These malpractices were high and went on without restrictions. Moreover, with the passage of time, the significance of innovations and applications and their protection, both, increased. The fast-changing pace of global trades and business practices has given rise to a global cutting-edge competition and short product cycle with rapid changes in technology. This competition has laid a great responsibility on Research and Development (R&D) to build new ideas—creating an Intellectual property (IP). It is also said that that is an idea "owned" by an individual or company and is therefore protectable under the law. IP law aims at encouraging innovation by giving the creators of new ideas ample time to profit from their ideas and recuperates their development costs.

Keywords: economy, India, intellectual property, patent, R&D

1. Introduction

Intellectual property (IP) includes rights to literary, artistic, inventions in all fields of human endeavor, scientific disclosures, industrial designs, trademarks, commercial names, etc. IPR can be held only by legal entities, i.e., who have the right to sell and purchase a property. IP allows the creators/owners of patents, trademarks, or copyrighted works to get benefits from their creation. Such rights are outlined in Art. 27 of the Universal Declaration of Human Rights, which provides for the right to benefit from the protection of moral and material interests resulting from authorship of scientific, literary, or artistic productions [1] (**Figure 1**).

2. IP rights at a glance

Intellectual properties denote novel makings of brain like invention, literary and art works, symbol(s), name(s), images, etc. generally seen in business. Intellectual property is categorized as follows:

Industrial property	Patents, trademarks, industrial designs, geographical indications

Copyright and related rights	Literary works—novels, poems and plays; films, music, art works (e.g., drawings, paintings, photographs, and sculptures) and architectural design. It also includes performances, recordings, and broadcastings

Figure 1.
Kinds of intellectual property rights.

2.1 Patent

Patent—an exclusive right given for an invention(s), which may be a product or a process. To get a patent, technical information about the invention must be disclosed to the public in a patent application. This right is provided for 20 years to the inventions which prove novelty, inventive step, and industrial application.

There are inventions which are non-patentable which are well described (*u/s* 3 a of Indian Patent Act 1970) [2]:

- Anything frivolous
- Contrary to law/morality or injurious to health
- A mere discovery of scientific principles, formulations, theories, etc.
- A mere discovery of a new property of a known substance
- Substance obtained with mere admixture resulting only in aggregation of properties of components
- A mere arrangement/rearrangement/duplication of known devices
- A method of agriculture or surgical entity

- Any process of medical, surgical, curative, prophylactic diagnostic, therapeutic, or other treatment of human beings or processes similar to the treatment of animals to free them from disease
- Plants and animals as a whole or any parts thereof other than microorganisms
- Mathematical or business methods or computer programs
- Literary, dramatic, musical, or artistic work or any esthetic creation
- A presentation of information
- Topography of integrated circuits
- Inventions related to atomic energy

2.2 Copyright and related rights

Copyright/author's rights—A legal term to describe the rights conferred for novel literary and artistic works created by an author/creator. Inventions that come under copyrights include books, musical compositions, portraits, films, computer programs, information databases, commercial advertisements, geographical maps, technical drawings, etc. Exhaustive lists of works covered by copyright are usually not to be found in legislation.

The two kinds of rights covered under copyright include:

Economic rights: It allows the owner to produce monetary rewards from the application of respective works

Moral rights: It protects the non-economic interests of the author(s).

The economic rights the owner of a work can exclude or allow:

- reproduction in any form
- public performance (play or musical work)
- recordings
- broadcasting
- translation into other languages
- adaptation (novel into a film/screenplay)

The Berne Convention is a landmark in copyright protection, where the copyright is granted automatically without registration. Most of the nations have a systematic structure for the registration of innovative works. Such registration arrangements can assist in resolving disputes over ownership or creation and facilitate the financial transactions and/or transfer of rights [3].

2.3 Trademark

A trademark is a "distinctive sign" that identifies certain goods or services as those produced or provided by a specific person or enterprise. Trademarks may be obtained for the brand name of a particular product or service.

The significance of trademark is mentioned as follows:

i. TM projects the actual origin of goods and services.

ii. It guarantees the identity of the origin of goods and services.

iii. It stimulates further buying tendencies.

iv. TM acts as a badge of loyalty.

v. It may enable consumer to make a lifestyle or fashion statement.

2.4 Registered design rights

Industrial designs constitute the esthetic aspect of designs. It comprises of 2D and 3D structures of articles. The owner of registered design rights prevents others from making, selling, licensing, and importing or copying the designs. The industrial design concerns more the aspect and esthetic of the device and also in the life sciences and biotechnology field.

2.5 Geographical indications

The geographical indications (GIs) are the signs used on the products that have some specific place of origin. The quality and characters of a product must be essentially due to its place of origin. It includes agri-products, foods, alcoholic drinks, handicraft items, and industrial products.

3. Implication of World Intellectual Property Organization (WIPO)

Established in 1970, the World Intellectual Property Organization (WIPO) is an international organization that ensures the maintenance of rights of inventors and owners of intellectual property worldwide, and they are appraised monetarily for their originality [4]. This international agency is recognized as an agency fostering creations of innovators, thus assisting the scientific world and literature. WIPO provides an edge to the dynamic industrial world by facilitating several revolutionary measures to international trade. WIPO acts meticulously with its member nations toward a guarantee that intellectual property system remains firm and in the benefit of IP assets across the globe.

Intellectual property (IP) rights are recognized as the yardstick of techno-economic growth of the country. This is because IP is directly proportional to the R&D divisions of the economy. Patents are a critical competitive arm in this cutting-edge competition, and a huge investment is needed for promoting and nurturing IP. Envisaging such facts, government's role, and initiative for an exhaustive environment are needed which would encourage innovation and commercialization [5]. In short, the economic benefits of the patent system are derived from its roles in promoting innovation and encouraging investment, economic growth, knowledge sharing, and the efficient use of resources.

In 1994, the General Agreement on Tariffs and Trade (GATT) conducted the Uruguay Round for international trade negotiations in line with Trade-Related Aspects of Intellectual Property Rights (TRIPS). Substantially, the member nations of World Intellectual Property Organization (WIPO) in 2000 agreed with the Patent Law Treaty. TRIPS transformed the regulation and the Patent Law Treaty, which primarily focused on rationalizing the procedural reforms.

WIPO is an organization for intellectual property (IP) services, policy formation and implementation, etc. This agency of the United Nations is supported by 192 member states. WIPO is established with under mentioned committees:

i. **The governing bodies:**

  i. The WIPO General Assembly and member states of each union (e.g., the PCT Union Assembly)

  ii. The WIPO Coordination Committee

  iii. The WIPO Conference

ii. **The permanent committees:**

  i. Program and Budget Committee (PBC)

  ii. Committee on Development and Intellectual Property (CDIP)

  iii. Intergovernmental Committee on Intellectual Property and Genetic Resources, Traditional Knowledge and Folklore (IGC)

  iv. Advisory Committee on Enforcement (ACE)

iii. **The standing committees:**

  i. Standing Committee on the Law of Patents (SCP)

  ii. Standing Committee on the Law of Trademarks, Industrial Designs, and Geographical Indications (SCT)

  iii. Standing Committee on Copyright and Related Rights (SCCR)

  iv. Committee on WIPO Standards (CWS)

4. India and IP system

India is a significant member of World Trade Organization (WTO) from 1995. It was a connection established to establish harmonization with IP standards [4]. The country signed different pacts to be included with:

- The Berne Convention, Copyrights Act, and Information Technology Act, 2000
- Patents: India's Patents Act of 1970 and 2003
- Industrial designs Act, 2000
- Geographical Indications of Goods Act, 1999

The National Intellectual Property Rights Policy is established in compliance with WTO's (World Trade Organization) agreement on TRIPS (Trade Related aspects of IPRs) aims to sustain entrepreneurship and to enhance the capabilities of Make in India program.

1947	Patent and Designs Act, 1911
1995	Indian—WTO pact
1998	India—Paris Convention (PCT)
1999	Patent Amendment Act
2005	Patent Amendment Act
2013	India—Madrid Protocol
2016	Indian IPR Policy

This activity aims at establishing a fact that IP is an asset and it promotes innovation and encourages entrepreneurship across the society. This organization also aims to ensure proper review, awareness, and enforcement of IP Laws [6].

5. Impact of IP and economic growth of country

Every year, WIPO IP Statistics Data Center publishes the statistics of IPs on varied grounds that project the innovation index of countries on varied basis. The key indicators for the assessment include:

a. Total applications

b. Applications by residents and non-residents

c. Applications by regions

d. Applications by income groups

e. IP rights in force

f. Patent—applications for the top 20 offices

g. Patent—Applications by filing route: direct and PCT system

h. Utility model—applications for the top 10 offices

i. Trademark—application class counts for the top 20 offices

j. Trademark—application class counts by filing route: direct and Madrid System

k. Industrial design—application design counts for the top 20 offices

l. Industrial design—application design counts by filing route: direct and Hague System

6. Research method

In this study, the analysis of patents' productivity was carried out using data from WIPO. The Total Patents Filed (*direct and PCT entries*) and Total Patent Grant (*direct and PCT entries*) were taken and analyzed for the year 2012–2017.

DOI: http://dx.doi.org/10.5772/intechopen.92605

Patent Office	**2012**		**2013**		**2014**		**2015**		**2016**		**2017**	
	Filed	***Granted***	***Filed***	***Granted***	***Filed***	***Granted***	***Filed***	***Granted***	***Filed***	***Granted***	***Filed***	***Granted***
China	652,777	217,105	825,136	207,688	928,177	233,228	1,101,864	359,316	1,338,503	404,208	1,381,594	420,144
North America	578,100	275,000	606,400	301,700	614,300	324,400	626,400	320,600	640,300	329,500	642,000	342,900
United States of America	542,815	253,155	571,612	277,835	578,802	300,678	589,410	298,407	605,571	303,049	606,956	318,829
Europe	345,900	159,100	346,000	161,900	346,300	161,800	360,200	165,400	354,900	195,900	355,700	203,600
Japan	342,796	274,791	328,436	277,079	325,989	227,142	318,721	189,358	318,381	203,087	318,479	199,577
Republic of Korea	188,915	113,467	204,589	127,330	210,292	129,786	213,694	101,873	208,830	108,875	204,775	120,662
European Patent Office	148,560	65,665	147,987	66,696	152,662	64,608	160,028	68,431	159,358	95,956	166,585	105,645
Russian Federation	44,211	32,880	44,914	31,638	40,308	33,950	45,517	34,706	41,587	33,536	36,883	34,254
Lower middle-income	71,600	16,600	72,500	17,000	73,100	19,100	77,100	18,700	76,900	23,300	78,900	24,500
Canada	35,242	21,819	34,741	23,833	35,481	23,749	36,964	22,201	34,745	26,424	35,022	24,099
Australia	26,358	17,724	29,717	17,112	25,956	19,304	28,605	23,098	28,394	23,744	28,906	22,742
Germany	61,340	11,332	63,167	13,858	65,965	15,030	66,893	14,795	67,899	15,652	67,712	15,653
India	43,955	4328	43,031	3377	42,854	6153	45,658	6022	45,057	8248	46,582	12,387

Average no. of patents filing *vs.* granting (2012–2017)
(*Patent Office-wise*)

Patent Offices	**Filed**	**Granted**	**%**
China	1,038,009	306,948	30
North America	617,917	315,683	51
United States of America	582,528	291,992	50
Europe	351,500	174,617	50
Japan	325,467	228,506	70
Republic of Korea	205,183	116,999	57
European Patent Office	155,863	77,834	50
Russian Federation	42,237	33,494	79
Lower middle-income	75,017	19,867	26
Canada	35,366	23,688	67
Australia	27,989	20,621	74
Germany	65,496	14,387	22
India	44,523	6753	15

Average no. of patents filing *vs.* granting (2012–2017) (*year-wise*)

Avg. patent	**2012**	**2013**	**2014**	**2015**	**2016**	**2017**
Filed	237,121	255,248	264,630	282,389	301,571	305,392
Granted	112,536	117,465	119,918	124,839	136,268	141,922
Percentage	**47%**	**46%**	**45%**	**44%**	**45%**	**46%**

The above **Figures 2** and **3** clearly depict the state of countries with reference to filing and granting of patents. Considering the state of filing, China was the leading country among all, whereas North America, United States of America, and Europe were lagging behind. On the other hand, the patent granted state projects a similar picture, where China was again leading in patent granted. This figure shows that approximately 46% of the patent filed were granted. On analyzing the average no. of patents filing *vs*. granting (2012–2017), it was found that Russia was leading with 79% patent granted, whereas India was far behind with only 15% granted patents. It clearly shows the state of innovations and its commercialization (**Figure 4**).

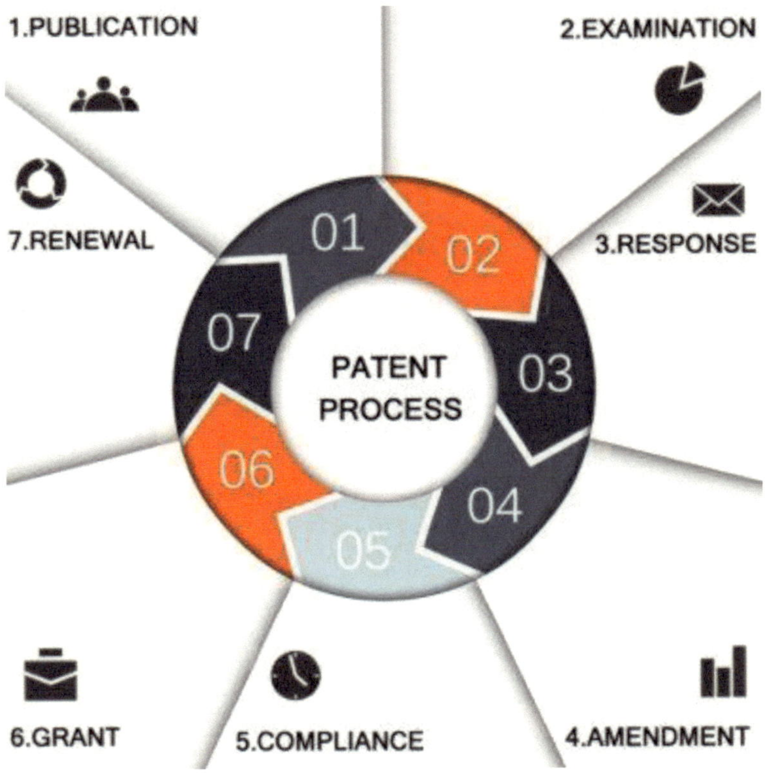

Figure 2.
Patenting process.

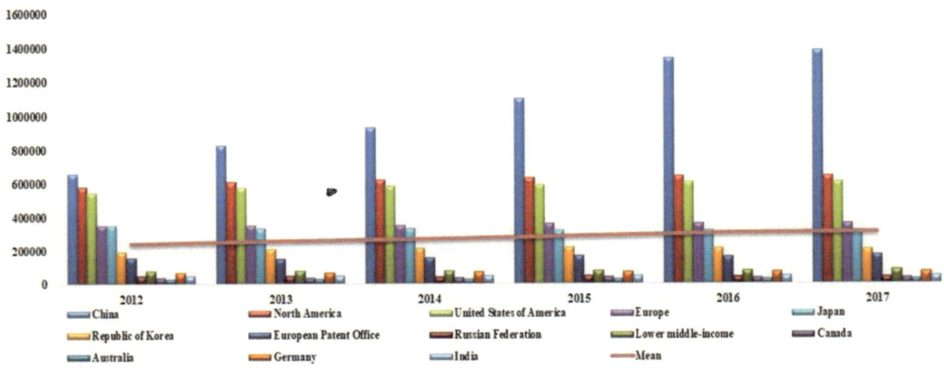

Figure 3.
No. of patents filed (2012–2017).

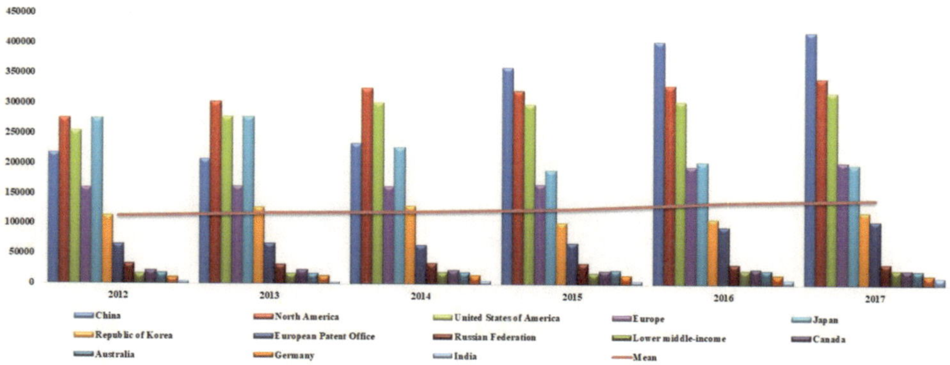

Figure 4.
No. of patents granted (2012–2017).

7. Conclusions

IPR is an important issue which raises a picture of innovation index and potential for commercialization of novel items. WIPO is an establishment that provides an edge to this regulatory system of innovation and legality. WIPO generates information regarding different kinds of IPR and their data with reference to fining and granting. This brief study provides an insight to the current state of patents (filed and granted) and their implication on globalization. In public, especially the innovators, the knowledge of IPR should be provided which would act as an act of mentoring them. It would provide the scope for protection of IPR and thus will create an avenue for protection of IPR and commercialization. This way, such activities would lead the country's economy with a fast pace.

Acknowledgements

The author would like to acknowledge entire fraternity of the Amity University Uttar Pradesh, Lucknow Campus, who provided an opportunity to teach and learn.

Conflict of interest

There is no conflict of interest.

Author details

Abhishek Kumar
Amity Institute of Biotechnology, Amity University Uttar Pradesh, Lucknow, India

*Address all correspondence to: kumarabhishek1302@gmail.com;
akumar2@lko.amity.edu

References

[1] Appendix L Consolidated Patent Laws—April 2019 Update

[2] Chapter 1 and 2: The Indian Patent Act; 1970

[3] Article 2: Berne Convention for the Protection of Literary and Artistic Works, Paris Act of July 24, 1971, as Amended on September 28, 1979

[4] Available from: http://www.wipo.int/about-ip/en/

[5] India as an Innovation Economy. The Role of IP and ICT, June 2018; 2018

[6] Innovation and Patents, Report IBEF; 2017

Chapter 8

Internal Relationship and Impact Path between Innovation and Entrepreneurship: Based on China's High-Tech Industry

Kai Zhao and Lixiang Wang

Abstract

Innovation is the source of entrepreneurship, entrepreneurship is the value embodiment of innovation, and the two are inseparable. At a time when dividends such as population, reform and opening up, and resources and environment are gradually disappearing, China urgently needs to accelerate scientific and technological innovation to support economic development, incubate scientific and technological enterprises, and ease labor market pressure with technological progress and efficiency improvement. This chapter focuses on China's high-tech industry, which is dominated by scientific and technological innovation. Starting from the overall, local, and regional perspectives, it organically integrates the traditional DEA, similar SFA, Malmquist index decomposition, chain multiple intermediary effect, and other multilevel research through cross-level analysis. Based on the research foundation of innovation efficiency after eliminating environmental and random factors, it deeply discusses the action path and impact mechanism of "double innovation" and provides targeted policy recommendations for the government and relevant local departments. The research confirms that the total effect of innovation on entrepreneurship is always positive, i.e., promoting "people-to-people innovation" is conducive to promoting "mass entrepreneurship" whether it is analyzed from the whole or from the part.

Keywords: Innovation, High-tech industry, DEA

1. Introduction

Innovation is the source of starting a business. In the process of starting a business, one needs to have a continuous and vigorous sense of innovation before one can produce creative ideas or schemes and explore new modes and outlets. Entrepreneurship is the embodiment of the value of innovation. The value of innovation mainly lies in transforming technology into productivity, and the fundamental way to realize this transformation is entrepreneurship. It can be seen that innovation and entrepreneurship are inseparable. Studying the internal relationship and mechanism between the two can not only provide an important theoretical basis and guidance for China to promote "double innovation" and prevent "deviation and deviation" in the middle of the process but also lead enterprises to carry out efficient innovation input and output, accelerate enterprises to adapt to the new normal, and provide power and guarantee for promoting innovation-driven strategy in depth.

With the accelerated process of economic globalization and the increasingly complicated and steep international market, China, as the largest developing country, urgently needs to play the role of a leader in scientific and technological innovation to support economic development, incubate scientific and technological enterprises, and relieve the pressure on the labor market at a time when its low-cost comparative advantages in production factors such as demographic dividend, reform and opening-up dividend, resources and environment dividend, and the resulting labor force no longer exist. Therefore, this chapter focuses on China's high-tech industry, which is dominated by scientific and technological innovation. Starting from the overall, local, and even regional perspectives, it attempts to organically integrate the traditional DEA, similar SFA, Malmquist index decomposition, chain multiple intermediary effect, and other multilevel research. Based on the research on innovation efficiency after eliminating environmental and random factors, it comprehensively and deeply discusses the action path and impact mechanism of "double innovation" and provides targeted policy recommendations for the government and relevant local departments.

This article will summarize and review the relevant literature from three aspects: innovation, entrepreneurship, and innovation and entrepreneurship.

First, about innovation. Scholars at home and abroad have conducted in-depth research on the innovation efficiency of China's high-tech industry from different perspectives. From the viewpoint of spatial economics, nonparametric DEA-Malmquist index method is used to explore the main factors affecting the innovation efficiency of China's high-tech industries [1]. Starting from the perspective of industry comparison, the panel stochastic frontier method (SFA) is used to evaluate the innovation efficiency of China's high-tech industry, and the influencing factors of innovation efficiency are analyzed [2]. The research proves that institutional innovation and the technicality of scientific researchers are the keys to improve the innovation efficiency of China's high-tech industry. From the perspective of value chain, Xiao et al. [3] empirically tested various factors that can affect innovation efficiency by using two-stage chain-linked DEA and Tobit models. The research shows that government support, financial environment, and other factors have a significant impact on innovation efficiency. And Chiu et al. [4], based on the value chain perspective, constructed a model combining research and development investment and operation process and measured the innovation efficiency of China's high-tech industry research and development value chain. In addition, there are many scholars from the SCP analysis perspective of industrial organization theory to study the impact of enterprise size, market power, technological opportunities, market process, and other factors on innovation efficiency [5, 6].

Second, about starting a business. Entrepreneurship is a social activity involving various phenomena, and scholars at home and abroad have conducted in-depth research on it from different angles such as economics, sociology, and management. Chen and Yang [7] based on microeconomics theory and from the perspective of industry differences analyzed the differences in the impact of various types of entrepreneurship on enterprise R&D incentives. Cao et al. [8] based on the social learning theory put forward a model of imitating entrepreneurial decision-making mechanism of high-tech industrial clusters. The study found that entrepreneurs implement entrepreneurial decision-making behavior under the stimulus of entrepreneurial motivation through observation and learning. Wang and Xue [9] set out from the theory of organizational learning to construct the framework of intellectual property entrepreneurship under the background of China's transformation and upgrading and take high-tech industry as an example to carry out empirical analysis to perfect the theory of intellectual property entrepreneurship. Franco and Filson [10] based on the innovation theory, on the basis of the knowledge spillover effect mechanism of employee flow diffusion, allow employees of current companies to imitate the behavior of their former employers, theoretically analyze the equilibrium conditions for Pareto optimality, and find out through simulation that derivative enterprises established by R&D personnel usually have higher R&D willingness and efficiency than other types of entrepreneurs.

Third, about innovation and entrepreneurship. At present, there are few studies abroad that can consider innovation and entrepreneurship together, and there are two completely opposite views. One view is that entrepreneurship is the process of realizing innovation, and innovation is the essential core of entrepreneurship [11]. From this point of view, innovation and entrepreneurship have an internal connection mechanism. However, another view is that entrepreneurship may involve innovation process, but it may not include innovation behavior [12], and there is no inevitable connection between innovation and entrepreneurship. Domestic scholars, mainly based on high-tech industries, empirically study the interaction between innovation and entrepreneurship. Based on the questionnaire survey data of China's high-tech industrial development zones, taking into account the dual effects of innovation activities and entrepreneurial activities within innovation clusters on the development of innovation clusters, this chapter makes an empirical analysis on the development of entrepreneurship, innovation, and innovation clusters in China's high-tech industries [13]. Jin and Xie [14], based on the actual development of China's high-tech industry, explored the role of government in the process of enterprise innovation and entrepreneurship.

Compared with previous literatures, the innovation of this chapter mainly includes the following two aspects: from the perspective of research content, the relationship between innovation and entrepreneurship studied in this chapter is a relatively blank research field, and the relevant research results at home and abroad are less, and the conclusions are quite different, while the research on the internal mechanism of innovation's impact on entrepreneurship combined with intermediary effect is even less, so this chapter is novel in content. From the perspective of research methods, this chapter firstly decomposes total factor productivity (TFP) based on DEA model excluding environmental and random factors and then uses chain multiple intermediary effect model to analyze the influencing process and mechanism among various variables and further analyzes the relationship between innovation and entrepreneurship in high-tech industries. Compared with the previous literature, this chapter emphasizes the application of cross-level analysis in methodology; organically combines the traditional DEA, similar SFA, Malmquist index decomposition, chain multiple intermediary effect, and other multilevel related researches; and further discusses the action path and influencing mechanism of double innovation in a more comprehensive and in-depth way.

2. Research methods

The research can be divided into the following four stages.

2.1 The first stage: traditional DEA

Referring to the related literatures on R&D input–output efficiency of high-tech industry, this chapter selects the input-oriented variable-scale BCC model to carry out the first phase of calculation. The main reason for choosing BCC model is its variable scale. Problems such as unequal competition and resource constraints in domestic high-tech industries may cause some decision-making units (DMU) to be unable to operate at the optimal scale, and the measurement of technical efficiency will be affected by scale efficiency. Considering this situation, BCC model adds convex conditions, allowing technical efficiency (TE) to be further decomposed into pure technical efficiency (PTE) and scale efficiency (SE), which is helpful to analyze the influencing factors of R&D input–output efficiency in China's high-tech industry in recent years.

2.2 The second stage: similar SFA

On the basis of the previous research stage, the difference between the actual input and the target input of the final accounting unit is calculated, i.e., the input slack, and a similar SFA model is constructed with the input slack as the dependent variable and the environmental factor as the independent variable, so as to separate the efficiency values affected by the external environment and random error factors and thus obtain the redundancy of the input of the decision-making unit caused only by the inefficiency of management.

2.3 The third stage: adjusted DEA and Malmquist index

According to the method proposed by Fried [15], the adjusted input data are substituted into BCC model again for efficiency analysis, thus obtaining the efficiency values of DMU after eliminating environmental factors and random factors. Compared with the traditional DEA model, the efficiency value thus obtained is closer to the real value. Since the data of DMU being evaluated is panel data including multiple time points, Malmquist TFP index can be used to analyze the effects of productivity changes, technical efficiency, and technological progress on productivity changes, respectively.

2.4 The fourth stage: chain multiple mediation effect

The total factor productivity excluding environmental and random factors is taken as the proxy variable to measure the innovation level in each region. The number of new ventures in high-tech industries, regional economic growth, and entrepreneurship in each region are included in the research framework, and an intermediary chain is formed according to the sequential characteristics of the intermediary variables. Through the intermediary effect model, the relationship between multiple variables and the process and mechanism of the influence between variables are analyzed simultaneously. This stage is mainly based on structural equation model (SEM) to carry out the above analysis. The following regression equations can be used to describe the relationship between variables:

$$\begin{aligned} Y &= c'X + b_1M_1 + b_2M_2 + e_1 \\ M_2 &= a_2X + a_3M_1 + e_2 \\ M_1 &= a_1X + e_3 \end{aligned} \tag{1}$$

The corresponding path of chain multiple mediation effect is shown in **Figure 1**.

As shown in **Figure 1**, the multiple mediation model includes two mediation variables M_1 and M_2; at this time, the multiple mediation effect analysis can be carried out from three angles. The first is to analyze from the total mediation effect, namely, $a_1b_1 + a_2b_2 + a_1a_3b_2$. Secondly, on the premise of controlling other

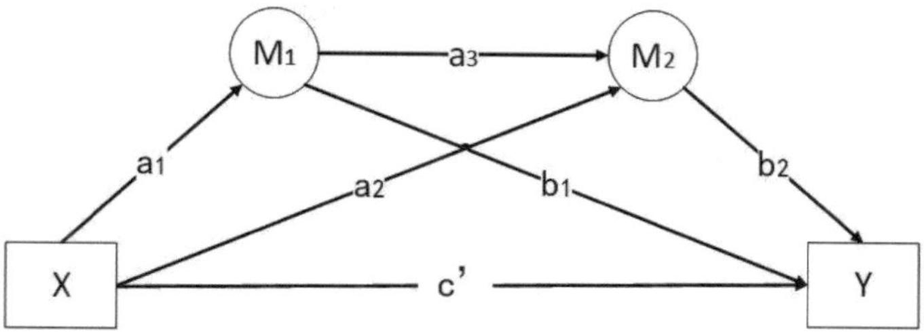

Figure 1.
Chain multiple mediation effect path diagram.

intermediate variables (such as control M_1), we can study the specific mediation effect of each intermediate variable, such as a_1b_1, a_2b_2, and $a_1a_3b_2$. Third, a comparative mediating effect can be obtained so as to be able to judge which of the effects of multiple mediating variables (e.g., a_1b_1, a_2b_2) is more effective, e.g., $a_1a_3b_2 - a_2b_2$, $a_1b_1 - a_2b_2$, and $a_1a_3b_2 - a_1b_1$ [16].

3. Variable selection and data description

3.1 Input–output indicators

Data on capital input, personnel input, and innovation output are all derived from China's High-tech Industry Statistical Yearbook. As capital investment data are often affected by price fluctuations, the relevant data should be reduced by using fixed asset investment price index (last year = 100) of corresponding years in all provinces and cities, and the provincial fixed asset investment price index data of each year comes from China Statistical Yearbook. In addition, Tibet and Xinjiang were excluded from the sample due to the serious lack of data. In order to eliminate the time lag between input and output and the difference between innovation activity cycles, this study chooses the time lag as 1 year, i.e., the input data is 2004–2013 and the output data is 2005–2014. In addition, because the internal expenditure of R&D funds, expenditure of new product development, and expenditure of technological transformation not only have an impact on the input–output efficiency of high-tech industries in the current period but also will have an important impact in some future periods, it is first necessary to convert the flow data into stock and then measure the impact of these three capital inputs on the innovation-output efficiency. Taking the calculation of R&D fund stock as an example, the method of permanent storage is used to deal with it.

$$x_{i,t} = (1 - \delta)x_{i.t-1} + e_{i,t-1} \quad (2)$$

In Eq. (2), $x_{i,t}$ and $x_{i,t-1}$ are the R&D expenditures of the t and $t-1$ years of the province i, respectively; $e_{i,t-1}$ is the R&D expenditure of the $t-1$ year after eliminating the price factor; δ is the depreciation rate; according to Griliches [17], it can be set to $\delta = 15\%$. Assuming that the average annual growth rate of R&D expenditures during the study period is g, the base R&D expenditure is

$$x_{i,o} = e_{\mathrm{i},0}/(g + \delta) \quad (3)$$

$e_{i,0}$ in Eq. (3) refers to the internal expenditure of R&D funds for the base period. On the basis of Eqs. (2) and (3), the R&D fund stock of each year can be obtained by using the perpetual inventory method. The above method can be used

Variable	Symbol	Unit	Definition
Innovation output 1	y1	Item	Number of patent applications
Innovation output 2	y2	Ten thousand yuan	Revenue from sales of new products
Innovation (personnel) input 1	x1	Person/year	Full-time equivalent of R&D personnel refers to the sum of the number of R&D full-time personnel plus part-time personnel converted into the current number of personnel according to the workload during the reporting year
Innovation (capital) investment 2	x2	Ten thousand yuan	The stock of R&D funds is calculated by the perpetual inventory method
Innovation (capital) investment 3	x3	Ten thousand yuan	The stock of new product development funds shall be accounted for by the perpetual inventory method
Innovation (capital) investment 4	x4	Ten thousand yuan	The stock of funds for technological transformation shall be accounted for by the perpetual inventory method

Table 1.
Description of input–output variables.

to process the funds for new product development and technological transformation, thus converting the flow data into stock. Input–output related variables are described in **Table 1**.

3.2 Environmental variables

Environmental variables are mainly used to reflect the geographic location of high-tech industries, macroenvironment, and government innovation support policies. Based on the relevant research foundation at home and abroad, and considering the characteristics of R&D and the availability of data, this chapter mainly selects the following indicators.

3.2.1 Regional real GDP

Real GDP can accurately reflect regional differences and the real level of regional economic development, so this chapter uses real GDP excluding price factors instead of nominal GDP. Generally speaking, the higher the regional economic development level, the more capable it is to invest in R&D innovation in high-tech industries and the higher the R&D innovation level.

3.2.2 Geographical location

Whether a region is located in a superior geographical position is crucial to the development of high-tech industries in the region. This chapter quantifies this variable by setting virtual variables, in which "1" is used to represent the eastern region, including Beijing, Tianjin, Hebei, Liaoning, Shanghai, Jiangsu, Zhejiang, Fujian, Shandong, Guangdong, and Hainan. "2" means the central region, including Shanxi, Inner Mongolia, Jilin, Heilongjiang, Anhui, Jiangxi, Henan, Hubei, and Hunan; "0" means the western region, including Chongqing, Sichuan, Guizhou, Yunnan, Shaanxi, Gansu, Qinghai, Guangxi, and Ningxia. Due to the serious lack of data in Xinjiang and Tibet, this article will not consider it for the time being.

3.2.3 Quality of local workers

In view of the availability of data, this chapter chooses the number of college students in the studied area as the characterization variable of laborer's quality. The higher the quality of local laborers, the more likely it is to provide more talents and intellectual support for the development of high-tech industries and the more conducive to the improvement of R&D efficiency.

3.2.4 Local government innovation support

Local government support has an important impact on the R&D and innovation process of high-tech industries. This chapter selects the government funds from the funds raised for scientific and technological activities to represent the innovation support of local governments. Generally speaking, local government support can provide guarantee for the infrastructure construction of high-tech industries in the region as well as financial support. The greater the support, the more conducive to R&D and innovation in high-tech industries.

3.2.5 Regional science and technology development level

Due to the spatial aggregation effect and spillover effect of high-tech industries, the degree of technological development in a region often plays an important role in the development of high-tech industries. This chapter chooses the number of high-tech industrial enterprises and the number of scientific and technological institutions to represent the degree of scientific and technological development in a region. In general, the more high-tech enterprises and scientific and technological institutions there are, the more conducive they are to R&D and innovation in high-tech industries.

Among the above environmental variables, except that the actual GDP of each region comes from China Statistical Yearbook, other data come from China High-tech Industry Statistical Yearbook. Descriptive statistics of relevant variables are shown in **Table 2**.

3.3 Mediating effect variables

Taking the total factor productivity (X) obtained by Malmquist index decomposition in the third stage as the independent variable. The dependent variable is

Variable	Symbol	Observed value	Mean value	Standard deviation	Minimum value	Maximum value
Regional real GDP	k_1	261	13,824.85	11,858	572.37	62,924.62
Geographical position	k_2	261	1	0.7894	0	2
Quality of local laborers	k_3	261	746,585	437,384.5	35,983	1,796,665
Local government innovation support	k_4	261	36,197.87	51,416.87	10	289,006.9
Number of high-tech industrial enterprises	k_5	261	853.29	1208.19	14	5874
Number of scientific and technological institutions	k_6	261	156.69	319.04	1	2474

Table 2.
Descriptive statistics of environmental variables.

the logarithm (Y) of the number of newly built entrepreneurs in individual and private enterprises in high-tech industries. The variable is obtained by using the difference between the number of private enterprises and individual workers in urban employment at the end of the year in the China Statistical Yearbook 2005–2014.The intermediate variables are, respectively, the logarithm of the number of new ventures (M1) and the logarithm of the actual GDP of each region (M2). Among them, the number of new ventures is obtained by year-on-year difference using the number of enterprises in the China Statistical Yearbook from 2005 to 2014. The actual GDP of each region comes from the China Statistical Yearbook.

4. Empirical analysis

4.1 Empirical analysis of traditional DEA in the first stage

DEAP software is used to preliminarily measure the comprehensive technical efficiency, pure technical efficiency, and scale efficiency of 29 provinces and cities in China from 2005 to 2014. The results are shown in **Tables 3–5**. According to the calculation results before adjustment, the average value of China's R&D comprehensive technical efficiency is 0.48–0.67 from 2005 to 2014, without considering the interference of external environment and random influence factors, which generally shows a rising trend. The average value of pure technical efficiency is 0.63–0.73, with room for improvement to varying degrees. The average value of scale efficiency is 0.753–0.926, and the overall efficiency level is relatively high. Generally speaking, the R&D efficiency of most provinces is below the efficiency frontier. As the result does not eliminate the influence of environmental factors and random interference factors, it cannot accurately measure the true level of the comprehensive technical efficiency of each province, so further adjustment and measurement are needed.

4.2 Regression analysis of SFA in the second stage

In order to separate the efficiency values influenced by external environment and random error factors, this chapter observes the influence of environmental factors and random error, respectively, by constructing similar SFA models in the second stage. SFA regression analysis is carried out by Frontier software. The relaxation values of each input variable obtained in the first stage are taken as dependent variables, and the selected six environmental variables are taken as independent variables to establish regression models to estimate the influence of environmental factors on the relaxation values of each input variable. If the regression coefficient is negative, it indicates that the positive change of environmental variables is conducive to reducing the input redundancy of high-tech industries, thus avoiding the loss and waste of input and improving the efficiency of research and development innovation. On the contrary, it will reduce the efficiency level of R&D innovation. The results of SFA regression analysis are shown in **Table 6**.

As can be seen from **Table 6**, the estimation results σ^2 and γ are both significant at the level of 1%, indicating that it is necessary to eliminate the influence of environmental variables in the model. Specifically, it can be seen from the following aspects: (1) Regional actual GDP has a significant negative impact on R&D personnel's FTE slack, new product development spending slack, and technological transformation spending slack. This shows that the higher the level of regional economic

Provinces		Year									
		2005	2006	2007	2008	2009	2010	2011	2012	2013	2014
Beijing	BA	0.27	0.30	1.00	1.00	1.00	1.00	1.00	1.00	1.00	1.00
	AA	0.45	0.45	1.00	1.00	1.00	1.00	1.00	1.00	0.97	0.92
Tianjin	BA	1.00	1.00	1.00	1.00	1.00	1.00	1.00	1.00	1.00	1.00
	AA	1.00	1.00	0.90	0.83	0.82	0.92	0.64	0.87	1.00	0.92
Hebei	BA	0.12	0.09	0.10	0.40	0.28	0.43	0.28	0.44	0.43	0.50
	AA	0.06	0.05	0.07	0.11	0.13	0.13	0.16	0.23	0.31	0.43
Shanxi	BA	1.00	1.00	1.00	1.00	1.00	1.00	0.83	0.95	0.87	0.52
	AA	0.01	0.02	0.05	0.04	0.04	0.08	0.08	0.13	0.17	0.12
Inner Mongolia	BA	1.00	0.41	0.05	0.27	1.00	0.61	0.56	0.57	0.56	0.34
	AA	0.01	0.00	0.00	0.00	0.02	0.02	0.02	0.02	0.03	0.03
Liaoning	BA	0.24	0.14	0.22	0.48	0.62	0.47	0.61	0.45	0.63	0.59
	AA	0.22	0.16	0.24	0.36	0.32	0.30	0.40	0.43	0.49	0.49
Jilin	BA	0.42	0.12	0.19	0.58	0.65	0.35	0.56	0.64	0.61	0.54
	AA	0.06	0.03	0.05	0.06	0.12	0.05	0.11	0.18	0.25	0.21
Heilongjiang	BA	0.50	0.06	0.08	0.23	0.19	0.21	0.24	0.30	0.29	0.45
	AA	0.13	0.04	0.05	0.07	0.09	0.10	0.17	0.20	0.25	0.32
Shanghai	BA	0.86	0.53	0.63	0.88	0.50	0.55	0.73	0.57	0.70	0.87
	AA	1.00	1.00	0.94	1.00	0.84	0.81	0.82	0.70	0.85	0.83
Jiangsu	BA	0.28	0.27	0.37	0.70	0.80	0.69	0.97	1.00	0.66	0.81
	AA	0.61	0.69	0.94	1.00	1.00	1.00	1.00	1.00	1.00	1.00
Zhejiang	BA	0.18	0.14	0.17	0.43	0.60	0.46	0.50	0.63	0.71	0.58
	AA	0.33	0.40	0.46	0.49	0.64	0.57	0.72	0.91	1.00	0.91
Anhui	BA	0.74	0.50	0.21	0.34	0.76	1.00	1.00	1.00	1.00	1.00
	AA	0.05	0.06	0.06	0.07	0.23	0.33	0.64	0.83	1.00	1.00
Fujian	BA	0.86	0.68	0.66	0.86	0.82	0.77	1.00	0.81	0.56	0.51
	AA	0.72	0.71	0.72	0.68	0.69	0.82	0.63	0.70	0.69	0.66
Jiangxi	BA	0.15	0.11	0.10	0.18	0.29	0.37	0.28	0.42	0.53	0.69
	AA	0.09	0.07	0.08	0.08	0.14	0.18	0.17	0.26	0.42	0.58
Shandong	BA	0.45	0.24	0.38	0.50	0.54	0.63	0.65	0.60	0.53	0.58
	AA	0.51	0.54	0.67	0.71	0.84	0.84	0.85	0.80	0.76	0.75
Henan	BA	0.15	0.12	0.17	0.69	0.51	0.71	0.48	0.51	1.00	1.00
	AA	0.08	0.09	0.14	0.20	0.30	0.33	0.44	0.51	1.00	1.00
Hubei	BA	0.16	0.13	0.16	0.36	0.54	0.50	0.54	0.52	0.55	0.52
	AA	0.16	0.11	0.17	0.18	0.38	0.37	0.44	0.58	0.68	0.58
Hunan	BA	0.19	0.15	0.12	0.70	0.94	0.86	1.00	1.00	1.00	0.85
	AA	0.04	0.04	0.05	0.11	0.27	0.26	0.56	0.59	0.79	0.86
Guangdong	BA	0.35	0.33	0.32	1.00	0.83	1.00	0.91	0.95	1.00	1.00
	AA	1.00	1.00	1.00	1.00	1.00	1.00	1.00	1.00	1.00	1.00

Provinces		Year									
		2005	2006	2007	2008	2009	2010	2011	2012	2013	2014
Guangxi	BA	0.56	0.15	0.11	0.55	0.49	0.41	0.52	0.53	0.68	0.57
	AA	0.04	0.02	0.03	0.03	0.05	0.04	0.08	0.11	0.17	0.16
Hainan	BA	1.00	1.00	1.00	1.00	1.00	1.00	1.00	1.00	1.00	0.85
	AA	0.00	0.00	0.01	0.00	0.05	0.02	0.07	0.12	0.14	0.15
Chongqing	BA	0.29	0.25	0.17	0.44	0.94	0.71	1.00	0.81	0.94	0.97
	AA	0.07	0.08	0.08	0.13	0.23	0.22	0.41	0.34	0.51	0.53
Sichuan	BA	0.21	0.23	0.25	0.29	0.54	0.35	1.00	0.82	0.70	0.98
	AA	0.29	0.33	0.44	0.38	0.53	0.41	0.55	0.80	0.84	0.90
Guizhou	BA	0.22	0.16	0.13	0.49	0.58	0.62	0.42	0.43	0.42	0.45
	AA	0.05	0.06	0.10	0.11	0.14	0.18	0.18	0.28	0.35	0.37
Yunnan	BA	1.00	0.20	0.46	1.00	1.00	0.80	0.92	0.81	0.76	0.64
	AA	0.08	0.02	0.08	0.03	0.07	0.04	0.09	0.14	0.13	0.14
Shaanxi	BA	0.09	0.07	0.08	0.17	0.21	0.23	0.27	0.25	0.29	0.24
	AA	0.16	0.15	0.21	0.20	0.19	0.22	0.29	0.32	0.44	0.37
Gansu	BA	0.53	0.27	0.17	0.48	0.42	0.94	0.46	0.68	0.59	0.63
	AA	0.02	0.01	0.01	0.02	0.03	0.05	0.05	0.08	0.08	0.11
Qinghai	BA	1.00	1.00	1.00	0.39	0.59	1.00	1.00	0.16	0.99	0.49
	AA	0.00	0.01	0.01	0.00	0.01	0.00	0.01	0.00	0.01	0.00
Ningxia	BA	0.13	0.24	0.10	0.28	0.31	0.41	0.69	0.69	1.00	0.35
	AA	0.01	0.01	0.01	0.02	0.02	0.03	0.04	0.04	0.08	0.03
Average value	BA	0.48	0.34	0.36	0.58	0.65	0.66	0.70	0.67	0.72	0.67
	AA	0.25	0.25	0.30	0.31	0.35	0.36	0.40	0.45	0.53	0.53

Note: "BA" means before adjustment; "AA" means after adjustment.

Table 3.
Technical efficiency estimation results of technological innovation.

development, the more conducive it is to reduce the redundancy of input variables, and the more effective it is to promote the improvement of R&D innovation efficiency in high-tech industries. (2) Geographical location has a positive effect on all input slack variables at a highly significant level, and compared with other environmental variables, geographical location has a stronger effect on all kinds of innovation input slack. The results show that the eastern region has higher investment redundancy than the central and western regions. This is mainly due to the greater demand for innovation in the eastern region, which often spends huge sums of money on research and development innovation, thus easily causing excessive investment in innovation. (3) The influence of regional workers' quality on four types of input slack variables also shows significant positive effects. The higher the number of college students in the region, the higher the quality of workers in the region. However, on the other hand, with the continuous improvement of China's education level, the number of talents engaged in high-tech industries is increasing and even reaching saturation, which to a certain extent increases the redundancy of

Provinces		Year									
		2005	2006	2007	2008	2009	2010	2011	2012	2013	2014
Beijing	BA	0.50	0.59	1.00	1.00	1.00	1.00	1.00	1.00	1.00	1.00
	AA	0.96	0.96	1.00	1.00	1.00	1.00	1.00	1.00	1.00	1.00
Tianjin	BA	1.00	1.00	1.00	1.00	1.00	1.00	1.00	1.00	1.00	1.00
	AA	1.00	1.00	1.00	1.00	1.00	1.00	1.00	1.00	1.00	1.00
Hebei	BA	0.13	0.28	0.15	0.44	0.34	0.48	0.28	0.45	0.44	0.50
	AA	1.00	1.00	1.00	1.00	1.00	1.00	1.00	1.00	0.99	1.00
Shanxi	BA	1.00	1.00	1.00	1.00	1.00	1.00	0.85	0.98	0.88	0.55
	AA	0.99	0.99	0.99	1.00	1.00	1.00	1.00	1.00	1.00	1.00
Inner Mongolia	BA	1.00	0.49	0.15	0.59	1.00	0.78	0.61	0.71	0.62	0.49
	AA	0.98	0.98	0.98	0.99	1.00	1.00	1.00	1.00	1.00	1.00
Liaoning	BA	0.59	0.29	0.27	0.48	0.75	0.53	0.61	0.46	0.66	0.60
	AA	1.00	0.99	1.00	1.00	1.00	1.00	1.00	0.99	1.00	0.95
Jilin	BA	0.44	0.32	0.40	0.59	0.67	0.35	0.56	0.65	0.63	0.57
	AA	0.99	0.98	0.97	0.97	0.97	0.97	0.97	0.97	0.98	0.96
Heilongjiang	BA	0.64	0.22	0.10	0.25	0.21	0.27	0.27	0.31	0.32	0.46
	AA	0.98	0.98	0.99	1.00	0.97	0.96	0.94	0.95	0.95	0.96
Shanghai	BA	1.00	1.00	0.91	1.00	0.73	0.70	0.77	0.57	0.75	0.88
	AA	1.00	1.00	0.99	1.00	0.90	0.89	0.96	0.89	0.93	0.99
Jiangsu	BA	0.60	0.36	0.78	1.00	1.00	1.00	1.00	1.00	1.00	1.00
	AA	0.98	0.87	0.98	1.00	1.00	1.00	1.00	1.00	1.00	1.00
Zhejiang	BA	0.38	0.38	0.55	0.57	0.83	0.63	0.74	0.90	1.00	0.88
	AA	0.91	0.85	0.81	0.79	0.91	0.80	0.85	0.92	1.00	0.91
Anhui	BA	0.91	0.51	0.28	0.64	1.00	1.00	1.00	1.00	1.00	1.00
	AA	0.98	0.99	0.99	1.00	1.00	1.00	1.00	1.00	1.00	1.00
Fujian	BA	0.88	0.68	0.78	0.93	0.91	0.89	1.00	0.81	0.57	0.52
	AA	1.00	0.98	0.98	1.00	0.99	0.99	1.00	0.94	0.81	0.77
Jiangxi	BA	0.23	0.22	0.12	0.20	0.29	0.38	0.29	0.42	0.53	0.70
	AA	0.97	0.99	0.99	0.99	0.96	0.95	0.93	0.90	0.91	0.98
Shandong	BA	0.87	0.58	0.73	0.65	0.65	0.78	0.72	0.69	0.66	0.66
	AA	1.00	1.00	1.00	0.95	0.95	0.99	0.94	0.87	0.84	0.78
Henan	BA	0.15	0.66	0.45	0.79	0.79	0.84	0.53	0.56	1.00	1.00
	AA	0.97	0.98	1.00	1.00	1.00	1.00	0.97	0.96	1.00	1.00
Hubei	BA	0.84	0.51	0.34	0.44	0.62	0.53	0.54	0.55	0.60	0.52
	AA	1.00	1.00	1.00	1.00	1.00	1.00	1.00	1.00	0.99	0.93
Hunan	BA	0.29	0.18	0.17	0.81	1.00	0.94	1.00	1.00	1.00	0.85
	AA	1.00	1.00	1.00	1.00	1.00	1.00	1.00	1.00	1.00	0.97
Guangdong	BA	1.00	1.00	1.00	1.00	1.00	1.00	1.00	1.00	1.00	1.00
	AA	1.00	1.00	1.00	1.00	1.00	1.00	1.00	1.00	1.00	1.00

Provinces		Year									
		2005	2006	2007	2008	2009	2010	2011	2012	2013	2014
Guangxi	BA	0.74	0.23	0.16	0.56	0.50	0.42	0.54	0.55	0.70	0.61
	AA	0.97	0.97	0.96	0.97	0.99	0.98	0.98	0.99	1.00	0.98
Hainan	BA	1.00	1.00	1.00	1.00	1.00	1.00	1.00	1.00	1.00	0.88
	AA	1.00	1.00	1.00	1.00	1.00	1.00	1.00	1.00	1.00	1.00
Chongqing	BA	0.31	0.49	0.27	0.61	0.96	0.77	1.00	0.81	0.94	0.98
	AA	0.95	0.94	0.94	0.95	0.98	0.98	1.00	0.97	0.99	1.00
Sichuan	BA	0.26	0.34	0.54	0.44	0.56	0.52	1.00	0.82	0.74	1.00
	AA	0.96	0.95	0.95	0.90	0.90	0.92	1.00	0.98	0.96	1.00
Guizhou	BA	0.25	0.73	0.39	0.71	0.69	0.67	0.45	0.43	0.42	0.46
	AA	0.93	0.94	0.95	0.94	0.96	0.96	0.94	0.91	0.90	0.90
Yunnan	BA	1.00	0.55	1.00	1.00	1.00	0.84	0.94	0.81	0.77	0.66
	AA	1.00	0.98	0.99	0.97	1.00	1.00	0.99	0.99	1.00	0.99
Shaanxi	BA	0.17	0.12	0.16	0.21	0.22	0.28	0.28	0.25	0.32	0.24
	AA	0.92	0.89	0.93	0.88	0.85	0.84	0.85	0.78	0.80	0.77
Gansu	BA	1.00	0.27	0.18	0.50	0.46	0.95	0.46	0.74	0.64	0.69
	AA	0.95	0.98	0.97	0.98	0.99	0.99	0.99	1.00	1.00	1.00
Qinghai	BA	1.00	1.00	1.00	1.00	1.00	1.00	1.00	1.00	1.00	1.00
	AA	0.96	0.97	0.96	0.97	0.98	0.98	0.98	0.99	1.00	1.00
Ningxia	BA	0.13	0.24	0.11	0.32	0.49	0.47	0.73	0.83	1.00	0.49
	AA	0.95	0.95	0.95	0.95	0.97	0.97	0.97	0.98	0.99	1.00
Average value	BA	0.63	0.53	0.52	0.68	0.75	0.73	0.73	0.73	0.77	0.73
	AA	0.98	0.97	0.97	0.97	0.98	0.97	0.97	0.96	0.97	0.96

Note: "BA" means before adjustment; "AA" means after adjustment.

Table 4.
Pure technical efficiency estimation results of technological innovation.

input variables and reduces the innovation efficiency level of China's high-tech industries (4). The number of enterprises in high-tech industries has a significant negative impact on the relaxation of R&D funds, new product development funds, and technological transformation funds, which shows that the increase of competition in the industry can effectively reduce the redundancy of capital investment and is beneficial to the improvement of R&D innovation efficiency (5). Local government innovation support has significant positive effects on four types of input slack variables, which indicates that the stronger the government's support for high-tech industries, the easier it is to increase the redundancy of each input, and the more unfavorable it is to improve innovation efficiency. This may be because some inappropriate subsidy policies adopted by the government distort the market, undermine the self-regulating function of the market, and hinder the improvement of innovation efficiency (6). The number of scientific and technological institutions has a significant positive effect on R&D personnel FTE slack variables, while it has a significant negative effect on R&D funds, new product development funds, and technological transformation funds. This shows that although the increase in the number of scientific and technological institutions will increase the redundancy of human capital investment and hinder the improvement of innovation efficiency, it

Provinces		Year									
		2005	2006	2007	2008	2009	2010	2011	2012	2013	2014
Beijing	BA	0.530 (drs)	0.510 (drs)	1.000 (crs)	1.000 (crs)	1.000 (crs)	1.000 (crs)	1.000 (crs)	1.000 (crs)	1.000 (crs)	1.000 (crs)
	AA	0.463 (irs)	0.469 (irs)	1.000 (crs)	1.000 (crs)	1.000 (crs)	1.000 (crs)	1.000 (crs)	1.000 (crs)	0.974 (irs)	0.923 (irs)
Tianjin	BA	1.000 (crs)	1.000 (crs)	1.000 (crs)	1.000 (crs)	1.000 (crs)	1.000 (crs)	1.000 (crs)	1.000 (crs)	1.000 (crs)	1.000 (crs)
	AA	1.000 (crs)	1.000 (crs)	0.900 (irs)	0.831 (irs)	0.824 (irs)	0.920 (irs)	0.637 (irs)	0.869 (irs)	1.000 (crs)	0.921 (irs)
Hebei	BA	0.944 (drs)	0.318 (drs)	0.672 (drs)	0.902 (drs)	0.820 (drs)	0.887 (drs)	0.988 (irs)	0.985 (irs)	0.989 (drs)	0.992 (irs)
	AA	0.058 (irs)	0.054 (irs)	0.071 (irs)	0.107 (irs)	0.130 (irs)	0.128 (irs)	0.160 (irs)	0.227 (irs)	0.314 (irs)	0.427 (irs)
Shanxi	BA	1.000 (crs)	1.000 (crs)	1.000 (crs)	1.000 (crs)	1.000 (crs)	1.000 (crs)	0.980 (irs)	0.974 (irs)	0.994 (drs)	0.944 (irs)
	AA	0.012 (irs)	0.022 (irs)	0.050 (irs)	0.036 (irs)	0.041 (irs)	0.081 (irs)	0.076 (irs)	0.127 (irs)	0.169 (irs)	0.118 (irs)
Inner Mongolia	BA	1.000 (crs)	0.838 (irs)	0.336 (irs)	0.451 (irs)	1.000 (crs)	0.781 (irs)	0.926 (irs)	0.793 (irs)	0.910 (irs)	0.691 (irs)
	AA	0.007 (irs)	0.003 (irs)	0.002 (irs)	0.002 (irs)	0.023 (irs)	0.015 (irs)	0.017 (irs)	0.015 (irs)	0.026 (irs)	0.025 (irs)
Liaoning	BA	0.414 (drs)	0.500 (drs)	0.807 (drs)	0.989 (drs)	0.831 (drs)	0.880 (drs)	0.999 (irs)	0.994 (irs)	0.951 (drs)	0.991 (irs)
	AA	0.218 (irs)	0.162 (irs)	0.239 (irs)	0.356 (irs)	0.319 (irs)	0.303 (irs)	0.399 (irs)	0.435 (irs)	0.490 (irs)	0.510 (irs)
Jilin	BA	0.949 (drs)	0.388 (drs)	0.468 (drs)	0.980 (drs)	0.969 (drs)	0.989 (drs)	0.989 (irs)	0.979 (irs)	0.962 (irs)	0.959 (irs)
	AA	0.062 (irs)	0.029 (irs)	0.052 (irs)	0.059 (irs)	0.118 (irs)	0.054 (irs)	0.113 (irs)	0.181 (irs)	0.257 (irs)	0.219 (irs)
Heilongjiang	BA	0.774 (drs)	0.272 (drs)	0.800 (drs)	0.912 (drs)	0.887 (drs)	0.762 (drs)	0.874 (drs)	0.990 (irs)	0.911 (drs)	0.978 (irs)
	AA	0.133 (irs)	0.036 (irs)	0.054 (irs)	0.072 (irs)	0.095 (irs)	0.105 (irs)	0.176 (irs)	0.211 (irs)	0.259 (irs)	0.338 (irs)
Shanghai	BA	0.862 (drs)	0.528 (drs)	0.690 (drs)	0.875 (drs)	0.690 (drs)	0.783 (drs)	0.958 (drs)	0.998 (irs)	0.928 (drs)	0.990 (drs)
	AA	1.000 (crs)	1.000 (crs)	0.952 (irs)	1.000 (crs)	0.934 (irs)	0.906 (irs)	0.852 (irs)	0.795 (irs)	0.913 (irs)	0.833 (irs)
Jiangsu	BA	0.470 (drs)	0.746 (drs)	0.472 (drs)	0.696 (drs)	0.795 (drs)	0.685 (drs)	0.974 (drs)	1.000 (crs)	0.657 (drs)	0.806 (drs)
	AA	0.625 (irs)	0.794 (irs)	0.962 (irs)	1.000 (crs)	1.000 (crs)	1.000 (crs)	1.000 (crs)	1.000 (crs)	1.000 (crs)	1.000 (crs)
Zhejiang	BA	0.462 (drs)	0.373 (drs)	0.319 (drs)	0.753 (drs)	0.729 (drs)	0.738 (drs)	0.681 (drs)	0.705 (drs)	0.708 (drs)	0.661 (drs)
	AA	0.363 (irs)	0.470 (irs)	0.566 (irs)	0.618 (irs)	0.708 (irs)	0.708 (irs)	0.839 (irs)	0.990 (irs)	1.000 (crs)	0.997 (irs)
Anhui	BA	0.820 (drs)	0.988 (drs)	0.765 (drs)	0.531 (drs)	0.758 (drs)	1.000 (crs)	1.000 (crs)	1.000 (crs)	1.000 (crs)	1.000 (crs)
	AA	0.050 (irs)	0.057 (irs)	0.063 (irs)	0.071 (irs)	0.226 (irs)	0.333 (irs)	0.641 (irs)	0.834 (irs)	1.000 (crs)	1.000 (crs)

Provinces		Year									
		2005	2006	2007	2008	2009	2010	2011	2012	2013	2014
Fujian	BA	0.978 (drs)	0.996 (drs)	0.846 (drs)	0.928 (drs)	0.908 (drs)	0.869 (drs)	1.000 (crs)	1.000 (crs)	0.978 (drs)	0.990 (drs)
	AA	0.725 (irs)	0.720 (irs)	0.729 (irs)	0.683 (irs)	0.696 (irs)	0.834 (irs)	0.634 (irs)	0.748 (irs)	0.846 (irs)	0.851 (irs)
Jiangxi	BA	0.621 (drs)	0.510 (drs)	0.806 (drs)	0.923 (drs)	0.984 (drs)	0.974 (drs)	0.994 (irs)	0.990 (irs)	0.997 (drs)	0.993 (irs)
	AA	0.090 (irs)	0.069 (irs)	0.080 (irs)	0.080 (irs)	0.148 (irs)	0.187 (irs)	0.186 (irs)	0.285 (irs)	0.467 (irs)	0.586 (irs)
Shandong	BA	0.522 (drs)	0.422 (drs)	0.520 (drs)	0.765 (drs)	0.837 (drs)	0.810 (drs)	0.905 (drs)	0.865 (drs)	0.807 (drs)	0.884 (drs)
	AA	0.505 (irs)	0.535 (irs)	0.666 (irs)	0.746 (irs)	0.881 (irs)	0.856 (irs)	0.908 (irs)	0.921 (irs)	0.904 (irs)	0.963 (irs)
Henan	BA	0.947 (drs)	0.186 (drs)	0.383 (drs)	0.871 (drs)	0.643 (drs)	0.839 (drs)	0.905 (drs)	0.905 (drs)	1.000 (crs)	1.000 (crs)
	AA	0.080 (irs)	0.090 (irs)	0.140 (irs)	0.200 (irs)	0.301 (irs)	0.326 (irs)	0.459 (irs)	0.532 (irs)	1.000 (crs)	1.000 (crs)
Hubei	BA	0.505 (irs)	0.259 (drs)	0.481 (drs)	0.824 (drs)	0.871 (drs)	0.935 (drs)	1.000 (crs)	0.946 (drs)	0.916 (drs)	0.999 (irs)
	AA	0.162 (irs)	0.109 (irs)	0.168 (irs)	0.175 (irs)	0.384 (irs)	0.370 (irs)	0.436 (irs)	0.581 (irs)	0.684 (crs)	0.620 (irs)
Hunan	BA	0.642 (drs)	0.839 (drs)	0.702 (drs)	0.866 (drs)	0.936 (drs)	0.911 (drs)	1.000 (crs)	1.000 (crs)	1.000 (crs)	0.999 (irs)
	AA	0.039 (irs)	0.042 (irs)	0.049 (irs)	0.105 (irs)	0.270 (irs)	0.260 (irs)	0.555 (irs)	0.592 (irs)	0.793 (irs)	0.886 (irs)
Guangdong	BA	0.354 (drs)	0.327 (drs)	0.322 (drs)	1.000 (crs)	0.833 (drs)	1.000 (crs)	0.911 (drs)	0.951 (drs)	1.000 (crs)	1.000 (crs)
	AA	1.000 (crs)	1.000 (crs)	1.000 (crs)	1.000 (crs)	1.000 (crs)	1.000 (crs)	1.000 (crs)	1.000 (crs)	1.000 (crs)	1.000 (crs)
Guangxi	BA	0.752 (drs)	0.642 (drs)	0.679 (drs)	0.976 (drs)	0.980 (drs)	0.976 (drs)	0.970 (irs)	0.964 (irs)	0.975 (irs)	0.942 (irs)
	AA	0.043 (irs)	0.016 (irs)	0.027 (irs)	0.035 (irs)	0.052 (irs)	0.038 (irs)	0.085 (irs)	0.115 (irs)	0.170 (irs)	0.160 (irs)
Hainan	BA	1.000 (crs)	1.000 (crs)	1.000 (crs)	1.000 (crs)	1.000 (crs)	1.000 (crs)	1.000 (crs)	1.000 (crs)	1.000 (crs)	0.966 (irs)
	AA	0.002 (irs)	0.001 (irs)	0.005 (irs)	0.003 (irs)	0.045 (irs)	0.022 (irs)	0.070 (irs)	0.116 (irs)	0.141 (irs)	0.150 (irs)
Chongqing	BA	0.934 (drs)	0.516 (drs)	0.631 (drs)	0.725 (drs)	0.973 (drs)	0.925 (drs)	1.000 (crs)	0.993 (irs)	0.999 (irs)	0.992 (irs)
	AA	0.076 (irs)	0.083 (irs)	0.088 (irs)	0.134 (irs)	0.235 (irs)	0.227 (irs)	0.413 (irs)	0.349 (irs)	0.519 (irs)	0.530 (irs)
Sichuan	BA	0.815 (drs)	0.675 (drs)	0.458 (drs)	0.664 (drs)	0.973 (drs)	0.672 (drs)	1.000 (crs)	0.999 (drs)	0.947 (drs)	0.984 (drs)
	AA	0.302 (irs)	0.344 (irs)	0.466 (irs)	0.419 (irs)	0.584 irs)	0.447 (irs)	0.552 (irs)	0.816 (irs)	0.873 (irs)	0.899 (irs)
Guizhou	BA	0.865 (drs)	0.224 (drs)	0.330 (drs)	0.691 (drs)	0.835 (drs)	0.924 (drs)	0.926 (drs)	0.997 (drs)	0.999 (drs)	0.990 (irs)
	AA	0.050 (irs)	0.060 (irs)	0.102 (irs)	0.114 (irs)	0.143 (irs)	0.188 (irs)	0.192 (irs)	0.312 (irs)	0.393 (irs)	0.418 (irs)

Provinces		Year									
		2005	2006	2007	2008	2009	2010	2011	2012	2013	2014
Yunnan	BA	1.000 (crs)	0.371 (drs)	0.458 (drs)	1.000 (crs)	1.000 (crs)	0.952 (drs)	0.980 (irs)	0.994 (irs)	0.987 (irs)	0.978 (irs)
	AA	0.082 (irs)	0.018 (irs)	0.080 (irs)	0.034 (irs)	0.072 (irs)	0.045 (irs)	0.087 (irs)	0.137 (irs)	0.132 (irs)	0.144 (irs)
Shaanxi	BA	0.525 (drs)	0.550 (drs)	0.493 (drs)	0.801 (drs)	0.935 (drs)	0.818 (drs)	0.957 (drs)	0.993 (irs)	0.933 (drs)	0.991 (irs)
	AA	0.175 (irs)	0.172 (irs)	0.221 (irs)	0.231 (irs)	0.229 (irs)	0.259 (irs)	0.340 (irs)	0.406 (irs)	0.550 (irs)	0.474 (irs)
Gansu	BA	0.529 (drs)	0.996 (irs)	0.924 (irs)	0.966 (irs)	0.910 (irs)	0.987 (drs)	0.994 (irs)	0.928 (irs)	0.914 (irs)	0.909 (irs)
	AA	0.024 (irs)	0.010 (irs)	0.008 (irs)	0.016 (irs)	0.026 (irs)	0.046 (irs)	0.045 (irs)	0.084 (irs)	0.083 (irs)	0.109 (irs)
Qinghai	BA	1.000 (crs)	1.000 (crs)	1.000 (crs)	0.387 (irs)	0.590 (irs)	1.000 (crs)	1.000 (crs)	0.162 (irs)	0.989 (irs)	0.490 (irs)
	AA	0.001 (irs)	0.011 (irs)	0.011 (irs)	0.000 (irs)	0.006 (irs)	0.005 (irs)	0.005 (irs)	0.001 (irs)	0.006 (irs)	0.003 (irs)
Ningxia	BA	0.946 (irs)	0.999 (crs)	0.946 (irs)	0.886 (irs)	0.641 (irs)	0.870 (irs)	0.946 (drs)	0.839 (irs)	1.000 (crs)	0.730 (irs)
	AA	0.010 (irs)	0.010 (irs)	0.011 (irs)	0.019 (irs)	0.021 (irs)	0.030 (irs)	0.036 (irs)	0.042 (irs)	0.042 (irs)	0.029 (irs)
Average value	BA	0.753	0.620	0.666	0.840	0.873	0.895	0.961	0.929	0.947	0.926
	AA	0.254	0.255	0.302	0.315	0.362	0.369	0.411	0.473	0.553	0.556

Note: "irs" indicates increasing scale efficiency; "crs" indicates that the scale efficiency is unchanged; "drs" indicates a decline in scale efficiency. "BA" means before adjustment; "AA" means after adjustment.

Table 5.
Estimate results of scale efficiency of technological innovation.

can effectively reduce the waste of R&D funds, new product development funds, and technological transformation funds, thus promoting the improvement of innovation efficiency.

To sum up, environmental variables have significant effects on input redundancy, and their effects are different. Therefore, it is necessary to eliminate the effects of environmental factors and random factors when studying the true level of innovation efficiency.

4.3 DEA empirical analysis and Malmquist index

Using DEAP software again, DEA analysis is conducted based on the original output data and the adjusted input variable data. Based on the results shown in **Tables 3–5** (after adjustment), the estimated outcomes are shown in **Table 6**.

Overall, the efficiency values before and after the adjustment have changed. The adjusted average technical efficiency is 0.25–0.53, the average pure technical efficiency is 0.98–0.96, and the average scale efficiency is 0.254–0.556.Compared with before adjustment, the average value of technical efficiency in different years has decreased, but the average value of pure technical efficiency has increased significantly, while the average value of pure technical efficiency is relatively stable, approaching 1.The average value of scale efficiency has not only dropped significantly, but also there are only two states after the adjustment: increasing scale

Variable	R&D personnel FTE slack variable	R&D funds slack variable	New product development funds slack variable	Funds for technological transformation slack variable
Constant term	−1.42E + 03*** (−2.97)	−2.94E + 05*** (−39647.79)	−4.14E + 05*** (−241,493.66)	−4.67E + 05*** (−455,599.32)
Regional real GDP	−3.39E − 01*** (−8.81)	−3.22E + 00 (−0.76)	−9.96E + 00** (−2.08)	−6.61E + 00* (−1.49)
Geographical position	1.05E + 03*** (2.23)	1.38E + 05*** (99,695)	2.27E + 05*** (215,428)	5.88E + 04*** (58,524)
Quality of local laborers	7.57E − 03*** (11.39)	3.62E − 01*** (6.34)	5.16E − 01*** (7.64)	5.74E − 01*** (7.07)
Number of high-tech industrial enterprises	−1.15E − 01 (−0.33)	−6.16E + 01*** (−2.8)	−5.64E + 01** (−2.2)	−1.14E + 02*** (−2.1)
Local government innovation support	2.30E − 02*** (4.03)	2.03E + 00*** (4.51)	2.20E + 00*** (3.81)	1.59E + 00*** (3.06)
Number of scientific and technological institutions	1.58E + 00* (1.45)	−1.64E + 02** (−1.76)	−1.61E + 02* (1.37)	−1.76E + 02** (−2.05)
σ^2	2.44E + 07***	1.43E + 11***	3.21E + 11***	4.09E + 11***
γ	7.52E − 01***	7.76E − 01***	8.46E − 01***	9.04E − 01***
Logarithmic likelihood function	−2.73E + 03	−3.98E + 03	−4.04E + 03	−4.00E + 03
Unilateral likelihood function	1.41E + 02	1.58E + 02	2.44E + 02	3.47E + 02

*Note: *** means $p < 0.01$; ** means $p < 0.05$; * means $p < 0.1$.*

Table 6.
Estimated results of SFA.

returns and constant scale returns. This shows that compared with the situation before the adjustment, China's high-tech industry does not actually have the problems of excessive scale and overcapacity. From a local point of view, the regions where the average value of technical efficiency has increased include Beijing, Shanghai, Jiangsu, Zhejiang, Shandong, Guangdong, and Shaanxi, indicating that the low efficiency of these provinces before adjustment is due to environmental factors. The average value of comprehensive technical efficiency in other regions has decreased, which indicates that the high level of innovation efficiency shown in these regions is mainly influenced by favorable environment and random factors.

In order to further investigate the changes in total factor productivity of China's high-tech industries, this chapter constructs Malmquist index model based on the DEA model adjusted in the third stage. The results are shown in **Tables 7–9**. The columns in the table are the index changes for every two consecutive years from 2005 to 2014 and the index changes for the whole period from 2005 to 2014. The last two rows are the arithmetic average and geometric average of the index, respectively. Generally, geometric mean is used to calculate average ratio and average speed, so this chapter uses this value to represent the average growth rate of total factor productivity, technical efficiency index, and technical progress index. **Table 10** summarizes Malmquist index and its decomposition index of technological innovation in order to meet the needs of total factor productivity of R&D innovation in various regions in subsequent research.

Provinces	Year									
	2005/ 2006	2006/ 2007	2007/ 2008	2008/ 2009	2009/ 2010	2010/ 2011	2011/ 2012	2012/ 2013	2013/ 2014	2005/ 2014
Beijing	1.144	2.691	0.999	0.958	0.952	1.049	1.181	0.871	1.087	1.141
Tianjin	1.066	0.878	0.869	0.93	0.977	0.843	1.276	1.314	0.952	0.999
Hebei	1.299	1.169	1.444	1.48	0.8	1.473	1.207	1.287	1.262	1.251
Shanxi	2.186	2.204	0.754	1.192	1.69	1.204	1.576	1.17	0.693	1.309
Inner Mongolia	0.556	0.8	0.565	19.297	0.534	1.56	0.771	1.589	0.977	1.191
Liaoning	0.817	1.451	1.498	0.93	0.801	1.588	1.015	1.049	0.933	1.085
Jilin	0.71	1.486	1.078	2.471	0.397	2.665	1.45	1.264	0.843	1.185
Heilongjiang	0.338	1.388	1.302	1.536	0.745	2.068	1.14	1.077	1.334	1.100
Shanghai	1.109	0.941	1.057	0.782	0.955	1.185	1.095	0.94	1.211	1.022
Jiangsu	1.181	1.357	1.211	0.853	0.858	1.54	0.97	0.917	1.077	1.086
Zhejiang	1.275	1.115	1.048	1.61	0.689	1.541	1.178	0.979	0.851	1.107
Anhui	1.191	1.113	1.193	3.639	1.006	2.247	1.214	1.054	1.147	1.388
Fujian	1.009	0.999	1.01	0.894	1.088	1.078	1.02	0.939	0.937	0.995
Jiangxi	0.953	1.111	1.04	1.829	1.136	1.214	1.326	1.498	1.309	1.246
Shandong	1.17	1.219	1.079	1.127	0.992	1.083	0.99	0.906	0.959	1.054
Henan	1.413	1.367	1.304	1.95	0.76	1.597	1.08	2.413	1.073	1.367
Hubei	0.965	1.405	1.07	2.174	0.883	1.476	1.21	1.02	0.853	1.177
Hunan	1.212	1.071	2.098	2.905	0.785	2.483	0.983	1.219	1.074	1.394
Guangdong	1.203	1.031	0.942	1.135	1.038	1.167	0.954	1.01	1.008	1.051
Guangxi	0.592	1.408	1.191	1.963	0.601	2.802	1.253	1.314	0.895	1.191
Hainan	1.002	3.76	0.529	18.576	0.354	3.899	1.534	1.082	1.051	1.647
Chongqing	1.179	1.023	1.63	1.674	0.902	2.46	0.772	1.327	1.041	1.256
Sichuan	1.18	1.337	0.94	1.273	0.604	1.635	1.65	0.904	1.112	1.134
Guizhou	1.704	1.517	0.933	1.707	0.957	1.185	1.474	1.102	1.197	1.278
Yunnan	0.343	4.176	0.381	2.515	0.55	2.368	1.471	0.865	1.056	1.102
Shaanxi	1.017	1.284	0.996	1.105	0.929	1.678	1.107	1.239	0.792	1.104
Gansu	0.699	0.734	1.9	1.925	1.369	1.216	1.744	0.872	1.306	1.225
Qinghai	34.988	0.943	0.03	20.816	0.527	1.452	0.187	5.327	0.506	1.259
Ningxia	1.232	1.087	1.807	1.065	1.281	1.608	1.077	1.642	0.376	1.150
Arithmetic average	2.232	1.451	1.100	3.459	0.868	1.702	1.169	1.317	0.997	1.189
Geometry average	1.117	1.317	0.946	1.922	0.820	1.596	1.107	1.202	0.967	1.182

Table 7.
Changes in total factor productivity index of technological innovation in high-tech industries.

Generally speaking, the average total factor productivity of R&D innovation in China's high-tech industries increased from 2005 to 2014, with an increase of 18.2%. Except that the total factor productivity index changes in 2007/2008, 2009/2010, and 2013/2014 are less than 1, the other annual average is greater than 1, which

Provinces	Year									
	2005/ 2006	**2006/ 2007**	**2007/ 2008**	**2008/ 2009**	**2009/ 2010**	**2010/ 2011**	**2011/ 2012**	**2012/ 2013**	**2013/ 2014**	**2005/ 2014**
Beijing	1.007	2.202	1	1	1	1	1	0.955	0.967	1.083
Tianjin	1	0.891	0.921	1.003	1.103	0.684	1.391	1.158	0.921	0.991
Hebei	0.97	1.286	1.473	1.313	1.008	1.266	1.351	1.437	1.309	1.257
Shanxi	1.878	2.314	0.7	1.157	2.015	0.952	1.675	1.319	0.683	1.294
Inner Mongolia	0.431	0.839	0.674	14.504	0.677	1.223	0.854	1.747	0.956	1.172
Liaoning	0.766	1.478	1.455	0.876	0.978	1.281	1.091	1.161	0.993	1.096
Jilin	0.474	1.733	1.137	2.073	0.457	2.135	1.606	1.428	0.818	1.151
Heilongjiang	0.262	1.565	1.307	1.303	1.064	1.738	1.209	1.219	1.302	1.106
Shanghai	1	0.934	1.071	0.84	0.941	0.995	0.881	1.163	1.024	0.979
Jiangsu	1.13	1.355	1.059	1	1	1	1	1	1	1.055
Zhejiang	1.173	1.21	1.042	1.316	0.865	1.273	1.251	1.094	0.907	1.115
Anhui	1.135	1.119	1.127	3.239	1.476	1.927	1.29	1.181	1	1.396
Fujian	0.978	1.02	0.945	1.006	1.196	0.775	1.112	0.989	0.934	0.989
Jiangxi	0.772	1.165	0.988	1.836	1.245	0.934	1.5	1.706	1.337	1.231
Shandong	1.084	1.244	1.045	1.166	1.009	0.931	0.989	1.015	0.969	1.046
Henan	1.131	1.587	1.397	1.622	1.084	1.369	1.147	1.896	1	1.331
Hubei	0.655	1.536	1.047	2.13	0.994	1.183	1.331	1.154	0.841	1.146
Hunan	1.082	1.146	2.123	2.691	0.965	2.131	1.063	1.329	1.074	1.411
Guangdong	1	1	1	1	1	1	1	1	1	1.000
Guangxi	0.378	1.633	1.318	1.523	0.711	2.409	1.372	1.486	0.898	1.163
Hainan	0.628	4.054	0.631	13.962	0.505	3.343	1.63	1.223	1.05	1.626
Chongqing	1.097	1.065	1.508	1.814	0.976	1.805	0.857	1.495	1.019	1.248
Sichuan	1.128	1.361	0.834	1.439	0.764	1.328	1.49	1.043	1.068	1.134
Guizhou	1.201	1.736	1.091	1.283	1.375	1.004	1.566	1.234	1.055	1.264
Yunnan	0.215	4.558	0.417	2.147	0.649	1.998	1.572	0.975	1.057	1.070
Shaanxi	0.891	1.335	0.99	1.011	1.106	1.328	1.052	1.407	0.827	1.088
Gansu	0.453	0.813	1.897	1.614	1.807	1.033	1.864	0.983	1.306	1.197
Qinghai	21.919	1.016	0.036	15.646	0.732	1.198	0.199	6.003	0.496	1.232
Ningxia	1.039	1.094	1.65	1.162	1.423	1.226	1.148	1.853	0.375	1.131
Arithmetic average	1.616	1.527	1.099	2.851	1.039	1.395	1.224	1.436	0.972	1.172
Geometric average	0.903	1.385	0.959	1.776	0.986	1.302	1.157	1.316	0.944	1.164

Table 8.
Changes in technological efficiency index of technological innovation in high-tech industries.

indicates that the innovation efficiency of China's high-tech industry is on the rise. Among them, the innovation efficiency in 2008/2009 increased the most, reaching 92.2%, while the innovation efficiency in 2009/2010 decreased the fastest, by 18%. Further according to the decomposed indexes, the pure technical efficiency

Provinces	Year									
	2005/2006	2006/2007	2007/2008	2008/2009	2009/2010	2010/2011	2011/2012	2012/2013	2013/2014	2005/2014
Beijing	1.136	1.222	0.999	0.958	0.952	1.049	1.181	0.912	1.124	1.054
Tianjin	1.066	0.986	0.943	0.928	0.886	1.231	0.918	1.135	1.033	1.009
Hebei	1.339	0.909	0.98	1.127	0.793	1.164	0.893	0.896	0.964	0.995
Shanxi	1.164	0.953	1.077	1.03	0.839	1.265	0.941	0.887	1.015	1.011
Inner Mongolia	1.289	0.953	0.838	1.33	0.788	1.275	0.902	0.91	1.021	1.016
Liaoning	1.067	0.981	1.029	1.061	0.819	1.24	0.93	0.903	0.94	0.990
Jilin	1.496	0.857	0.949	1.192	0.868	1.248	0.903	0.885	1.03	1.029
Heilongjiang	1.29	0.887	0.996	1.179	0.701	1.19	0.943	0.883	1.025	0.995
Shanghai	1.109	1.008	0.987	0.931	1.015	1.191	1.243	0.809	1.183	1.044
Jiangsu	1.045	1.001	1.144	0.853	0.858	1.54	0.97	0.917	1.077	1.029
Zhejiang	1.086	0.921	1.006	1.223	0.796	1.21	0.942	0.895	0.938	0.993
Anhui	1.049	0.995	1.058	1.124	0.682	1.166	0.941	0.892	1.147	0.994
Fujian	1.032	0.98	1.069	0.889	0.91	1.391	0.917	0.95	1.003	1.007
Jiangxi	1.235	0.953	1.052	0.996	0.912	1.299	0.884	0.878	0.979	1.012
Shandong	1.08	0.98	1.033	0.966	0.983	1.163	1.001	0.893	0.99	1.007
Henan	1.248	0.862	0.934	1.203	0.701	1.166	0.941	1.273	1.073	1.027
Hubei	1.473	0.915	1.023	1.021	0.888	1.248	0.91	0.884	1.014	1.027
Hunan	1.121	0.934	0.988	1.08	0.813	1.165	0.925	0.917	1	0.988
Guangdong	1.203	1.031	0.942	1.135	1.038	1.167	0.954	1.01	1.008	1.051
Guangxi	1.567	0.862	0.904	1.289	0.846	1.163	0.913	0.884	0.997	1.025
Hainan	1.596	0.928	0.838	1.33	0.702	1.166	0.941	0.885	1.001	1.013
Chongqing	1.075	0.96	1.081	0.923	0.924	1.363	0.901	0.888	1.021	1.006
Sichuan	1.046	0.983	1.126	0.884	0.791	1.231	1.108	0.867	1.041	1.000
Guizhou	1.42	0.874	0.855	1.33	0.696	1.18	0.941	0.893	1.135	1.011
Yunnan	1.596	0.916	0.913	1.171	0.847	1.185	0.936	0.888	0.998	1.030
Shaanxi	1.142	0.962	1.006	1.092	0.841	1.263	1.051	0.881	0.957	1.014
Gansu	1.542	0.903	1.002	1.192	0.757	1.176	0.935	0.887	1	1.023
Qinghai	1.596	0.928	0.838	1.33	0.72	1.212	0.941	0.887	1.019	1.023
Ningxia	1.186	0.993	1.095	0.917	0.9	1.312	0.938	0.887	1.005	1.017
Arithmetic average	1.252	0.953	0.990	1.093	0.837	1.228	0.960	0.916	1.025	1.015
Geometry average	1.237	0.951	0.986	1.082	0.831	1.225	0.957	0.913	1.024	1.015

Table 9.
Changes in technological progress index of technological innovation in high-tech industries.

decreased by 0.003%, while the scale efficiency increased by 16.8%. The increase in scale efficiency offsets the decrease in pure technical efficiency, thus increasing technical efficiency. This shows that the increase in technical innovation efficiency in China's high-tech industries in recent years is due to the improvement in

Provinces	TFP	TP	TEC	PTE	SE
Beijing	1.141	1.054	1.083	1.003	1.08
Tianjin	0.999	1.008	0.991	1	0.991
Hebei	1.251	0.995	1.257	1	1.257
Shanxi	1.309	1.011	1.294	1	1.294
Inner Mongolia	1.191	1.016	1.172	1.002	1.171
Liaoning	1.085	0.99	1.096	0.994	1.102
Jilin	1.184	1.029	1.151	0.996	1.156
Heilongjiang	1.101	0.995	1.106	0.999	1.107
Shanghai	1.022	1.044	0.979	0.999	0.98
Jiangsu	1.086	1.029	1.055	1.002	1.053
Zhejiang	1.107	0.993	1.115	1	1.114
Anhui	1.388	0.994	1.395	1	1.395
Fujian	0.995	1.007	0.989	0.972	1.018
Jiangxi	1.246	1.012	1.231	1	1.231
Shandong	1.054	1.007	1.046	0.973	1.075
Henan	1.367	1.027	1.331	1.002	1.328
Hubei	1.177	1.027	1.146	0.992	1.155
Hunan	1.394	0.988	1.41	0.997	1.415
Guangdong	1.05	1.05	1	1	1
Guangxi	1.191	1.025	1.163	1	1.163
Hainan	1.647	1.013	1.625	1	1.625
Chongqing	1.256	1.006	1.248	1.004	1.244
Sichuan	1.134	1	1.134	1.006	1.128
Guizhou	1.278	1.011	1.264	0.993	1.272
Yunnan	1.102	1.03	1.07	1	1.071
Shaanxi	1.104	1.014	1.088	0.979	1.112
Gansu	1.225	1.023	1.197	1.005	1.191
Qinghai	1.26	1.023	1.232	1.003	1.229
Ningxia	1.151	1.017	1.131	1.003	1.128
平均值	1.182	1.015	1.164	0.997	1.168

*Note: TFP, TP, TEC, PTE, and SE in the table, respectively, represent total factor productivity, technological progress, technological efficiency, and pure technological efficiency. And TFP = TP * TEC, and TEC=PTE * SE.*

Table 10.
Malmquist index of technological innovation in high-tech industry and its decomposition.

management level and technical efficiency. In addition, from a local point of view, except for Tianjin, Shanghai, and Fujian, where the total factor productivity has not increased significantly, the total factor productivity in other places has increased by different ranges, with Hainan having the largest growth range, reaching a growth rate of 64.7%. Except Hebei, Liaoning, Heilongjiang, Zhejiang, Anhui, and Hunan, the index of technological progress in other regions showed slow growth, with Beijing having the largest growth rate, with a growth rate of 5.4%.

DOI: http://dx.doi.org/10.5772/intechopen.90869

4.4 Chain multiple mediation effect analysis

In order to clarify the internal mechanism of China's high-tech industry innovation and "mass entrepreneurship" and find the key to accelerate the process of "double innovation," this chapter adopts a multichain intermediary effect model to analyze the direct effect and various indirect effects between innovation and entrepreneurship from the overall, regional (east, middle, and west), and local (provinces and cities) perspectives.

4.5 Overall and regional

The overall analysis results of the multiple chain intermediary effect model are shown in **Figure 2**, and the effect results are shown in **Table 11**.

The analysis results of the east, middle, and west regions are shown in **Figure 3** and **Table 12**.

On the whole, the total effect of innovation on entrepreneurship is 1.769, that is, the increase of total factor productivity is conducive to the increase of the number of new entrepreneurs. However, from a further perspective, the direct effect of innovation on entrepreneurship is shown as inhibition ($c' < 0$), while the mediating effect through different paths shows a significantly higher promotion effect (a_1b_1, a_2b_2, and $a_1a_3b_2$ are significantly positive). This shows that the promotion effect of innovation on entrepreneurship is not a simple direct effect. The government cannot rely solely on improving innovation efficiency to promote entrepreneurship so as to relieve the pressure on China's labor market. Instead, it should promote entrepreneurship by increasing new ventures and promoting economic growth on the basis of promoting innovation drive.

From the point of view of the east, middle, and west regions, the total effect of innovation on entrepreneurship is promotion, and the promotion in the east region is obviously stronger than that in the middle and west regions, which may be caused

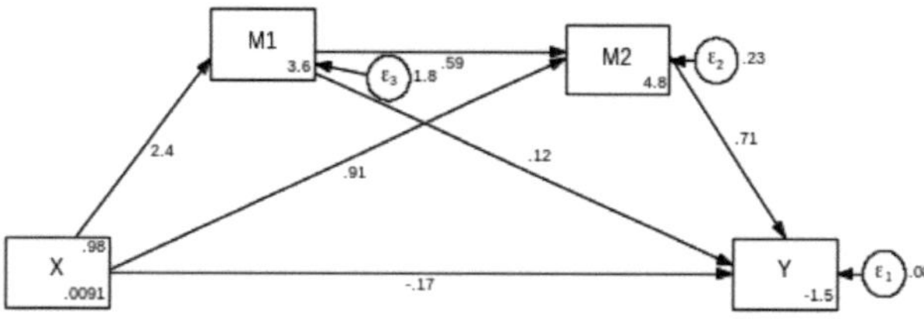

Figure 2.
Multiple chain mediating effect based on the whole.

	Effect path	Calculation	Effect value
Indirect	X → M1 → Y	a_1b_1	0.288***
	X → M2 → Y	a_2b_2	0.646***
	X → M1 → M2 → Y	$a_1a_3b_2$	1.005***
Direct	X → Y	c'	−0.17
Total indirect effect		$a_1b_1 + a_2b_2 + a_1a_3b_2$	1.939
Total effect		$c' + a_1b_1 + a_2b_2 + a_1a_3b_2$	1.769

*Note: *** means $p < 0.01$; ** means $p < 0.05$; * means $p < 0.1$.*

Table 11.
Results of direct and indirect effects (overall).

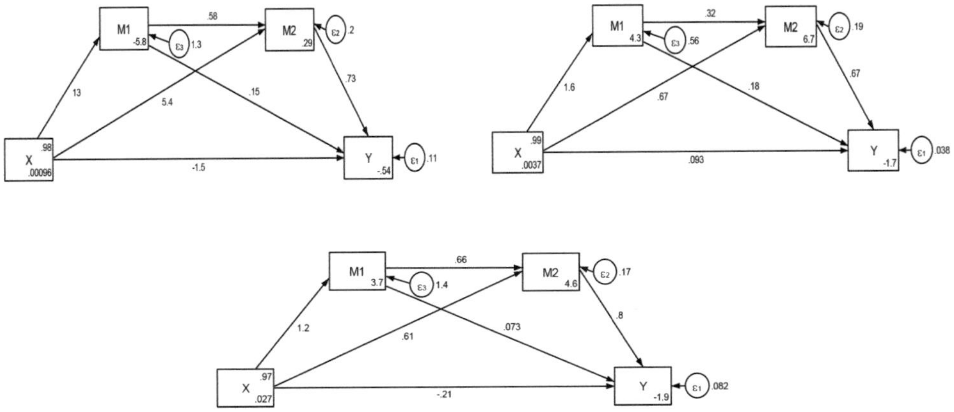

Figure 3.
Multiple chain mediating effects in east, central, and west regions.

Region	Direct effect	Indirect effect			Total indirect utility	Total utility
East	-1.5^{**}	1.95^{***}	3.942^{**}	5.5042^{*}	11.3962	9.8962
In	0.093^{**}	0.288^{**}	0.4489^{**}	0.3430^{**}	1.07994	1.17294
West	-0.21^{*}	0.792^{*}	0.488^{**}	0.6336^{**}	1.9136	1.7036

*Note: *** means $p < 0.01$; ** means $p < 0.05$; * means $p < 0.1$.*

Table 12.
Direct and indirect effects of east, middle, and west regions and their effect values.

by the superior geographical position and relatively developed economic level of the east region. The direct effects in the east and west are significantly negative, indicating that innovation will play a restraining role in the direct path of entrepreneurship. However, the indirect effects are significantly positive, especially the path in the eastern region, whose influence is much stronger than other paths, which shows that the eastern region mainly promotes entrepreneurship through the path of "innovation → enterprise increase → economic growth → entrepreneurship." For the central region, whether it is a direct or indirect path, the impact of innovation on entrepreneurship always presents a significant positive effect.

4.6 Provinces, cities, and regions

The analysis results of direct effect, indirect effect, and total effect of innovation on entrepreneurship in various provinces and cities are shown in **Table 13**.

The direct effects of Beijing, Shanxi, and Jilin are significantly positive, while the direct effects of Yunnan, Hainan, Guangdong, and Fujian are significantly negative, while the direct effects of most other provinces are not significant. On the contrary, in terms of indirect effects, most provinces have significant positive effects, while only Beijing, Shanxi, and Shanghai have negative effects.

5. Conclusions and policy recommendations

This chapter decomposes total factor productivity on the basis of DEA model excluding environment and random factors and then analyzes the influencing process and mechanism among variables by using chain multiple intermediary effect model and further analyzes the relationship between innovation and

ID	Province	Direct	Indirect		
		c'	a_1b_1	a_2b_2	$a_1a_3b_2$
1	Beijing	**5.201*** (1.757)**	−6.559 (6.288)	−2.633 (4.822)	**−0.831*** (0.173)**
2	Tianjin	−4.307 (3.513)	3.616 (3.377)	**11.984** (5.399)**	−0.998 (0.615)
3	Hebei	1.264 (2.751)	2.260 (4.549)	1.628 (3.650)	**0.794*** (0.180)**
4	Shanxi	**0.862*** (0.103)**	−0.406 (1.834)	1.251 (2.184)	**−2.682*** (0.732)**
5	Inner Mongolia	−0.451 (0.180)	0.303 (0.596)	0.257 (0.883)	**2.882** (1.433)**
6	Liaoning	−0.680 (0.486)	2.317 (3.019)	−0.502 (2.617)	−0.418 (0.452)
7	Jilin	**1.114* (0.607)**	−4.547 (3.793)	−1.757 (5.084)	**1.941** (0.939)**
8	Heilongjiang	−0.506 (0.613)	0.007 (0.264)	**5.044*** (1.948)**	−0.014 (0.504)
9	Shanghai	1.899 (1.190)	2.565 (4.491)	1.379 (4.168)	**−0.555** (0.226)**
10	Jiangsu	0.342 (0.337)	−2.641 (5.668)	0.969 (5.130)	**0.885*** (0.189)**
11	Zhejiang	−1.569 (1.558)	0.370 (2.733)	**9.835** (4.488)**	−0.067 (0.497)
12	Anhui	0.355 (1.166)	3.088 (3.405)	5.097 (3.229)	**0.775*** (0.085)**
13	Fujian	**−5.648*** (1.088)**	2.330 (4.915)	**17.260** (7.653)**	**2.214*** (0.837)**
14	Jiangxi	2.282 (1.500)	−2.912 (7.217)	0.205 (4.388)	**1.012*** (0.111)**
15	Shandong	0.184 (1.825)	−4.029 (10.165)	3.385 (7.460)	**1.338*** (0.352)**
16	Henan	−0.216 (0.557)	2.915 (1.946)	2.947 (1.832)	**1.457*** (0.114)**
17	Hubei	0.581 (0.432)	−2.694 (2.279)	−3.573 (2.799)	**1.261*** (0.472)**
18	Hunan	0.309 (0.966)	3.751 (4.610)	3.298 (3.883)	**1.950*** (0.145)**
19	Guangdong	**−4.674** (1.930)**	9.218 (6.795)	9.520 (7.017)	**0.982** (0.456)**
20	Guangxi	−0.333 (0.516)	1.835 (3.313)	3.344 (3.186)	**1.176* (0.639)**
21	Hainan	**−0.785*** (0.223)**	0.596 (0.799)	1.846 (1.243)	−1.546 (1.133)
22	Chongqing	0.326 (0.732)	6.575 (4.528)	7.843 (5.252)	**1.216*** (0.219)**
23	Sichuan	0.092 (0.512)	−2.002 (2.406)	0.041 (1.602)	**1.050*** (0.324)**
24	Guizhou	0.299 (0.949)	−0.035 (0.357)	2.873 (3.699)	0.114 (0.767)

ID	Province	Direct	Indirect		
		c'	a_1b_1	a_2b_2	$a_1a_3b_2$
25	Yunnan	**−1.977*** **(1.170)**	0.098 (0.624)	−2.534 (4.542)	−0.214 (0.907)
26	Shaanxi	2.643 (3.316)	−1.189 (5.848)	2.710 (5.332)	**3.571***** **(0.694)**
27	Gansu	−0.189 (0.375)	1.510 (2.146)	−2.794 (2.800)	**0.831**** **(0.392)**
28	Qinghai	0.056 (0.049)	0.206 (0.190)	**0.112*** **(0.067)**	**0.361**** **(0.170)**
29	Ningxia	−0.550 (0.710)	0.652 (0.917)	0.186 (1.056)	0.795 (0.513)

*Note: *** means $p < 0.01$; ** means $p < 0.05$; * means $p < 0.1$.*

Table 13.
Direct, indirect, and total effects of provinces and cities.

entrepreneurship in high-tech industries. The research confirms: (1) Before environmental factors and random interference are eliminated, the comprehensive technical efficiency and scale efficiency of R&D in China's high-tech industry are obviously overestimated, while the pure technical efficiency is underestimated. Therefore, it is necessary to eliminate environmental and random factors and increase the credibility of the research. (2) No matter from the overall or partial analysis, the total effect of innovation on entrepreneurship has always been positive, that is, promoting "people-to-people innovation" is conducive to promoting "mass entrepreneurship." (3) In most cases, innovation does not directly promote entrepreneurship but indirectly promotes entrepreneurship through a micro–macro combination path.

5.1 Relevant policy recommendations

Generally speaking, the government can encourage China's high-tech industry to explore new market areas and gain competitive advantages by formulating relevant industrial policies and promoting innovation, thus providing motive force for innovation drive. Through continuous entrepreneurship, innovative achievements will be continuously transformed into real productive forces to promote the sustainable development of high-tech industries and social economy. We should strengthen the combination of "production, study, and research" and focus on improving the "double-creation" mechanism and the "double-creation" environment.

First of all, as the direct effect of innovation on entrepreneurship is positive in Beijing, Shanxi, and Jilin, the government and relevant local departments can appropriately increase the amount of financial allocation for research and development of high-tech products and conquering high-end technologies, strengthen the government's financial support, and give full play to the policy's guidance and support for innovation by strengthening the government's innovation subsidies and tax incentives, thus realizing a "double harvest" of innovation and entrepreneurship on the basis of effectively improving the innovation efficiency of high-tech industries in the region. Secondly, in Fujian, Guangdong, Hainan, and Yunnan, the government should make great efforts to promote the development of other industries while developing high-tech industries, so that the local advantageous industries and characteristic industries can develop continuously and steadily and all kinds of industries will be put together. Thirdly, in Tianjin, Heilongjiang, Zhejiang, Fujian, and Qinghai, the government should actively promote economic development. While making great efforts to improve GDP, it should also pay attention to the per capita level of GDP, scientific and technological content, and green degree and strive to provide a good macroenvironment for promoting "double innovation" by correctly grasping the "three improvements." Finally, in Beijing, Shanghai, and Shanxi, the number of new high-tech enterprises should be controlled to ensure that a reasonable market structure can not only bring into play economies of scale but also promote effective competition, thus effectively stimulating the improvement of innovation efficiency and entrepreneurship scale.

Author details

Kai Zhao* and Lixiang Wang
School of Statistics, Huaqiao University, China

*Address all correspondence to: kai.zhao@hotmail.fr

References

[1] Bao GH. Spatial econometric analysis of innovation efficiency and its influencing factors in China's high-tech industry. Economic Geography. 2014;**6**: 100-107

[2] Jing H. Research on innovation efficiency of China's high-tech industry-empirical analysis based on SFA method. Scientific Research. 2010;**3**:467-472

[3] Renqiao X, Li Q, Zhongwei C. Research on innovation efficiency of China's high-tech industry and its influencing factors. Management Science. 2012;**5**:85-98

[4] Chiu Y, Huang C, Chen Y. The R&D value-chain efficiency measurement for high-tech industries in China. Asia Pacific Journal of Management. 2012; **29**(4):989-1006

[5] Kui-Zao D, You-Jin L. The Impact of marketization on innovation efficiency and industry differences-based on the empirical test of China's high-tech industry. Financial Research. 2013; **39**(5):4-16

[6] Wu Yanbing R, Stock D. Knowledge function and production efficiency. Economics (Quarterly). 2006;**3**: 1129-1156

[7] Yanying C, Wenlu Y. Knowledge workers' entrepreneurial entry and R&D incentives for incumbent enterprises-evidence from China's high-tech industry. Scientific Research. 2012;**11**:1707-1714

[8] Xiaohong C, Li C, Shujuan M. Study on decision mechanism of imitation entrepreneurship based on high-tech industrial clusters. Scientific Research. 2008;**4**:739-748

[9] Chongming W, Yuanhao X. Theoretical construction and empirical analysis of intellectual property entrepreneurship: A multi-case study based on high-tech enterprises. Journal of Zhejiang University (Humanities and Social Sciences Edition). 2014;**3**:58-70

[10] Franco AM, Filson D. Spin-outs: Knowledge diffusion through employee mobility. The Rand Journal of Economics. 2006;**37**(4):841-860

[11] Aldrich H, Zimmer C. Entrepreneurship through social networks. The Art and Science of Entrepreneurship. 1986;**22**:3-23

[12] Lester RH, Certo ST, Dalton CM. Initial public offering investor valuations: An examination of top management team prestige and environmental uncertainty. Journal of Small Business Management. 2006; **44**(1):1-26

[13] Bin C, Xu W, Wang Q. Summary of research on innovation, entrepreneurship and innovation cluster development [J]. Scientific and Technological Progress and Countermeasures. 2014;**9**:157-160

[14] Bei J, Xiaoxia X. Entrepreneurship and innovation mechanism of high-tech industry in the United States and its enlightenment. Management World. 2001;**4**:63-70

[15] Fried HO. Accounting for environmental effects and statistical noise in data envelopment analysis. Journal of Productivity Analysis. 2002;**17**: 157-174

[16] Preacher KJ, Hayes AF. Asymptotic and resampling strategies for assessing and comparing indirect effects in multiple mediator models. Behavior Research Methods. 2008;**40**:879-891

[17] Griliches Z. Patent statistics as economic indicators: A survey. Journal of Economic Literature. 1990;**28**:1661-1707

Section 3

Commercial Application

Chapter 9

Activities Pivotal for the Sustainability of Newly Established Technology Transfer Offices: A Case Study of Publicly Financed South African Universities

Sebua S. Semenya

Abstract

The activities with potential to sustain new technology transfer offices (TTOs) within the publicly financed South African universities (PFSAU) and elsewhere are poorly examined. The current chapter thus aims to lay out a series of simple strategic activities which the referred universities can execute to ensure the sustainability of their newly formed TTOs. Data were collected via strategic conversations with intellectual property (IP) experts, and active academic researchers from PFSAU. The activities considered vital for the sustainability of newly formed TTOs in this study encompass extensive training of TTOs staff, IP awareness within and outside the universities, compliance with relevant legislations, learning from well-established TTOs, establishment of IP and innovation policy as well as IP and innovation modules, collaboration with formal and informal sectors outside the universities, execution of applied and industry-driven research by academics and finally, protection and commercialisation of IP. Overall, efficacious executions and implementations of these activities as discussed in the present study will not only contribute towards the sustainability of newly established TTOs within PFSAU but also aid in achieving some of this universities' shared goals such as community engagement, research with economic impact, teaching and learning. However, some of the referred activities can be achieved either over a short or medium periods, but together are crucial stepping stones to continual achievements of long-term goals of TTOs in PFSAU.

Keywords: intellectual properties, innovation, South Africa, technology transfer office

1. Introduction

Intellectual property (IP) is the application of the mind by any individual to develop or invent something new and original, either an innovative technology or invention that can be legally protected from being exploited by people without the owner's/inventor's consent [1–3]. This protection can be in terms of a particular country's legislation or a foreign law. The World Intellectual Property Organization [2] describes an innovative technology as a means of creating something novel that improves a product, process or service. Furthermore, it defines an invention as new research results that can both solve a problem and be exploited commercially. According to Kalanje [4], innovative technologies and inventions generally stand a better chance of successfully reaching the marketplace if IP is used strategically.

Various types of IP that can be used to legally protect the innovative technologies and inventions include patents, copy rights, designs, trademarks, geographical indications, trade secrets/know-how and plant breeder's rights [5–8]. By copyright, the author of the present paper refers to a bundle of rights granted automatically (in South Africa) by law to creators of the original work [9]. However, the work must be fixed in a tangible medium (i.e. copies and phonorecords) for protection under this IP. Typical examples of materials that can be copyrighted encompass artistic, dramatic, literary and musical works, sound recordings, broadcasts and films [10, 11]. Unlike copyright, registered designs are granted as a form of formal IP and are classified as either aesthetic or functional [12]. According to the National Intellectual Property Management Office [6], aesthetic designs protect the visual attractiveness of a product, and functional designs protect features of an article that are necessitated by the function the article is to perform. These designs must be new and original, and not common in the state of the art at the time of registration or protection. It should be stated that a sole product may be registered as both a functional and aesthetic design. With regard to trademarks, their primary functions are to distinguish different sources of products or providers of services from each other, but they may also have other connotations [13, 14]. A trademark can take many forms including amongst others, words, pictures or even smells [15]. Geographical indications are forms of IP that identify the geographical origin of a product where a given quality, reputation or other characteristic of such product is essentially attributable to its geographical origin [16]. Generally, geographical indications are protected by means of sui generis systems or via conventional IP rights, mainly as a form of trademark. A trade secret is any confidential and commercially valuable information that provides a company with a competitive advantage, such as customer lists, methods of production, marketing strategies, pricing information and chemical formulae [17]. Protection of these secrets may extend indefinitely, lasting as long as the subject matter of the trade secret is commercially valuable and is kept confidential. In contrast, a patent is the legal right of an inventor to exclude others from making or using an invention, and this right is customarily limited in time to 20 years from the priority date in most countries [18]. To qualify for patent protection, inventions must be new, nonobvious and commercially applicable.

Intellectual properties are becoming increasingly important tools for sustainable development in developing countries [19]. Most developing countries that are found in various regions of Africa such as Namibia [20], Nigeria [21], Kenya [22], Mozambique [23], Uganda [24], Tanzania [25] and Egypt [26] amongst the others have developed IP policies to foster economic and social development. South Africa is not excluded and the IP Rights from Publicly Financed Research and Development Act, Act 51 of 2008 (IPR Act), was established by the government to encourage these developments. The objectives of this Act are to encourage the identification, protection, utilisation and commercialisation of all IP emanating from publicly financed research and development, for the benefit of the people of the Republic.

As part of an effort to achieve these, the South African government has recently established technology transfer offices (TTOs) in various publicly financed universities and other state-owned enterprises to carry out the above-stated objectives. The government provides the start-up finance for a certain number of years (3 years for start) to ensure the establishment of these offices, and thereafter, it is the responsibility of the host institution to sustain the referred office. It should be stated that the performance of university TTOs in South Africa and elsewhere has been studied, and a wide range of Data Envelopment Analysis metrics including TTO revenue, number of IP/invention disclosures, number of patent applications, patents granted, licences signed, start-up companies formed and new commercial products, employment and productivity growth of start-up partners amid others have been selected to assess the performance and success of TTOs based at the universities [27, 28]. However, studies looking at the strategic activities with potential to contribute towards achieving these metrics which are curial to the sustainability of newly formed TTOs within the publicly financed South African universities (PFSAU) are lacking. It is fundamental that continual effective strategic activities that encourage the innovative ideas and disclosures of actionable IP be put in place to ensure that these offices achieve the objectives of IPR and become self-supporting.

The present study is thus aimed at investigating some of these strategic activities. Importantly, the stated Data Envelopment Analysis approach highlighted earlier is regarded as the most suitable and acceptable way of measuring university-based TTO efficiency. However, such approach is not applicable to newly established TTOs, as the offices need to engage in strategic activities that will in a long run enable them to build a strong IP/invention and commercialisation portfolio to allow the application of such approach. Therefore, the strategic activities can be considered performance measurement necessary to determine whether newly established TTO is on the right track to achieve their goals or not.

2. Research methods

Information presented in this chapter was gathered using strategic conversation with IP experts and active academic researchers in PFSAU who are knowledgeable about IP and technology transfers. Furthermore, the author also extracted copious notes through listening to strategic conversations amongst local and international IP experts who presented at World Intellectual Property Organisation Summer school, held at the University of the Western Cape (Cape Town, South Africa, 27 November to 08 December 2017), under the theme 'Advanced Intellectual Property and Transfer of Technology'. According to Kyprianou et al. [29], strategic conversations are any naturally occurring, as opposed to scripted or interview-based, interactions (including talk and non-verbal cues) amongst the targeted population. Godfrey and Hill [30] wrote that strategic conversation data are distinct from archival and interview data and are likely to generate insights into otherwise unobservable and neglected aspects of strategy because conversations are (1) unscripted, naturally occurring and fluid and (2) include multiple voices and perspectives. Generally, all the personnel from whom the authors obtained information via strategic conversation are referred in this study as 'participants', except in few cases were they are specified (i.e. academic researchers in PFSAU). Overall, content analysis was used to analyse data gathered. According to Krippendorff [31], this type of analysis provides new insights, increases a researcher's understanding of a particular phenomenon and informs practical actions. Simple descriptive statistics, namely percentage, were used were necessary.

3. Results

The present study documented the following activities with potential to sustain newly established TTOs within PFSAU;

3.1 Extensive training of technology transfer offices staff

An extensive training of staff from newly established TTOs via workshops and short courses was perceived by all participants as critical to ensure that the office functions swiftly and efficiently. Furthermore, they reported that the success of any strategic activity depends upon motivated, knowledgeable as well as empowered staff. However, they stressed that relevant workshops and courses that are in line with the office's strategic goals should be prioritised. Some of the participants were also of the view that newly established TTO staff must not attend all technology transfer or IP-related courses/workshops. This was based on the fact that the duties of TTO staff are both university-based and outside-university based. For instance, they asserted that the staff must educate the researchers and students within the university about the various technology transfer issues including IP protection and commercialisation, and also search and approach/visit potential funders for IP commercialisation outside the university.

3.2 Intellectual property awareness within and outside the universities

Intellectual property awareness was stated by the vast majority (n = 16, 80%) of participants as one of the critical factors that might encourage the researchers and students within the university and formal and informal sectors outside the university to disclose IP and innovative ideas with potential for commercialisation to newly formed TTOs within PFSAU. Based on the researcher's understanding of participants' descriptions of these sectors, informal sectors in this study refer to community members including those who are involved in the informal trading of creations and innovative products. The formal sector includes institutions outside the university which are known or more likely to develop products with potential IP for commercialisation or composed of individuals with ideas that might lead to the identification of these IP. According to participants, IP campaigns and awareness amid both formal and informal sectors outside the university are crucial, because the sustainability of newly established TTO within PFSAU cannot wholly rely on IP disclosure from academics within the university. Similar campaigns and awareness were also mentioned by participants (n = 16, 80%) as imperative amongst researchers in the universities. About 57.2% (n = 9) of these participants specifically those from PFSAU stated that very few of their academic co-workers know about the IP protection and commercialisation; thus, IP awareness in this regard is fundamental. Workshops (n = 16, 80%) and media outlets (n = 8, 40%) such as prints-outs in the form of posters, pocket manuals and flyers, and Internet specifically social networks such as Facebook and radio were generally perceived by interviewees as important innovative ways of increasing awareness of IP.

3.3 Intellectual property and innovation policy

Only seven participants (35%) regarded the development of IP and innovation policy as essential key strategic activity for the sustainability of newly established TTOs within PFSAU. They stated that the primary aim of this policy should be to promote a culture of innovation, IP protection and commercialisation within the universities, and in both formal and informal sectors outside the universities, while protecting IP rights. For instance, most of the participants (n = 4, 20%) stressed the need for IP and innovation policy to endorse execution of applied and industry-driven research as well as innovations amongst the researchers within the universities and in both these sectors. The rest of the interviewees (15%, n = 3) reported that for this policy to contribute towards the sustainability of newly established TTOs, it must encourage the strategic collaboration between local and/or international business and these offices. Furthermore, they pointed out that such policy must specify the terms and conditions for funding of collaborative research or innovative programmes, including the ownership of IP or innovative idea.

3.4 Compliance with relevant legislations

Extensive knowledge of various IP and innovative laws as well their compliance by newly established TTO's staff was highlighted by some participants (n = 20) as essential to the office's sustainability. This will, according to some of these participants, assist the newly established TTOs within PFSAU to avoid the financial penalties and damages to the office's reputation allied to infringement. Furthermore, they were of the view that staff from this office must keep track of any legislation or regulation changes and appraise how they may affect the office's various operational areas.

3.5 Learning from well-established technology transfer offices

One participant reported that staff from newly established TTOs within PFSAU should consult with well-established TTOs to get advice and to observe their activities. This participant was of the view that the latter offices are now able to do the following: (i) eliminate projects and processes that do not work and (ii) identify potential or real problems and search for new working strategies or approaches to solve them. Subsequently, newly formed TTOs within PFSAU can benefit by learning from experienced TTOs.

3.6 Intellectual property and innovation modules

This activity was highlighted by one participant who stated that an introduction of compulsory IP and innovation modules within the South African higher institutions of learning and elementary schools would be one of the key activities to sustain the newly formed TTOs within PFSAU. According to this participant, IP and innovation education can support and capacitate students and learners in becoming IP creators or inventors.

3.7 Collaboration with formal and informal sectors outside the universities

As one of the imperative strategic action to sustain newly formed TTOs within PFSAU, an overwhelming majority (n = 16, 80%) of participants recommended establishment of alliance between these offices and informal as well as formal sectors (as defined in this study). This collaboration was viewed as having great potential to produce economically viable and beneficial innovations, which would contribute meaningfully to sustaining the newly formed TTOs within PFSAU as more IP and innovative ideas from both personnel within the universities and outside will be disclosed to offices. Therefore, participants suggested the identification of people possessing innovative ideas or who are involved in innovative business (formal or informal) outside the universities by newly formed TTO staff and collaborate with them.

3.8 Execution of applied and industry-driven research by academics

As expected, an execution of applied and industry-driven researches or projects was disclosed by all participants as a vital activity to sustain newly formed TTOs within PFSAU. Participants emphasised the need for researchers and academics within these universities to avoid conducting research that is basic or does not consider the identification and protection of IP with potential for commercialisation. According to the participants, this can be achieved by conducting IP and innovative awareness focusing exclusively on the significance of conducting research/project with potential IP for commercialisation. However, in addition to this, they suggested the initiations of activities with an objective to coerce academics to execute research projects that might lead to the identification of IP with potential for commercialisation. In this regard, the vast majority (n = 14, 70%) of these participants emphasised the need for a clear innovation and IP policy underlining the attractive and adequate incentives for researchers who disclosed the IPs with potential for commercialisation to TTOs. They stressed the need for this policy when taking into consideration the long duration of obtaining a patent as opposed to the benefit of publishing research work (including those with potential IP for commercialisation) in the journals accredited by the South African Department of Higher Education and Learning. Such benefits according to participants include generous financial remuneration (depending on the institution) and contribution to job promotion. Another strategic action suggested (n = 8, 40%) to coerce researchers within PFSAU to conduct research with commercial impact is to formalise a compulsory extensive patent and novelty search prior to the initiation of research projects. Therefore, the research proposal templates of all faculties within the universities should be amended to include novelty and potential IP section. Research proposals without this section should not be approved by the relevant committee.

3.9 Intellectual property protection and commercialisation

As anticipated, the protection and commercialisation of IP and innovative materials was mentioned by all participants as a compulsory or 'must do' activity to ensure the sustainability of newly established TTOs within PFSAU. However, for this to be a success, it was emphasised that either some of the earlier mentioned strategic activities or the combinations of these activities should be implemented successfully. These activities included collaboration with formal and informal sectors outside the universities, compliance with relevant legislations, execution of applied and industry-driven research by academics, extensive training of TTO staff, IP and innovation policy, IP and innovation modules, IP awareness within and outside the universities, and learning from well-established TTOs.

4. Discussion and perspectives

Strategic planning is critical to the success of any newly established office, and TTOs are not an exception, chiefly because this kind of a planning indicates where an institution wants to go and how it will get there [32, 33]. However, prior initiations of strategic plans of any office within the institutions, clear goals and associated strategic objectives for the office must be a priority written [34, 35]. Subsequently, strategic objectives must outline an office's intended activities designed to achieve inscribed strategies and, ultimately, goals. With reference to PFSAU, their common goals include, enhancing teaching and learning, research and community engagement/public services. Consequently, it is acceptable to state that the establishment of TTO within the above-stated universities must directly contribute to some of these goals.

As highlighted earlier, in South Africa, the primary and common goal of TTOs within the PFSAU is to identify IP and thereafter protect and commercialise it for the benefit of the people of the republic as mandated by the IP Rights from Publicly Financed Research and Development Act, Act 51 of 2008 [6]. Therefore, continual accomplishment of these goals will automatically aid in the sustainability of newly established TTOs. However, such attainment will in turn depend on the execution of effective strategic activities. Participants in the present study mentioned the following as some of the key strategic activities that South African publicly financed universities can use as tools to achieve the aforesaid goals and ultimately the sustainability of their newly formed TTOs: (i) collaboration with formal and informal sectors outside the universities, (ii) compliance with relevant legislations, (iii) execution of applied and industry-driven research by academics, (iv) extensive training of TTOs staff, (v) IP and innovation policy, (vi) IP and innovative modules, (vii) IP awareness within and outside the universities and (viii) learning from well-established TTOs. These activities were considered by participants as vital determinants of newly based university TTO productivity and sustainability. Therefore, it can be said that the sustainability of this kind of TTOs relies on short or medium strategic activities (or both activities) that build on each other's accomplishments, to ensure long-term goals of the offices and continued progress.

4.1 Extensive training of technology transfer office staff

An extensive training of newly established TTO staff via relevant workshops and short courses to ensure efficient functioning of the office as stated by participants in this study is partially supported by various studies [36–39]. These studies demonstrated the effectiveness of staff empowerment at work place via relevant workshops or courses. In support of finding from the current study, Perera et al. [40] revealed that lack of relevant skills, knowledge and experience amongst most officers who are responsible for the development of research, commercialisation and marketing in a Government Research Organizations of Sri Lanka hindered an effective technology transfer and commercialisation process. A similar finding was noted in Ghana [41] and elsewhere [42, 43]. Indeed, Van Looy et al. [44] found that there is a positive association between university technology transfer efficiency, knowledge and relevant experience of TTO staff. Therefore, extensive training of staff via workshops as well as short courses might be crucial as it can capacitate the workforce with appropriate professional skills and knowledge, especially since there are no formal educational qualifications for technology transfer. Meanwhile, TTO staff are expected to have a variety of educational backgrounds useful in carrying out the office's goals, and in this regard, initiatives such as workshops and short courses as reported in this study are key to achieving this. These initiatives should however encompass skills focusing on flexibility of dealing with academic staff and students, because the successful transfer of technology (i.e. IP protection and commercialisation) within the universities depends in large part on the IP disclosures to TTOs by these personnel. Sibanda [45] observed that key ingredients for successful technology transfer within the South African public research institutions stem from an effective and trustworthy relationship between TTO staff and the inventors, based on the ability of the first personnel to engage with the latter and demonstrate empathy with their challenges, as well as being able to proactively assist them to extract the maximum value from their research.

However, it is very crucial to emphasise that not all newly established TTO staff within PFSAU require training. For instance, newly appointed vast experienced employees with relevant skill set, networks and depth of knowledge usually have worked long enough to understand technology transfer culture and thus can add instant value to the office. Hiring such people can therefore also help cut down on training cost, as the focus can only be on mandatory training. Generally, to ensure swift proper functioning of newly established TTOs (including effective technology transfer management) and ultimately its sustainability, first priority should be given to highly experienced professionals in the field of technology transfer when recruiting staff for newly established TTOs within PFSAU. Importantly, for inexperienced employees who need to be capacitated with appropriate professional skills and knowledge, there must be a balance between course/workshop attendance and day-to-day activities of the office. Accordingly, the relevancy of each course/workshop to be attended by such employees must be determined against the office's principal strategic goals prior approval and financing. This however, should not be misconstrued, because there are some courses/workshops that are not directly contributing to the office's strategic goals, but can assist the staff to better execute and rapidly understand matters that are directly linked to the office's mandate. Therefore, a sound motivation should be given for attending such courses/workshops.

4.2 Intellectual property awareness within and outside the universities

The success of the IP system depends very much on the public's level of awareness [46]. According to Doerte [47], this kind of awareness generally influences and changes public opinion and behaviour on an issue, because it serves as an educational tool to assist people to better understand a particular issue or topic and ultimately develop an interest. As such, it is not surprising that a sizable number of participants in the present study mentioned IP awareness amongst academics and students within the university and other people not affiliated to the universities (referred in this study as formal and informal sectors) but who are involved in innovative creations as a potential activity to contribute to the sustainability of newly established TTO within PFSAU. In support of this view, Tartari et al. [48] found that researchers who are aware of the significance of research commercialisation are more likely to be involved in IP protection and collaborative projects with industries. Likewise, a study by Risaburo et al. [49] revealed that Indian academic institution patent application increased drastically after the institutions became aware of the importance of protecting IP and dissemination of knowledge through patents.

On the other hand, Alessandrini et al. [50] who interviewed personnel dedicated to technology transfer at PFSAU found that low levels of IP awareness (including of the benefits of protecting and commercialising research) amongst researchers have contributed to the low number of actionable IP/invention disclosures and the low conversion of patents to commercial products or licences. These authors also revealed that top management within the universities is vital for success of newly established TTOs and consequently suggested that a top-down approach would be most beneficial by promoting awareness of IP amongst the executives. Certainly, the top management holds the power to set tone, and thus they play a principal role in whether the institution will actively engage in IP protection and commercialisation or not. Therefore, IP awareness by newly established TTO staff within the PFSAU must not only follow bottom-up approach (i.e. conducting IP awareness amongst academics and students) as suggested by participants in this study, but should also adopt top-down approach (i.e. conducting IP awareness amongst councils and management). The latter approach should be the first because once the university top executives are aware of the value of IP protection and commercialisation to the institution and South Africa at large, it will be instrumental in spreading the message across the executives (i.e. faculty deans and heads of departments), who will in turn inform the researchers.

The recommendations made by participants in the present study regarding execution of IP awareness amid formal and informal sectors as one of the strategic activities to sustain newly established TTOs have merit. For instance, Szogs [51] who studied a collaboration between the University of Dar es Salaam's College of Engineering and Technology (Tanzania) and informal and informal sectors regarding the transfer of technology found that some of the inventions created by students in the colleges were initially developed by informal and formal sectors. The research by Kawooya [52] revealed active interactions in Automotive Engineering (i.e. sharing of innovations, solutions to problems and product designs as well as models) between the personnel from formal university research institution and informal-sector in Kampala (Uganda). In South Africa, most commercialised geographical indications and pharmaceutical products [44, 53–60] invented/developed by academic researchers were either inspired by traditional knowledge in informal sectors or developed with the help of people in this sector. It therefore makes sense that participants in the current study perceive IP awareness amid academics and students within the university and informal sectors as having potential to ensure that newly formed TTOs receive commercialisable IP and innovative disclosures from people affiliated to the university and those who are not. This is crucial especially since the IP Rights from Publicly Financed Research and Development Act, No. 51 of 2008 only oblige the South African university staff (i.e. academics, researchers and supports) and students to disclose innovative and IP ideas they created using institution's resources to TTOs [61], without coercing them to execute projects that might lead to the identifications of these ideas. In other words, academics within the PFSAU are not compelled to conduct projects that might lead to the identification of the referred ideas. Therefore, educating both informal and formal sectors about IP as well as innovations including allied benefits, in addition to people affiliated to the university, is more likely to increase IP disclosure to the university's newly established TTO. However, for this to happen, staff from this office must during IP awareness advice people to work with them as far as IP protection and commercialisation are concerned.

Although there is logic in conducting IP awareness in the formal and informal sectors as one of the strategic activity to sustain newly established TTOs as discussed above, it should however be noted that establishing beneficial partnership with these sectors will not be an easy task and cost-free. This is especially true when looking at the strategic activities such as workshops, media outlets including Internet (via the development of Website spreading the word about the importance of IP protections and commercialisations), radio and print-outs such as poster, pocket manual and flyers, disclosed by interviewees as part of IP awareness. For instance, print-outs reporting on IP and innovation to be distributed to people should be written in both local and English dialects, to accommodate people (especially in the informal sector) who cannot read and understand the latter language. Similarly, to cover a larger number of audiences in informal and formal sectors using radio broadcast will require IP information to be communicated in various languages to accommodate diverse South African ethnic groups, and this will be very costly for newly established TTOs. It will therefore be more practical and cost-effective for these offices to firstly focus on informal and formal sectors located near the universities. In this regard, the use of local community radio station and print-outs to convey IP information will be less expensive. In addition, the newly established TTO staff can identify potential people or groups within informal and formal sectors and arrange with them to provide a short talk on matters of IP.

Though not mentioned by participants in this study, initiation of IP and innovation competitions with attractive prices and rewards for the winners could also increase awareness and eventually IP portfolio within newly established TTOs. This initiative is not a new suggestion and has proved to be beneficial in encouraging innovation and commercialisable inventions [62–64]. Such initiatives as mentioned by participants in this study could therefore inspire academics, people in both formal and informal sectors, to disclose potentially commercialisable inventions and innovative ideas to newly established TTOs. However, there must be terms and conditions, whereby winners of prize/s in such competitions must have, at least, disclosed a single IP or innovative idea that meets the legal requirements for protection by these offices. The criterion for determining the winners can be outlined by TTO personnel. This will in the long-run create a strong rapport between this personnel and inventors within the universities, as well as informal and formal sectors, and will in due course encourage them to voluntarily disclose their ideas that are worth protecting to the office.

4.3 Intellectual property and innovation policy

The significance of a relevant and sound policy in sustaining and assisting an institution to achieve its role cannot be overemphasised [65, 66]. Some participants in the current study suggested the development of IP and innovation policy as one of the crucial key strategic activity for the sustainability of newly established TTOs within PFSAU. Similar findings were IP policy were less valued by academics in these institutions as fundamental to transfer technology and commercialise research output was reported in Botswana [67]. According to the participants in the present study, IP and innovation policy must promote the following: (1) the execution of applied and industry-driven research as well as innovations amongst the researchers within the universities and in both formal and informal sectors, (2) encourage the strategic collaboration between local and/or international business and newly established TTOs, and (3) it must specify the terms and conditions for funding of collaborative research including the ownership of IP.

The latter need careful attention; Bansia and Karunanidhi [68] found that most academics affiliated to a PFSAU strongly disagreed with the provision of IP Rights from Publicly Financed Research and Development Act, Act 51 of 2008, regarding the ownership of IP, that if a researcher has conducted research with publicly financed funding, the ownership of the IP produced from such research resides with the institution the researcher is affiliated to. Comparable finding was reported by Ramika [69]. Thus, a very generous financial reward via IP and innovation policy will go a long way in encouraging academics within the universities and personnel in informal and formal sectors to disclose IP for possible protection to newly established TTOs. It is worth mentioning that IP and innovation policy that encourage the strategic collaboration between local and/or international business and this offices, as reported in this study, is supported by other studies [70, 71] which demonstrated that such partnership is key to the successful transfer of technology from universities to industry/market. Nevertheless, for sustainable newly established TTO-business partnerships, effective engagement mechanisms beneficial to both parties must be enacted.

However, participants' recommendations that IP and innovation policy must promote the execution of applied and industry-driven research as well as innovations amongst the researchers within the universities and in both formal and informal sectors will be very complex and time-consuming for newly established TTOs. For instance, such policy must provide a climate beneficial for industry-driven research and innovations by advocating extensive training and opportunities for increasing skills and marketplace awareness amongst researchers/innovators, to guide research/innovation direction on industry requirements [72]. Therefore, the referred policy can be effective and beneficial activity in several years. This is especially true, when taking into account the diversity of IP and an innovation with potential value for commercialisation that might arise from the academic staff.

Importantly, the academic staff should be involved in policy development as they will be implementing it on almost daily basis. In this regard, newly established TTO IP and innovative policy draft must be made available to them for comments and approval. Same policy draft must be accessible to the public within informal and formal sectors for inputs. The involvement of all potential partners with newly established TTOs in institutional policy development will advocate a sense of ownership, less dissatisfaction and greater obligation to implementation. This will ultimately build trust and strong rapport between the TTO staff and potential partners in IP protection and the drive to commercialisation. However, the success of the referred policy must be reviewed and revised more often in line with newly established TTO strategic goals, to permit the office to respond and deal with unexpected changes in industrial structures.

4.4 Compliance with relevant legislations

Studies showed that legal compliance with relevant legislations and regulations is one of the cornerstones for the sustainability and success of any office [73–75], and as such newly established TTOs are not exception. The increased need for TTO staff to be aware of the latest developments in various IP law and related regulations cannot be over-emphasised [76]. This is because IP rights (including legal compliance) and infringement are generally thorny issues in the technology transfer process [77, 78].

In the present study, some participants stated that newly established TTO staff must be knowledgeable about various IP and innovative laws and ensure that they comply with them to avoid the financial penalties and damages to the office's reputation allied to infringement. Certainly, as far as technology transfer processes are concerned, TTO staff are key human resources in carrying out all compliance activities on behalf of the PFSAU. Furthermore, they are also responsible for the improvement or amendment of the institutional policies relating to the management and commercialisation of IP. Therefore, it is very fundamental for newly established TTO staff to identify legislations and regulations (locally and internationally) that apply to the office and assess how each affect the day-to-day work of the office. This must be continual activity to ensure that the office also meets its legal obligations in various operational areas to mitigate its risks. It is therefore suggested that newly established TTOs within PFSAU must either have a highly experienced legal expert to handle and/or oversee legal matters or must work closely with the university's legal office and seek advice or clarity prior to committing/signing any deal or agreement, especially those that are legally binding. The latter will cut cost of using external legal consultants for some services.

4.5 Learning from well-established technology transfer offices

While TTOs are still new in some PFSAU, there are universities and science councils formally carrying out technology transfer activities which are considered well-established, having been in operation for a number of years [79]. These are institutions that learned effectively from their own failures and from the failures of others over time [80] and have likely commercialised more IP and facilitated numerous patents and licence agreements. One participant in the current study stated that staff from newly established TTOs should consult with employees of well-established TTOs to get advice on the running of the office including the strategic activities. In the same view, Friedman and Silberman [81] observed that the length of time a TTO has existed can measure any learning or experience effects within it and that established networks as well as relationships created over time, which are vital in the success of TTO, come with experience. Similarly, Weckowska [82] has shown that the university TTOs learn through experimentation and failure and by sharing these experiences with other TTOs, thereby improving the technology transfer process. Therefore, the newly formed TTO within PFSAU can be efficient by benchmarking its own performance against well-established TTOs and seeking advices where necessary in order to set up a roadmap for improvement. Although this might contribute to the survival and adaptation of newly established TTO as imperative information for learning, it does not mean that employees from this office 'must do things similarly to well-established TTOs' even if prior rights/consent are attained. Case studies have shown that universities' TTOs vary in size, resource allocated and scope of their technical specialisation [83–85]. As such, if not cautious, newly formed TTOs may adopt strategic actions that are not compatible with the configuration of their resources and academic environment, all which according to Lafuente and Berbegal-Mirabent [86] translate into ineffective changes in the TTOs' technology transfer operations and, consequently, poor productivity results.

Accordingly, excursions to well-established TTOs for advice by newly formed TTOs staff as reported in this study must be viewed primarily as a vehicle to assist in observing actions from divergent perspectives and subsequently to develop novel and original ideas/activities that can addresses their goals. It is therefore recommended that as part of learning from experienced TTOs, staff from newly established TTOs should ask questions related to the short and long-term challenges that are likely to be faced by the office, the failure of some of the projects including the root cause of failure and mitigation measures used. This will assist the staff from newly established TTOs to avoid similar challenges from occurring, and/or to know which effective solution to apply when they come across such hitches, and subsequently allow the introduction of changes that enhance productivity levels.

4.6 Intellectual property and innovation modules

Education in every sense is one of the fundamental factors of development [87], because it raises people's productivity and creativity and promotes entrepreneurship as well as technological advances. However, only one participant in this study stated that an introduction of compulsory IP and innovation modules within the South African higher institutions of learning and elementary schools would be one of the key strategic activities with potential to sustain newly established TTOs based on the universities. University researchers in Pakistan also highlighted the need of IP property rights in the educational system of this country for effective IP and commercialisation [88]. Comparable finding was noted in Brazil [89] and Australia [90]. Indeed, as reported by European Union Intellectual Property Office [91], IP education has great potential to capacitate learners/academic staff with skills and competences that would enable them to become familiar with IP, understand its potential to generate income and economic growth and lead them to respect IP rights, whether their own or those of others. A study conducted by the National Union of Students [92] found that most students in Higher Education and Further Education institutions of the

United Kingdom who had studied designs, design rights and trade marks in their current course recognised the importance of IP education as a key to exploit ideas commercially and want IP issues to be included from the early stages of their course. The same organisation has also shown evidence that IP teaching earlier in students' education motivates their greater interest in technology transfer issues.

While an introduction of compulsory IP and innovation modules within the South African elementary schools has potential to instil innovation culture amongst learners, its contribution towards the sustainability of newly established TTOs based in the universities will only materialise over years when learners go to tertiary institution wherein they are expected to develop a comprehensive understanding of the IP which will motivate them to become inventors or innovators in their respective fields of study. Similarly, the contribution of compulsory IP and innovation modules within the South African higher institutions will only benefit newly established TTOs in a long run. For instance, the development of module curriculum (and its accreditation) might take longer, as it must be tailored to particular needs of students in different disciplines across the university, covering theoretical teachings and practical approaches through real life case studies. However, once programme is up and running, students will be able to rapidly and prematurely recognise and explore their own creative ideas/IP worthy of legal protection and commercialisation and disclose them to TTOs.

4.7 Execution of applied and industry-driven research by academics

All participants in this study suggested an execution of applied and industry-driven researches by academics as imperative activity to sustain newly established TTOs within PFSAU. This finding does not strike as surprising since augmentation of research-related revenues is one of the goals embraced by many universities [93]. In agreement with participants of the current study, Asuako [41] also emphasised the need for academics within the Ghanaian government owned Universities to undertake industry-oriented research to successfully transfer technology and ultimately support the needs of society. Researchers in South Africa [69] and Norway [94] also accentuated this. Interestingly, Mansfield [95] found that 11 and 9% of new products and processes, respectively, in 76 United States firms were initially from academic research. Similarly, Tijssen [96] who questioned inventors in the Netherlands reported that 20% of patented technologies that became innovations were based on publicly funded research executed by academics. With particular reference to the present study, execution of applied and industry-driven research by academics will indeed contribute towards the sustainability of newly established TTOs within PFSAU. However, for some TTOs located in the universities dominated by scientists who carry out research of a basic nature, the referred sustainability will be achieved over a period of time. This is because supporting these scientists to think creatively and conduct novel industry-driven researches is a complex process that cannot be achieved in a short period of time and will depend on the nature of the project.

One fundamental factor that discourages academic researchers to conduct industry-driven researches mentioned by participants in this study is the lack of IP and research commercialisation awareness. It is worth stating that encouraging academics to execute applied and industry-driven researches via IP awareness alone has shortcomings, as newly established TTO staff have very little influence on the quality and type of researches conducted by academics. When asked about actions to take if IP awareness fail, most of the participants highlighted the need for initiations of activities with an objective to both encourage and coerce academics to conduct research with potential IP for commercialisation. They disclosed that a universities' policy reflecting better benefits (i.e. generous financial remuneration and contribution to job promotion) of protecting and commercialising research work compared to the benefits offered by publishing in the accredited journals will go a long way in encouraging academics to both initiate and actively participate in IP projects with potential for commercialisation and ultimately disclose them to newly established TTOs. Indeed, studies [85, 97] showed that researchers' retaliation to take part in technology transfer activities within institutions of higher learning is a weak system of incentives.

Another strategic activity reported by participants for encouraging academics to conduct industry-driven research is to do an extensive patent and novelty search prior initiation of projects. The significance of this action towards increasing the probability of implementing projects with commercial value cannot be overemphasised [97–99] and will certainly assist the academics as well as students to avoid the likelihoods of duplicating research projects. However, for this to work, researchers should keep up-to-date with the latest developments in their respective professional fields to ensure that their researches are new and original. One way to achieve this is for newly established TTOs to encourage/initiate joint research projects to foster university-to-industry technology transfer. In addition, some participants recommended the amendments of the research proposal templates of all faculties within the universities to include novelty and potential IP section. Subsequently, suggested disapproval of research proposals without information relating to this section. In this regard, it makes sense that newly established TTO staff must form part of the university's research proposal-approval committee (perhaps at departmental level) and assess projects with potential IP for commercialisation. This will afford TTO staff an opportunity to provide advices to researchers on how the office can assist in commercialising their researches and to guards against activities that might affect the legal requirements of protecting potential IP from such projects.

Although not stated by the participants in this study, staff from newly established TTOs within PFSAU should write industry-driven proposals in collaboration with appropriate academics/researchers and apply for funding. Subsequently, funded research projects encompass the following: (1) aim and objectives and (2) expected outcomes with potential to address newly established TTOs objectives. The terms and conditions of the project must be allocated to interested postgraduate students. This approach will increase the probability of discovering protectable IP with potential for commercialisation and most importantly afford newly established TTO staff more influence on the research areas or projects conducted by university employees and students. Also, an establishment of a multidisciplinary journal run by these offices that accepts the manuscripts reporting on protected innovations and inventions (amongst others) in all fields of study recognised by the South African Department of Higher Education will contribute significantly in generating money (i.e. via publication fees) for newly established TTOs. In addition, the journal policy should compel the authors whose manuscripts are accepted for publications to transfer the copyright to the journal. This will give the TTOs an exclusive monopoly over all the accepted articles or published articles, including the right to trade as collection of articles or book based on a series of papers. Newly established TTOs in PFSAU can furthermore capitalise financially from the government funding initiatives (such as Technology Innovation Agency Seed Funding, amid others) which are mainly administered by the office to fund the academic projects with 'potential' IP for commercialisation. In this regard, TTO personnel with the consent of funders can amend institutional IP and innovation policy to compel funding recipients to at least write and publish an article in accredited journals in case commercialisable IP was not attained as expected. Subsequently, a considerable proportion of financial reimbursement for publication offered by the government should go to newly established TTOs.

4.8 Protection and commercialisation

As anticipated, the protection and commercialisation of IP and innovative ideas was mentioned by all participants as a compulsory activity to ensure the sustainability of newly established TTOs within PFSAU. This finding was expected for a sole obvious reason that TTOs within these institutions were established with the primary aim of protecting IP and commercialising it for the benefit of people of the republic [6]. There is a growing body of research [98, 100, 101] indicating that the universities' commercialisation performance depends partly on the abilities of their respective TTOs to facilitate exploitation of academic inventions in commercial applications. However, the investigator of the present study shares similar sentiments with his participants that the successful protection and/or commercialisation of IP/innovative creations by newly established TTOs within PFSAU will depend on the positive outcomes of the earlier listed and discussed strategic activities. In other words, these offices stand a better chance of identifying protectable IPs/innovations and successfully commercialise them if these activities are effectively applied. Each of the referred activity has different benefits with potential to launch the office forward towards achieving its principal mandate, which include the introduction of IPs/innovations in markets and thereafter generate income and job creations.

5. Conclusions and perspective

This study concludes that the sustainability of newly established TTOs within PFSAU requires integrated incessant strategic activities, subjected to continual monitoring to ensure their effectiveness. The success of each strategic activity can be easily monitored quarterly and annually by its impact towards contributions to the offices' objectives and ultimately universities' strategic goals. Overall, efficacious implementations of strategic activities proposed in the current study will not only contribute towards the sustainability of newly established TTOs within PFSAU, but will also aid in achieving some of these universities' shared goals such as community engagements, research with economic impact, teaching and learning. For instance, IP awareness as discussed in this study as well as introduction of compulsory IP course within the universities will contribute towards achieving the institutions' teaching and learning goal. Collaboration with informal and formal sectors (as defined in this study) outside the universities as earlier discussed is directly linked to the institution's mission of engaging with the public/community, and lastly, the execution of applied and industry-driven research by academics will contribute to the university's goals of conducting research projects with economic impact. Therefore, all the proposed strategic activities in this study if implemented successfully can be used as an effective tool to sustain newly established university-based TTOs and direct them towards accomplishing the overall goals of the university. However, it should be emphasised that some of the strategic activities documented in this study can be achieved over short, medium or long-term periods, but together they can be utilised as stepping stones to continually achieve the overall goals of newly established TTOs within the publicly financed South African universities.

Acknowledgements

The author is grateful to all participants who participated in this study.

Author details

Sebua S. Semenya
Technology Transfer Office, Research Administration and Development Department, University of Limpopo, Sovenga, South Africa

Address all correspondence to: sebua.semenya@ul.ac.za

References

[1] Pouris A, Pouris A. Patents and economic development in South Africa: Managing intellectual property rights. South African Journal of Science. 2011;**107**:11-12

[2] World Intellectual Property Organization. 2017. Available from: http://www.wipo.int/edocs/pubdocs/en/intproperty/450/wipo_pub_450.pdf [Accessed: 03 August 2018]

[3] Companies and Intellectual Property Commission. 2017. Available from: http://www.cipc.co.za/index.php/trade-marks-patents-designs-copyright/what-ip/ [Accessed: 01 August 2018]

[4] Kalanje CM. Role of Intellectual Property in Innovation and New Product Development. 2018. Available from: http://www.wipo.int/sme/en/documents/ip_innovation_development_fulltext.html [Accessed: 27 July 2018]

[5] Knudso W. An Introduction to Patents, Brands, Trade Secrets Trademarks, and Intellectual Property Rights Issues. Michgain State University: Product Centre of Agriculture and National Resources; 2006

[6] National Intellectual Property Management Office. A Guide to Intellectual Properties for Researchers. Pretoria: The Innovation Hub; 2013

[7] Dagne TW. Place-based intellectual property strategies for traditional and local agricultural products: Acting locally to participate globally in a rights-based approach. Drake Journal of Agricultural Law. 2013;**17**:3-4

[8] De Beer J, Armstrong C, Oguamanam C, Schonwetter T. Innovation and Intellectual Property Collaborative Dynamics in Africa. University of Cape Town, South Africa: UCT Press; 2013

[9] Society of Composers, Authors and Music Publishers of Canada. 2017. Available from: http://www.socan.ca/files/pdf/Copyright%20101%20Eng.pdf [Accessed: 28 July 2018]

[10] Southern African Research and Innovation Management Association. A Guide to Intellectual Properties for Researchers. Pretoria: CSIR Campus; 2013

[11] Bollier D, Bradford G, Racine L, Sohn GB. So What—About Copyright? What Artists Need to Know about Copyright and Trademarks: For Filmmakers, Visual Artists, and Writers. United States of America: LuLu Enterprises; 2013

[12] Organisation for Economic Co-operation and Development. Enquiries into Intellectual Property's Economic Impact Chapter 1. Synthesis Report. Paris, France: Directorate for Science, Technology and Innovation Committee on Digital Economy Policy; 2015

[13] Qinghu A. Well-known marks and China's system of well-known mark protection. Official Journal of the International Trademark Association. 2005;**95**:706-772

[14] Kudrjavceva J. Issues surrounding registration of colour trademarks [MSc dissertation]. University of Latvia; 2012

[15] Jackson L. Solicitor with the Commercial and ICT Unit of Leman Solicitors. 2012. Available from: http://www.leman.ie/ [Accessed: 24 July 2018]

[16] World Intellectual Property Organization. Geographical Indications: An Introduction. 2012. Available from: http://www.wipo.int/edocs/pubdocs/en/geographical/952/wipo_pub_952.pdf [Accessed: 29 July 2018]

[17] Yeh BT. Protection of Trade Secrets: Overview of Current Law and Legislation. Congressional Research Services; 2016

[18] Hall BE. Contribution to the New Palgrave: A Dictionary of Economics. 2nd ed. 2007. Available from: https://eml.berkeley.edu/~bhhall/papers/BHH06_Patents_Palgrave.pdf [Accessed: 28 July 2018]

[19] Fink CM, Maskus KE. Why we study intellectual property rights and what we have learned. In: Fink CM, Maskus KE, editors. Intellectual Property and Development. Lessons from Recent Economic Research. Washington, D.C.: The World Bank; 2002. pp. 1-15

[20] Mengistie G, Halm N, Kaakunga RA. Intellectual Property Audit Report of Namibia. Multi-Stakeholders Workshop: Validation of the National Intellectual Property Strategy for Namibia. Windhoek: Nampower Convention Centre; 2016

[21] Nwokocha U. Nigerian intellectual property: Overview of developments and practice. Journal of Intellectual Property. 2016;**6**:110-116

[22] Nzomo V. Laws Governing Intellectual Property (IP) in Kenya. 2011. Available from: https://ipkenya.wordpress.com/2011/09/09/laws-governing-intellectual-property-ip-in-kenya/ [Accessed: 28 July 2018]

[23] USAID. An Assessment of Mozambique's Intellectual Property System. Nathan Associates Inc., United States Agency for International Development; 2009

[24] Spennemann C. Development Dimensions of Intellectual Property in Uganda: Transfer of Technology, Access to Medicines and Textbooks. United Nation; 2010

[25] Lugwisa AH. Intellectual Property Rights in Tanzania. 2017. Available from: http://yakubuchambers.com/wp-content/uploads/2016/07/a-paper-on-intellectual-property-in-Tanzania.-3.pdf [Accessed: 03 August 2018]

[26] US-Egypt Business Council. Intellectual Property Rights in Egypt. 2017. Available from: http://www.usegyptcouncil.org/wp-content/uploads/2010/08/USEBC-Intellectual-Property-White-Paper-Oct-15.pdf [Accessed: 01 August 2018]

[27] Kim J, Anderson J, Daim J. Assessing university technology transfer: A measure of efficiency patterns. International Journal of Innovation and Technology Management. 2008;**5**:495-526

[28] Tseng A, Raudensky M. Performance evaluations of technology transfer offices of major US research universities ampere. Journal of Technology Management and Innovation. 2014;**9**:93-102

[29] Kyprianou C, Graebner ME, Rindova V. Strategic conversations: Methods for data collection and analysis. In: Elsbach K, Kramer R, editors. The Handbook of Qualitative Organizational Research. Routledge; 2016. pp. 272-285

[30] Godfrey PC, Hill CWL. The problem of unobservables in strategic management research. Strategic Management Journal. 1995;**16**:519-533

[31] Krippendorff K. Content Analysis an Introduction to its Methodology. London, United Kingdom: Sage Publications Ltd; 2004

[32] Gates LP. Strategic Planning with Critical Success Factors and Future Scenarios: An Integrated Strategic Planning Framework. Technical Reports. Carnegie Mellon University; 2010

[33] Pirraglia W. Why is Strategic Planning Important to a Business? 2017.

Available from: http://smallbusiness.chron.com/strategic-planning-important-business-2671.html [Accessed: 22 July 2018]

[34] Chartered Institute of Purchasing and Supply and US Organization the National Institute of Governmental Purchasing. Public Procurement Practice: Strategic Procurement Planning. 2012. Available from: https://www.nigp.org/ [Accessed: 20 July 2018]

[35] Holmes AT. How to Facilitate the Strategic Planning Process. 2018. Available from: http://www.drtyroneholmes.com/uploads/2/0/3/4/20346297/how_to_facilitate_the_strategic_planning_process_-_final.pdf [Accessed: 03 August 2018]

[36] Mahmudi RK, Kargaran JM. The effect of in-service training on empowerment of staff at the University of Tabriz. International Journal of Humanities and Cultural Studies. 2001;**1**:1-7

[37] European Commission. Improving Knowledge Transfer between Research Institutions and Industry across Europe. Belgium; 2007

[38] Maxfield RC, Flumerfelt S. The empowering principal: Leadership behaviours needed by effective principals as identified by emerging leaders and principals. International Journal of Teacher Leadership. 2009;**2**:39-48

[39] Voegtlin C, Boehm S, Bruch H. How to empower employees: Using training to enhance work units' collective empowerment. International Journal of Manpower. 2015;**36**:354-373

[40] Perera HSC, Darshana M, Liyanage C. A Case Study of Technology Transfer Process in a Government Research Organization in Sri Lanka. Technical Reports. Department of Management of Technology, University of Moratuwa Sri Lanka; 2015

[41] Asuako EL. Constraints of industrialization and technology transfer in Ghana [MSc dissertation]. Ghana: Kwame Nkrumah University of Science and Technology; 2015

[42] Swamidass PM, Vulasa V. Why university inventions rarely produce income? Bottlenecks in university technology transfer. The Journal of Technology Transfer. 2009;**34**:343-363

[43] Jorgensen B. Out of the lab and into the market: Universities and businesses struggle with technology transfer issues. Electronic Business. 2005;**31**:13

[44] Van Looy B, Landoni P, Callaert J, Van Pottelsberghe B, Apsalis E, Debackere K. Entrepreneurial effectiveness of European universities: An empirical assessment of antecedents and trade-offs. Research Policy. 2011;**40**:553-564

[45] Sibanda M. Intellectual property, commercialisation and institutional arrangements at South African public research institutions. In: The Economics of Intellectual Property in South Africa. Geneva, Switzerland: World Intellectual Property Organization (WIPO) 1013(E); 2009

[46] Ahmed S, Varun PK. Awareness regarding intellectual property rights a survey amongst the P.G. and Ph.D. students of Babasaheb Bhimrao Ambedkar University, Lucknow. International Journal of Law. 2017;**4**:184-190

[47] Doerte P. Media Campaigns—Posters and Flyers (WD). 2017. Available from: https://www.sswm.info/ [Accessed: 01 August 2018]

[48] Tartari V, Perkmann M, Salter A. In good company: The influence of peers on industry engagement by

academic scientists. Research Policy. 2004;**43**:1189-1203

[49] Risaburo N, Kiang CS, Ganguli P, Nithad K, Nishio K, Tansinsin LG, et al. Technology Transfer, Intellectual Property and Effective University-Industry Partnerships: The Experience of China, India, Japan, Philippines, the Republic of Korea, Singapore and Thailand. Geneva: World Intellectual Property Organization; 2018

[50] Alessandrini M, Klose K, Pepper MS. University entrepreneurship in South Africa: Developments in technology transfer practices. Innovation: Management, Policy and Practice. 2013;**15**:205-214

[51] Szogs A. Technology Transfer and Technological Capability Building in Informal Firms in Tanzania. CIRCLE, Lund University; 2010

[52] Kawooya D. Informal–formal sector interactions in automotive engineering, Kampala. In: De Beer J, Armstrong C, Oguamanam C, Schonwetter, T (Editors). Innovation and Intellectual Property: Collaborative Dynamics in Africa. UCT Press, University of Cape Town, Cape Town; 2014

[53] Levy D. Continuities and changes in Ndebele beadwork: C. 1883 [MA dissertation]. Johannesburg: University of the Witvatersrand; 1990

[54] Van Wyk B-E. A broad review of commercially important southern African medicinal plants. Journal of Ethnopharmacology. 2008;**119**:342-355

[55] Maharaj VJ, Fouche G, Senabe J, Nthambeleni R, Kotze F. Agro-processing opportunities identified through a novel mosquito repellent from a medicinal plant. In: Proceedings of the 2nd CSIR Biennial Conference on Science Real and Relevant; Pretoria, South Africa; 2008. Available from: http://hdl.handle.net [Accessed: 26 July 2018]

[56] Singh Y. Systematics of Hypoxis (Hypoxidaceae) in southern Africa [PhD thesis]. Pretoria: University of Pretoria; 2009

[57] Van Wyk B-E. The potential of South African plants in the development of new food and beverage products. South African Journal of Botany. 2011;**77**:857-868

[58] Van Wyk B-E. The potential of South African plants in the development of new medicinal products. South African Journal of Botany. 2011;7:812-829

[59] Aboyade OM, Styger G, Gibson D, Hughes G. Sutherlandia frutescens: The meeting of science and traditional knowledge. Journal of Alternative and Complementary Medicine. 2014;**20**:71-76

[60] Department of Science and Technology. Intellectual Property and Technology Transfer at Publicly Funded Research Institutions: Inaugural Baseline Study: 2008-2014. 2017. Available from: http://www.sarima.co.za/wp-content/uploads/2017/05/SA-IPTT_BASELINE-SURVEY-REPORT-2017.pdf [Accessed: 12 August 2018]

[61] Department of Science and Technology. Intellectual Property Rights from Publicly Financed Research and Development Act, No. 51 of 2008. Department of Science and Technology, Government Printer, Pretoria; 2017

[62] Mokter H, Ilkka K. Competition-based innovation the case of the x prize foundation. Journal of Organization Design. 2014;**3**:46-52

[63] Moser P, Nicholas T. Prizes, publicity and patents: Non-monetary awards as a mechanism to encourage

innovation. The Journal of Industrial Economics. 2003;**61**:763-788

[64] The Knowledge Round Table. Using Innovation Competitions to Motivate Students. 2018. Available from: https://www.theknowledgeroundtable.com/using-innovation-competitions-to-motivate-students/ [Accessed: 25 August 2018]

[65] Conti A, Gaule P. Is the US outperforming Europe in university technology licensing? A new perspective on the European paradox. Research Policy. 2011;**40**:123-135

[66] Department of Agriculture. Policy on Agriculture in Sustainable Development a Discussion Document. 2018. Available from: http://www.nda.agric.za/docs/Policy/SustainableDev.pdf 8th [Accessed: 20 July 2018]

[67] Njoku OA. Perspectives on intellectual property from Botswana's publicly funded researchers. In: De Beer J, Armstrong C, Oguamanam C, Schonwetter T, editors. Innovation and Intellectual Property: Collaborative Dynamics in Africa. University of Cape Town, Cape Town: UCT Press; 2018

[68] Bansia R, Karunanidhi R. Intellectual property from publicly financed research and intellectual property registration by universities: A case study of a university in South Africa. Procedia—Social and Behavioral Sciences. 2015;**181**:185-196

[69] Ramika B. Commercialization of university innovation in South Africa [PhD thesis]. KwaZulu Natal: Durban University of Technology; 2016

[70] Van Zyl A, Amadi-Echendu A, Bothma TJD. Nine drivers of knowledge transfer between universities and industry R&D partners in South Africa. South African Journal of Information Management. 2007;**9**:1-22

[71] Chávez JR. University Industry Technology Transfer in Canada (online). 2010. Available from: http://rnee.umich.mx/index.php/RNEE/article/view/61 [Accessed: 17 July 2018]

[72] Baxter R. Innovation and Inventors Interest. New York: Free Press; 2011

[73] Benedek P. Compliance management—A new response to legal and business challenges. Acta Polytechnica Hungarica. 2012;**9**:135-148

[74] Losiewicz-Dniestrzanska E. Monitoring of compliance risk in the bank. Procedia Economics and Finance. 2015;**26**:800-805

[75] Vadastreanu AM, Maier D, Maier A. Is the success possible in compliance with ethics and deontology in business? Procedia Economics and Finance. 2015;**26**:1068-1073

[76] Maskus KE. Encouraging International Technology Transfer. UNCTAD/ICTSD Issue Paper No. 7 (Geneva: UNCTAD/ICTSD). Geneva, Switzerland: International Centre for Trade and Sustainable Development (ICTSD); 2004

[77] Sikoyo GM, Nyukuri E, Wakhungu JW. Intellectual Property Protection in Africa: Status of Laws, Research and Policy Analysis in Ghana, Kenya, Nigeria, South Africa and Uganda. Nairobi, Kenya: ACTS Press; 2006

[78] Song X, Balamuralikrishna R. JOTS v27n1—The Process and Curriculum of Technology Transfer. 2018. Available from: https://scholar.lib.vt.edu/ejournals/JOTS/Winter-Spring-2001/song.html [Accessed: 01 August 2018]

[79] Wolson RA. The role of technology transfers offices in building the South African biotechnology sector: An assessment of policies, practices and

impact. The Journal of Technology Transfer. 2007;**32**:343-365

[80] Madsen PM, Desai V. Failing to learn? The effects of failure and success on organizational learning in the global orbital launch vehicle industry. Academy of Management. 2010;**53**:3451-3476

[81] Friedman J, Silberman J. University technology transfer: Do incentives, management, and location matter? The Journal of Technology Transfer. 2003;**28**:17-30

[82] Weckowska DM. Learning in university technology transfer offices: Transactions focused and relations-focused approaches to commercialization of academic research. Technovation. 2015;**41**:62-74

[83] Sellenthin MO. Technology transfer offices and university patenting in Sweden and Germany. The Journal of Technology Transfer. 2009;**34**:603-620

[84] DRS P, Vidal VS, Zen AC, Barros HM. Management of Intellectual Property in Brazilian Universities: A Multiple Case Study. Rua Washington Luiz: Federal University of Rio Grande do Sul (EA/UFRGS); 2013

[85] Vinig T, Lips D. Measuring the performance of university technology transfer using meta data approach: The case of Dutch universities. The Journal of Technology Transfer. 2015;**40**:1034-1049

[86] Lafuente E, Berbegal-Mirabent J. Assessing the performance of technology transfer offices: An analysis of the relevance of TTO's outcome configuration and aspiration performance. Paper presented at the 4th Workshop on Efficiency in Education, Politecnico di Milano; October 20-21 2016. In: Proceedings of the 4th Workshop on Efficiency in Education; 2016. pp. 1-24

[87] Ozturk I. The Role of Education in Economic Development: A Theoretical Perspective. 2008. Available from: https://ssrn.com/abstract=1137541 or http://dx.doi.org/10.2139/ssrn.1137541 [Accessed: 3 August 2018]

[88] Hina K, Batool S, Khalique M, Iqbal Z. Intellectual property rights in education of Pakistan: Review of constitution, current status and expectations. The Dialogue. 2017;**12**:136-147

[89] Gimenez AMN, Bonacelli MBM, Carneiro AM. The challenges of teaching and training in intellectual property. Journal of Technology Management and Innovation. 2012;**7**:176-188

[90] Monotti A. Maximising the benefits from intellectual property in universities: Awareness of our rights and obligations. Australian Universities Review. 2000:23-31

[91] European Union Intellectual Property Office. Intellectual property and Education in Europe: Study on IP Education in School Curricula in the EU Member States with Additional International Comparisons. Alicante, Spain: Office for Harmonization in the Internal Market; 2015

[92] National Union of Students. Student Attitudes Towards Intellectual Property National Union of Students. London, UK; 2012

[93] Warshaw JB, Hearn JC. Leveraging university research to serve economic development: An analysis of policy dynamics in and across three U.S. states. Journal of Higher Education Policy and Management. 2014;**36**:196-211

[94] Rasmussen E, Rice MP. A framework for government support mechanisms aimed at enhancing university technology transfer: The Norwegian case. International

Journal of Technology Transfer and Commercialization. 2012;**11**:1-25

[95] Mansfield E. Academic research and industrial innovation. Research Policy. 1991;**20**:1-12

[96] Tijssen RJ. Science dependence of technologies: Evidence from inventions and their inventors. Research Policy. 2002;**31**:509-526

[97] Markman G, Gianiodisa P, Phan P, Balkin D. Innovation speed: Transferring university technology to market. Research Policy. 2005;**34**:1058-1075

[98] Graf SG. Improving patent quality through identification of relevant prior art: Approaches to increase information flow to the patent office. Lewis and Clark Law Review. 2005;**495**:502-504

[99] Loizides F, Diallo B, Pollard A, Mavri A. Increasing the Discovery and Use of Non-Patent Literature (NPL): Scientific Publications in Patent Examination. IOS Press; 2017. DOI: 10.3233/978-1-61499-769-6-211 [Accessed: 13 July 2018]

[100] Alexander AT, Martin DP. Intermediaries for open innovation: A competence-based comparison of knowledge transfer offices practices. Technological Forecasting and Social Change. 2013;**80**:38-49

[101] Siegel DS, Waldman DA, Atwater LE, Link AN. Toward a model of the effective transfer of scientific knowledge from academicians to practitioners: Qualitative evidence from the commercialization of university technologies. Journal of Engineering and Technology Management. 2004;**21**:115-142

Chapter 10

Dissemination of Distributed Energy Technologies

Arkady Trachuk and Natalia Linder

Abstract

At present, the electric power industry is undergoing a cardinal transformation all over the world, the main driver of which is technological innovations, which determine the possibilities for the transition of this sphere to a fundamentally new stage of development. The purpose of this chapter is to analyze the amplification of distributed power generation technologies among industrial companies, as well as the factors for the adoption of new technologies by industrial companies in Russia. The following steps were taken for the analysis of the most significant factors of the adoption of distributed power generation technology by industrial companies: in-depth semi-structured interviews with large industrial company representatives (8 companies) and survey of industrial companies (69 companies). The results obtained allow us to conclude that for analyzed companies, technical feasibility, the cost of electricity, and perceived benefits are critical factors in deciding on the use of distributed power generation technologies. Obtaining cheap electric and thermal energy, a gradual increase in energy capacities and evenness of investment with fast energy generation for industrial and household needs are possible today due to the use of energy-efficient solutions based on distributed power generation technologies.

Keywords: electric power industry, distributed power generation, new technologies, factors of innovation adoption, energy efficiency

1. Introduction

At the moment, the sphere of electric power industry is undergoing a cardinal transformation all over the world, the main driver of which is technological innovations, which determine the possibilities for transition of this sphere to a fundamentally new stage of development. Avoiding a centralized energy supply is a global trend, for example, the global market for distributed energy technologies (small distributed power generation, demand management, storage, energy efficiency, etc.) is growing at a rate of about 6–9% per year. It is expected that by year 2025, the input volume of distributed power generation capacity will exceed the input volume of centralized power generation three times. According to the International Energy Agency, distributed energy will provide up to 75% of new connections during global electrification until 2030.

In Russia, the spread of distributed generation technologies is proceeding at a much lower rate; therefore, the factors of its expansion require a deeper analysis.

The purpose of this chapter is to analyze the spread of distributed energy technologies among industrial companies, as well as the factors for the adoption of new technologies by industrial companies in Russia. For the analysis of the most significant factors of distributed power generation technology adoption, industrial companies conducted in-depth semi-structured interviews with representatives of large industrial companies (8 companies) and a survey of industrial companies (69 companies). A regression model was used for the analysis, which allows determining the strength and significance of the influence of selected factors on the companies' decision-making on their own power generation.

The results obtained allow us to conclude that for analyzed companies, technical feasibility, the cost of electricity, and perceived benefits are critical factors in deciding on the use of distributed power generation technologies. The risk factor turned out to be insignificant, which the companies explained in the in-depth interviews by the fact that distributed power generation systems reduce the occurrence of the listed adverse effects to a minimum. Obtaining cheap electric and thermal energy, a gradual increase in energy capacities and evenness of investment with fast energy generation for industrial and household needs are possible today due to the use of energy-efficient solutions based on distributed power generation technologies.

2. Technologies of distributed energy and their structure

Distributed energy technologies (distributed energy resources, DER) in the world practice [1] include a wide range of technologies:

- Distributed generation
- Demand management (demand response)
- Energy efficiency management
- Microgrids
- Distributed power storage systems
- Electric cars

The basic characteristic of all these technologies is proximity to the energy consumer. Distributed generation is a set of power plants located close to the place of energy consumption and is connected either directly to the consumer or to the distribution electrical network (in the case when there are several consumers). The type of primary energy source used by the station (e.g., fossil fuel or renewable energy), as well as the station's relevance to consumer, generating or grid-supplying company, or a third party, does not matter. In foreign practice there is a tendency to limit the power of distributed generation power plants by the top bar, depending on the technology used. For example, Navigant Research uses a 500 kW boundary for wind, 1 MW for solar, 250 kW for gas turbines, and 6 MW for gas piston and diesel power plants. The European Distributed Energy Partnership Project (EU-DEEP) used similar boundaries: thermal power plants (steam, gas turbines, piston engines) up to 10 MW, microturbines up to 500 kW, wind power stations up to 6 MW, and solar up to 5 MW.

In Russia, there is no consensus on this issue, and there are no restrictions in regulatory documents. On the other hand, the 25 MW total for all technologies is sometimes used (which "separates" the power plants from the retail and wholesale electricity and capacity markets). Some experts insist that distributed generation cannot have power limitations—in this logic, distributed power generation should include all power plants owned by consumers, including large industrial combined heat and power plants (CHP) with a capacity of more than 200 MW (located near large factories and plants). There is no consensus about the distributed generation of heating CHP plants with a capacity of more than 25 MW located in cities and towns (the capacity of some of them exceeds 1000 MW).

Among the criteria for the classification of distributed generation types, they also distinguish the type of fuel (from gas to secondary energy resources, for example, blast furnace gas, associated petroleum, and coke oven gas), generation technology (from steam power plants to wind generators), location, the amount of energy consumption by the main ("anchor") consumer (stations), mode factor, voltage level of network connection, and many others.

In this study, we see distributed generation including power plants located close to the consumer, connected to a distribution grid (110 kV and below) or directly supplying electricity to the consumer. The limitation on power and technology is not taken into account (if this is not specified separately). Autonomous power supply zones and isolated power systems are not the focus of this study.

Demand management is the change in energy consumption and power consumption by final users relative to their normal load profile due to changes in electricity prices needed to reduce system-wide costs in exchange for incentive payments from the energy market. For this study, it is important that demand management reduces the magnitude of peak loads in the power system and, accordingly, the system's need for installed capacity of power plants in the short term (day, week), medium term (1 year), and long term (e.g., during long-term power take 4 years ahead).

Energy efficiency and energy saving in this study are considered as a set of actions on the side of electricity consumer and lead to a long-term decrease in its energy demand. The focus of the study is on energy-saving measures that reduce the need for energy at times of power system peak loads and, accordingly, reduce the system's requirements for the given capacity of power plants.

Microgrid is an integrated power system consisting of distributed energy resources and several electrical loads (consumers), operating as a sole managed object in parallel with an existing electrical network or in island mode.

Distributed power storage systems (accumulators) are a set of storage systems installed at ultimate customer's side and at distribution network facilities and providing, among other things, backup and demand management capabilities.

Electric cars are considered as one of the types of distributed energy resources, since they play a role not only to energy consumers but also to distributed accumulators (vehicle-to-grid technology).

The power systems of Russia and foreign countries starting from the second half of the twentieth century historically developed in a similar logic. Large power plants were usually built near fuel extraction sites (in Russia, peat and coal, later—gas and fuel oil) or close to transport corridors along which this fuel was transported, as well as near large bodies of water or rivers. The more powerful was a power plant (scale effect), the cheaper was its construction (per 1 kW of power)—therefore, the average unit capacity of the stations grew steadily, increasing 500 times and more from the 1920s to the 1980s. The stations were often located at a considerable distance from large cities, for environmental reasons. In Russia, combined heat and power plants (CHP), built in close proximity to the consumer of thermal energy (city, plant, etc.) and electrical energy (industrial CHP), became an exception to this practice.

The transmission of electrical energy from the stations to consumers was carried out through the construction of trunk lines (voltage 220–500 kV and above to reduce transmission losses) and through the distribution electrical networks with a total length of hundreds of thousands of kilometers. At the same time, at the level of medium- and low-voltage distribution networks (35 kV and below), the consumer, as a rule, was at the end of the chain and, unlike larger consumers of supergrids, did not always have a backup power source from the power grid.

For several decades, this power system architecture has remained generally unchanged. Centralized power systems successfully, reliably, and at a reasonable price provided consumers with electricity. But by the end of the twentieth century, the scale effect stopped working; it had been working back in the 1950s, and the oil crisis of the 1970s sharply increased the interest of energy-importing countries in new energy-efficient power generation technologies.

The catalyst for change was distributed generation, namely, the emergence of new electricity production technologies in the 1970s and 1980s in the USA and Europe—gas turbine, gas piston, and combined cycle—that allowed creating low-cost and efficient power plants of small capacity from tens of kW to tens of MW (**Figure 1**).

This immediately led to an increase in distributed generation usage (**Figure 2**).

In addition to distributed generation, new opportunities for energy-saving technologies and demand management have opened up in the electric power industry. A classic example is the "Energy Demand Management" program, launched in the 1970s in the USA, aimed at saving electricity by encouraging consumers to reduce energy consumption during peak periods of demand or to shift energy consumption to off-peak demand periods.

In the first decade of the twenty-first century, the rapid development of renewable energy sources began. Governments in Europe, the USA, and other countries, striving for carbon-free energy and reducing dependence on energy exports, adopted large-scale and long-term programs to support renewable energy, after which the cost of solar and wind energy systems dropped several times with a significant increase in their technological efficiency. Thus, the present value of electricity from solar and wind power plants in 2009–2017 decreased by 67–86% (**Figure 3**).

As a result, in just 20–30 years, a consumer from a situation of deterministic centralized energy power supply came to choose from a wide range of alternative solutions that allow using them in an optimal proportion, based on individual priorities of cost, reliability, and quality of power supply.

The experience of the Northern European countries shows that it is better to develop distributed generation in conjunction with distributed heat supply, using cogeneration—the technology of co-production of heat and electricity in a single

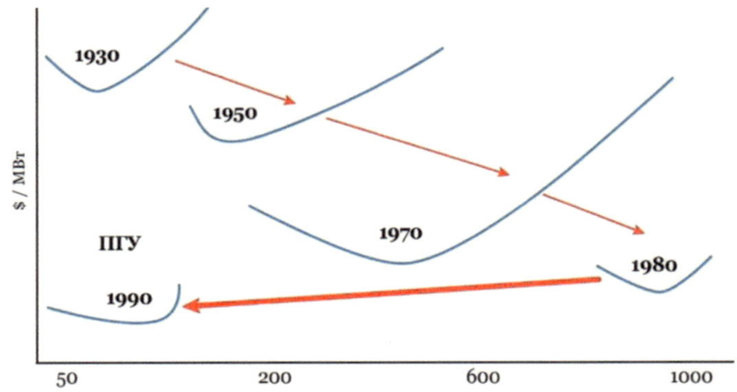

Figure 1.
Illustration of the scale effect (and its exhaustion) in the cost of the gas power plant construction in 1930–1990 depending on their power (MW). Source: Hunt et al. [2].

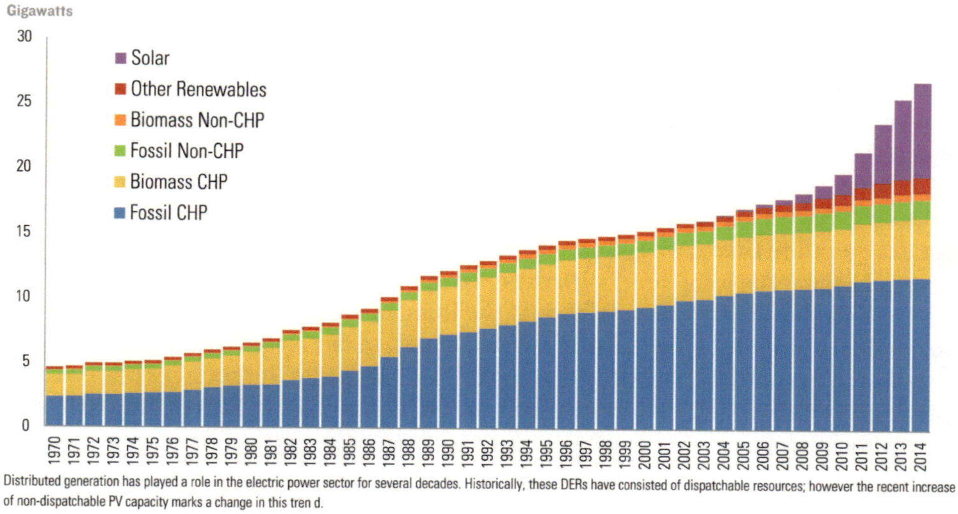

Figure 2.
Dynamics of distributed generation development in the USA (GW). Source: Rhodium Group [3].

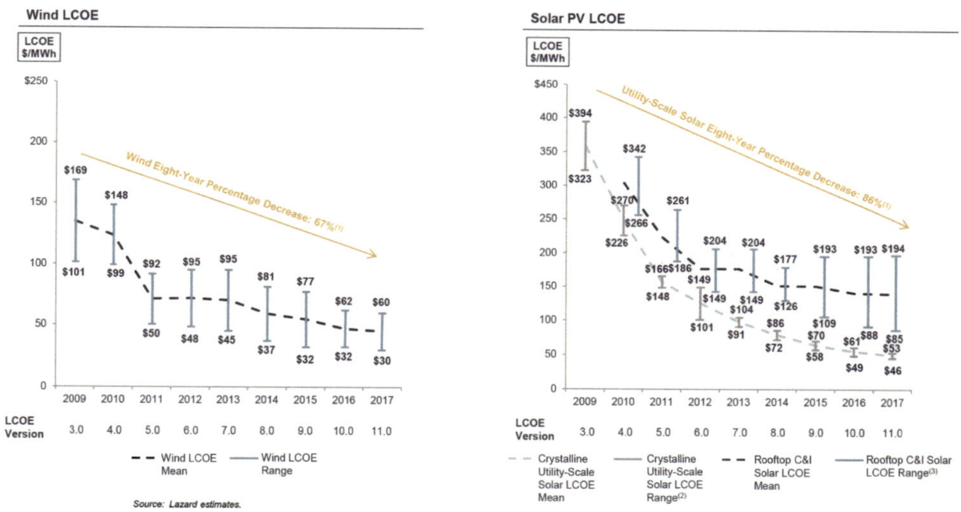

Figure 3.
Dynamics of levelized cost of electricity (LCOE) from solar and wind power plants in 2009–2017, USD/MWh. Source: Lazard's Levelized Cost of Energy Analysis, version 11.0 [4].

cycle. Distributed cogeneration in these countries has become the first step toward effective decentralization of power systems and, among other things, has reduced the cost of maintaining the supergrids and eliminating irrational energy losses. For example, in Denmark, the system of supporting measures for mini-CHP led to the emergence of hundreds of small natural gas and biomass energy centers in only 10–20 years. In addition, the number of wind power plants has increased.

According to the Danish Energy Agency, the development of distributed cogeneration reduced the annual consumption of primary energy in Denmark by 11% and reduced CO_2 emissions by 4.5 million tons per year.

The appearance of many new small generators has complicated the processes of their integration into the unified power grid and management and regulation processes. That situation demanded new technologies of flexible network construction and intelligent control of them, which later became known as the smart grid. The consumer of electricity begins to play an increasing role in the energy system, mastering new roles—generator and accumulator of electricity. Freedom of consumer choice is increasing. At the same time, there are many opportunities for demand management and energy efficiency both at the level of a specific household and at the level of the economy as a whole.

In order to carry into effect these possibilities, the states are changing the models of electricity and capacity markets toward their liberalization. It can be said without exaggeration that a necessary basis is being formed for building a competitive environment at the retail level with the development of distributed energy.

The entry of distributed energy into the Russian energy system became noticeable in the 2000s, but over the past 17 years, in fact, it was limited to only distributed generation. The development of this process in Russia takes place at a much lower rate, which requires a deep study of the spreading factors of distributed energy technologies.

3. Development of research model and hypotheses

Companies will switch to sources of their own generation when they are able to perceive them and are ready for their use. Therefore, the basis for studying the possibilities of using distributed generation technologies is their acceptability or perception on the part of industrial companies.

The use of factor analysis involves the study of factors that have the greatest influence on the industrial companies' decision to adopt new technology.

In the literature, there are a fairly limited number of studies on the adoption of new technologies by industrial companies. The most famous models are:

- Perceived organizational e-readiness (POER) model is used to measure the intraorganizational factors for the adoption of new technologies. This model was proposed by Molla and Licker in 2002 [5] for analyzing the intraorganizational environment factors, including personal characteristics of company's employees, system of internal assistance in the company, and attitude of employees to innovation.

- Perceived external e-readiness (PEER) model is used to analyze external factors. The PEER model [5] analyzes the factors of competitive pressure in the industry, influence of regulators, and technological changes in the industry.

Table 1 presents the intraorganizational and external factors affecting the adoption of new-generation technologies by companies.

Thus, we can formulate the first hypothesis of our study.

Hypothesis 1. Industrial companies' adoption of distributed energy technologies is influenced by intraorganizational factors: (a) technical feasibility, (b) availability of human resources, (c) perceived risks, (d) perceived advantage, (e) connection costs, (f) electricity costs and external costs, (g) market pressure, (h) pressure of the regulator (government), and (i) technological changes in the industry.

To identify the specific characteristics of distributed energy technologies that influence their adoption by companies, we used research results [15–21] and identified the most significant specific factors (**Table 2**).

The conducted analysis allowed us to formulate the second hypothesis of the study.

Hypothesis 2. The decision on the use of distributed energy technologies is influenced by specific factors: (a) the presence of by-products that can be used as

Adoption factors	Studies confirming the importance of the relevant factor
Perceived organizational e-readiness (POER) model	
Technical feasibility (integration, scalability, remote access, infrastructure, complexity, etc.)	Wu [6] Trachuk [7]
Availability of human resources	Vorozikhin [8] Bhowmik et al. [9]
Perceived risks (safety, investment)	Wu [6] Trachuk et al. [10] Bhowmik et al. [9]
Perceived benefits and need for alternative energy sources	Seo et al. [11] Brandon et al. [12]
Cost (transaction fee)	Brandon et al. [12]
Costs	Seo et al. [11]
Perceived external e-readiness (PEER) model	
Market changes affecting the company's decision to use new technologies	Subhes [13] Seo et al. [11] Trachuk et al. [7] Trachuk et al. [10]
Decisions of regulators (authorities), affecting the company's decisions to use new technologies	Subhes [13] Michael et al. [14] Brandon et al. [12] Trachuk et al. [7]
Technological changes in the industry affecting the company's decisions	Subhes et al. [13] Michael et al. [14]

Table 1.
Factors affecting the adoption of new technologies by companies.

fuel, (b) high efficiency, (c) lack of energy transmission costs, (d) lack payments for technological connection to electric networks, (e) the existing ratio of prices for electric energy and natural gas, (f) possibility of changing the volume of generated electricity and heat when economic situation changes, (g) reduced need for energy transmission over long distances, and (h) increased share of local energy resources.

At the next stage, the index was calculated for the main factors influencing the decision on self-generation for intraorganizational factors (technical feasibility; availability of human resources; perceived risks; perceived benefits and the need for alternative energy sources; cost of electricity; costs for construction and installation of distributed sources generation) and external factors (changes in the market that affect the company's decision to use innovation; decisions of regulators (authorities), affecting the decisions of companies on the use of new technologies; technological changes in the industry, affecting decisions of company) by summing up the references to individual items from the questionnaire (**Table 3**).

The frequency of mentioning specific factors is calculated in the same way (**Table 4**).

Then, nonparametric Spearman correlation coefficients (ρs) were calculated for the ranked data. To recognize the relationship between the components of the model as significant, the correlation coefficient had to exceed a threshold value of 0.50.

3.1 Description of variables

For the quantitative phase of the study, questions were formulated, measuring the most significant factors. The questions were formulated as follows: "How much do you agree with the statements below?". The 7-point Likert scale was used for answers (1 "I completely disagree," 4 "I do not know if I agree or disagree," 7 "I completely agree").

The "technical feasibility" factor was measured using a scale consisting of two questions that determine the company's ability to install distributed generation facilities taking into account the existing infrastructure. To assess the "perceived advantage" factor, questions were to evaluate higher rates of distributed generation efficiency than UNEG services. The factor "construction costs and installation of distributed

Adoption factors	Studies confirming the importance of the relevant factor
Specific factors	
Availability of by-products that can be used as fuel	Juan et al. [16]
High efficiency (provided that the generating facility is designed to meet the needs of a specific industrial production in both electrical and thermal energy)	Zhang [21]
No cost for power transmission	Berg et al. [15] Yingyuan et al. [19]
No payment for technological connection to electric networks (if the object of generation is isolated from the power system)	Berg et al. [15]
The existing ratio of prices for electric energy and natural gas indicates a high gas potential	Juan et al. [16]
Ability to change the volume of generated electrical and thermal energy when economic situation changes	Li et al. [18]
Energy production takes place in the immediate vicinity of the consumption points, which leads to less need for energy transmission over considerable distances	Kazemi et al. [17]
Increasing the share of local energy resources	You et al. [20]

Table 2.
The most significant specific factors for companies to adopt new technologies for distributed energy.

	Intraorganizational factors	Percentage of mentioning
1	Technical feasibility (integration, scalability, remote access, infrastructure, complexity, etc.)	61.6
2	Availability of human resources	19.3
3	Perceived risks (safety, investment)	45.9
4	Perceived benefits and need for alternative energy sources	76.3
5	Electricity cost	74.1
7	Costs of building and installing distributed generation sources	81.5
	External factors	
9	Market changes affecting company's decision to use innovation	62.7
10	Decisions of regulators (authorities), affecting company's decisions to use new technologies	96.3
11	Technological changes in the industry affecting company's decisions	73.5

Table 3.
Frequency of mentioning internal and external factors of distributed energy technology acceptance by companies.

		Percentage of mentioning
1	Availability of by-products that can be used as fuel	41.5
2	High efficiency (provided that the generating facility is designed to meet the needs of a specific industrial production in both electrical and thermal energy)	48.4
3	No cost of power transmission	58.9
4	No payment for technological connection to electric networks (if the object of generation is isolated from the power system)	79.4
5	Existing ratio of prices for electric energy and natural gas indicates a high gas potential	42.6
6	Ability to change the volume of generated electrical and thermal energy when economic situation changes	41.2
7	Energy production takes place in the immediate vicinity of the consumption points, which leads to a reduction of needed energy transmission over considerable distances	34.6
8	Increasing proportion of local energy resources	55.6

Table 4.
Frequency of mentioning specific factors of distributed energy technology adoption by industrial companies.

generation sources" was measured using two questions that characterize the need to pay back the construction of our own generation in the medium term or the absence of a significant impact of construction costs on the cost structure of the company.

Measuring the external factors of adopting distributed generation technologies was based on three groups of questions. First, market pressure was measured in accordance with the answers to questions about competitive pressure, comparing the technologies used. Second, technological changes in the industry were evaluated. They were measured by assessing the possibility of equipment repair and equipment operation during peak hours of load. Third, decisions of regulators were measured in the absence of administrative obstacles and support for distributed generation.

Similarly, a questionnaire was formed to analyze the specific factors of the distributed energy technology adoption.

3.2 Description of the data analysis procedure

In conducted analysis, the reliability factors (Cronbach's alpha) were first evaluated for all variables, measured on a scale of several questions. The calculated coefficients corresponded to the recommended minimum level of reliability −0.75. At the next stage, the factor analysis was carried out using the method of principal components for nine questions describing four aspects of intraorganizational factors and six questions describing three aspects of external factors.

The analysis of specific factors affecting the distributed generation technology adoption by distribution network companies was conducted for 15 questions.

In total, four specific factors explained 73.8% of the variation in the answers to questions from companies, which corresponds to the recommendations for explaining 70% of the variation in structural models.

A factor analysis based on the method of principal components with orthogonal rotation revealed the presence of four intraorganizational factors and two environmental factors that described a total of 72.8% of the variation in questions. The values of the factors obtained were used to form a final set of factors influencing the distributed generation technology adoption by companies, which were then included in the regression analysis.

Using the maximum likelihood method, standardized and non-standardized regression coefficients were determined. Non-standardized coefficients were used to test hypotheses, and standardized factors were used to determine factors that influenced the distributed generation adoption by companies more.

4. Results of the study

Tables 5 and **6** demonstrate the regression analysis results showing the influence of various factors on the distributed energy technology adoption by industrial companies (the company's internal characteristics and environmental factors), as well as the influence of specific factors. We evaluated the impact of these independent variables on the adoption of distributed energy technologies using the maximum likelihood method.

Independent factors	**Hypotheses**	**Non-standardized coefficients**	**Standardized coefficients**
Invariable (β_0)		0.191 (0.0134)	
Intraorganizational characteristics			
Technical feasibility (integration, scalability, infrastructure, complexity, etc.) (Ti)	Hypothesis 1(a)†	0.264^{***} (0.098)	0.281^{***}
Perceived risks (safety, investment) (RKi)	Hypothesis 1(c)	0.166^{***} (0.015)	0.185
Perceived advantages and need for alternative sources of generation (URi)	Hypothesis 1(d)	0.451^{**} (0.104)	0.454^{**}
Electricity cost (COSTi)	Hypothesis 1(e)	0.598^{***} (0.062)	0.599^{***}
Costs of building and installing distributed generation sources (Ci)	Hypothesis 1(f)	-0.387^{***} (0.209)	-0.385^{***}
Environmental factors			
Market Pressure (EASEi)	Hypothesis 1(g)	-0.196^{**} (0.118)	-0.394^{**}
Technological changes in the industry (TRi)	Hypothesis 1(h)	0.153^{***} (0.201)	0.254^{***}
Decisions of regulators (authorities) affecting decisions of companies on the use of new technologies (GRi)	Hypothesis 1(i)	-0.393^{***} (0.023)	-0.194^{***}
Adjusted R-square		0.709	
Number of observations		69	

†Hereinafter, the designation of the hypothesis corresponds to its formulation in the text.
**Significance of the coefficient p < 0.10.*
***Significance of the coefficient p < 0.05.*
****Significance of the coefficient p < 0.01.*
Standard errors are given in brackets.

Table 5.
Acceptance of distributed energy technology by industrial companies: the impact of internal organizational characteristics and environmental factors.

Independent factors	Hypotheses	Non-standardized coefficients	Standardized coefficients
Invariable (β_0)		0.216 (0.031)	
Specific factors			
Availability of by-products that can be used as fuel	Hypothesis 2(b)†	0.421*** (0.023)	0.419***
High efficiency (provided that the generating facility is designed to meet the needs of a specific industrial production in both electrical and thermal energy)	Hypothesis 2(c)	0.324*** (0.127)	0.327*
No cost for power transmission	Hypothesis 2(e)	0.378** (0.212)	0.381***
No payment for technological connection to electric networks (if the object of generation is isolated from the power system)	Hypothesis 2(h)	0.321** (0.041)	0.323
Existing ratio of prices for electric energy and natural gas indicates a high gas potential	Hypothesis 2(g)	0.016*** (0.091)	0.009***
Ability to change the volume of generated electrical and thermal energy when economic situation changes	Hypothesis 2(i)	0.163* (0.037)	0.168*
Energy production takes place in the immediate vicinity of consumption points, which leads to a reduction of needed energy transmission over considerable distances	Hypothesis 2(j)	0.211*** (0.009)	0.209***
Adjusted R-square		0.628	
Number of observations		69	

†Hereinafter, the designation of the hypothesis corresponds to its formulation in the text.
**Significance of the coefficient p < 0.10.*
***Significance of the coefficient p < 0.05.*
****Significance of the coefficient p < 0.01.*
Standard errors are given in brackets.

Table 6.
Adoption of distributed generation technologies: the impact of specific factors.

In general, the results of the regression analysis confirmed the hypotheses of the study. The models based on the regression equations were able to explain 63% of the variation of internal organizational and external factors in the distributed energy technology adoption by companies and 57% of specific factors.

When modeling the distributed energy technology adoption by companies (**Table 5**), it turned out that technical feasibility ($\beta = 0.264$; $p < 0.05$), comparative advantage of using distributed generation ($\beta = 0.451$; $p < 0.10$), and cost of electricity ($\beta = 0.598$; $p < 0.10$) positively affect the adoption of distributed energy technologies. The factor "perceived risks" ($\beta = 0.166$; $p = 0.01$) does not have a significant impact on the growth in the number of distributed energy users. And, the factor "costs for construction and installation of distributed generation sources" ($\beta = -0.387$; $p < 0.10$) has a negative influence on the decision to use distributed energy technologies.

Among the external factors, regulators' decisions have a significant impact on the distributed energy technology adoption by companies ($\beta = 0.393$; $p < 0.05$).

Market pressure and technological changes in the industry do not have a significant negative impact on the rate of distributed energy technology adoption by companies.

Thus, the technical feasibility, comparative advantage, and cost of electricity are the main factors for the growth in the number of distributed energy technology users in the studied sample.

Table 6 shows the regression analysis results of the specific factors that have influence on the distributed energy technology adoption.

All specific factors had a positive effect on the distributed generation technology adoption by companies with a probability of error p of no more than 0.05. The coefficient β with the variable "efficiency" was 0.324 ($p < 0.01$); for the factor "no energy transfer costs" was β = 0.378 ($p < 0.05$); and for the factor "absence of payment for technological connection to electric networks" was β = 0.321 ($p < 0.05$). At the same time, the factors "the existing price ratio for electric energy" (β = 0.016; $p > 0.10$) and "the possibility of changing the volumes of generated electric and thermal energy when economic situation changes" (β = 0.163; $p > 0.10$) did not have a significant impact.

The results of testing hypotheses are the following. According to Hypothesis 1, which described the factors influencing the distributed energy technology perception by companies, it was partially confirmed for intraorganizational factors, (a) technical feasibility (β = 0.264; $p < 0.05$); (d) perceived benefits (β = 0.451; $p < 0.01$), and (e) electricity cost (β = 0.598; $p < 0.05$), and environmental factor, (i) the regulator's decision (β = 0.396; $p < 0.05$). The factors (f) costs of building and installing distributed generation sources (β = −0.387; $p < 0.01$) and (g) market pressure (β = −0.196; $p < 0.01$) have a negative impact on the distributed energy technology adoption. For factors (c) perceived risks (β = 0.166; $p < 0.01$) and (h) possibility of changing the volumes of generated electrical and thermal energy (β = 0.153; $p < 0.01$), the hypothesis was not confirmed.

According to Hypothesis 2, companies' perception of distributed energy technologies is influenced by specific factors. This hypothesis is partially confirmed for common factors: (b) the presence of by-products that can be used as fuel (β = 0.421; $p < 0.01$); (d) high efficiency (β = 0.324; $p < 0.10$); (e) no costs for energy transfer (β = 0.316; $p < 0.01$); and (h) lack of payment for technological connection to electric networks (β = 0.363; $p < 0.01$). The influence of factors (g) existing ratio of prices for electric energy and natural gas (β = 0.016; $p < 0.01$); (i) possibility of changing the volume of generated electrical and thermal energy (β = 0.163; $p = 0.45$); and (j) a reduction in need for energy transmission over considerable distances (β = 0.211; $p < 0.01$) has not been confirmed.

Thus, the proposed model of analysis is successful, describing various factors of adoption of technologies of distributed energy by industrial companies. Standardized coefficients not only allow testing hypotheses but can also be used to compare the influence of various characteristics of distributed energy facilities on the likelihood of their acceptance by industrial companies.

5. Conclusions

Thus, according to the obtained results, when deciding on the company's own generation, the main factors are technical feasibility (β = 0.421), perceived advantages (β = 0.363), electricity cost (β = 0.324), and the decision of regulators (β = − 0.309). It can be concluded that for analyzed companies, technical feasibility, cost of electricity, and perceived benefits are critical factors in deciding on the use of distributed generation technologies. The risk factor turned out to be insignificant (β = 0.209), which, when conducting in-depth interviews, the companies explained by the fact that distributed generation systems reduce the occurrence of the listed adverse effects to a minimum. Obtaining cheap electric and thermal energy, a gradual increase in energy capacities and evenness of investment with fast energy for industrial and household needs are possible today due to the use of energy-efficient solutions based on distributed generation technologies.

5.1 Limitations of the study

It is necessary to note some of the limitations of this study. It was not possible for us to interview the entire totality of Russian companies due to limited data collection opportunities. However, our sample of companies covers a representative part by sector, sales revenue, and company size. In the future, researchers would be able to analyze the factors of distributed generation technology adoption in a larger sample of companies.

The results of a sample of 69 companies confirm the practicability of a comprehensive assessment of the distributed generation technology adoption factors. Within the framework of this study, the selected internal, external, and specific factors were measured empirically and used to analyze the distributed generation technology adoption by companies.

The qualitative stage of research allowed us to draw initial conclusions about the significance of certain aspects of distributed generation technology adoption. Thus, in accordance with the results of the theoretical base analysis, it was empirically confirmed that when companies adopted distributed generation, the cost of electricity and technical compatibility were of greatest importance. At the qualitative stage, the majority of respondents named these aspects of adoption as the most important.

Conflict of interest

There is no conflict of interest.

Author details

Arkady Trachuk* and Natalia Linder
Department of Management, The Financial University under the Government of the Russian Federation, Moscow, Russia

*Address all correspondence to: atrachuk@fa.ru

References

[1] Navigant Research. Global DER deployment forecast Database. 4Q 2017

[2] Hunt S, Shuttleworth G. Competition and Choice in Electricity. England: John Wiley & Sons; 1996

[3] Rhodium Group. The State of the Art in Valuing Distributed Energy Resources. New York, NY: Columbus Circle. 2017. Resources: https://rhg.com/wp-content/uploads/2017/01/RHG_WhatsItWorth_Jan2017.pdf

[4] Lazard's Levelized Cost of Energy Analysis, version 11.0. 2017

[5] Molla A, Licker PS. Perceived e-readiness factors in e-commerce adoption: An empirical investigation in a developing country. International Journal of Electronic Commerce. 2005;**10**(1):83-110

[6] Wu J. Control technologies in distributed generation system based on renewable energy. In: 2009 3rd International Conference on Power Electronics Systems and Applications, PESA 2009; 2009

[7] Трачук АВ. Реформирование электроэнергетики и развитие конкуренции (монография). Москва: 2010

[8] Ворожихин В. Организационно-экономические механизмы развития энергетики. LAP LAMBERT Academic Publishing изд. Saarbrücken: LAP LAMBERT Academic Publishing; 2013. c.245

[9] Bhowmik A, Schatz J, Maitra A, Halpin S. Determination of allowable penetration levels of distributed generation resources based on harmonic limit considerations. IEEE Transactions on Power Delivery. 2003;**18**(2):619-624

[10] Trachuk A, Linder N. Technologies of the distributed generation: Empirical evaluations of the innovations acceptance. Strategic Decisions and Risk Management. 2018;(1):32-48. DOI: 10.17747/2078-8886-2018-1-32-48. (In Russ.) Resources: https://www.jsdrm.ru/jour/article/view/750?locale=en_US#tab1

[11] Seo H, Park M, Kim G, Yu I, Ali M. A study on the performance analysis of the grid-connected pv-af system. In: Proceeding of International Conference on Electrical Machines and Systems ICEMS; 2007

[12] Brandon D, Humayun T, Robert U. The Smart Grid and the Promise of Demand-side Management. McKinsey & Company; 2010. Available from: http://www.calmac.com/documents/MoSG_DSM_VF.pdf

[13] Subhes C. Bhattacharyya Energy Economics Concepts, Issues, Markets and Governance. UK: University of Dundee, Springer; 2011. 645 p

[14] Grubb M, Jamasb T, Pollitt MG. Delivering a Low Carbon Electricity System. Technologies, Economics and Policy. University of Cambridge, UK: Cambridge University Press; 2008. 536 p

[15] Berg A, Krahl S, Paulun T. Cost-efficient integration of distributed generation into medium voltage networks by optimized network planning. In: IET Seminar Digest; 2008. pp. 12380

[16] Lujano-Rojas JM, Monteiro C, Dufo-Lopez R, Bernal-Agustın JL. Optimum residential load management strategy for real time pricing demand response programs. Energy Policy. 2012;**45**:671-679

[17] Kazemi A, Sadeghi M. Distributed generation allocation for loss reduction and voltage improvement. In: 2009 Asia-Pacific Power and Energy

Engineering Conference, APPEEC 2009 Proceedings; 2009

[18] Li H, Leite H. Increasing distributed generation using automatic voltage reference setting technique. In: IEEE Power and Energy Society 2008 General Meeting: Conversion and Delivery of Electrical Energy in the 21st Century; PES. 2008

[19] Yingyuan Z. Liuchen C, Meiqin M, Ming D. Study of energy management system for distributed generation systems. In: 3rd International Conference on Deregulation and Restructuring and Power Technologies DRPT; 2008

[20] You S, Jin L, Hu J, Zong Y, Bindner HW. The danish perspective of energy internet: From service-oriented flexibility trading to integrated design, planning and operation of multiple cross-sectoral energy systems. Zhongguo Dianji Gongcheng Xuebao. 2015;**35**(14):3470-3481. DOI: 10.13334/j.0258-8013.pcsee. 2015.14.001

[21] Zhang X. A framework for operation and control of smart grids with distributed generation. In: IEEE Power and Energy Society 2008 General Meeting: Conversion and Delivery of Electrical Energy in the 21st Century; PES. 2008

Chapter 11

Business Incubator and Economic Development

José Moleiro Martins, António Abreu and João M.F. Calado

Abstract

This chapter aims to (i) understand the functioning and importance of incubators in supporting the creation of new business and local economic development, as they help locally engage young entrepreneurs and thus retain expertise, for example, in regions farthest from large urban centers, (ii) realize the importance of incubators and science parks in the development of start-ups, (iii) understand the role of education in promoting entrepreneurship, and (iv) understand the competitive environment as it becomes more complex and dynamic, as there are opportunities to serve customers who are dissatisfied; thus the threats that large companies experience offer small business opportunities.

Keywords: incubators, start-ups, small business, economic development, education

1. Economic importance of incubators

An incubator is a way for the community to help entrepreneurs who have good ideas but do not have the resources to start their activities independently.

Small business incubators are a way of boosting economic development, whose practice began in the United Kingdom since the 1970s as artists' cooperatives, often being located in historic buildings. In the USA, incubators have been used, for example, to (i) assist the recovery of ruined and impoverished neighborhoods, (ii) promote scientific innovation by linking partnerships between universities and business, and (iii) help entrepreneurs who want to expand their specialist knowledge through interaction with other small business owners [1–3].

1.1 The role of small businesses in the local economy

Interest in incubators lies partly in the role that small businesses play in most local economies, for example, in the jobs created and the innovation generated. Furthermore, small businesses can be developed in greater numbers faster than the larger companies often not local.

Incubators are a vehicle of aid to local entrepreneurs as they constitute the local economy and are more likely to maintain their activity locally than multinational enterprises. In addition, supporting the creation of small local businesses can help locally engage young entrepreneurs by avoiding the loss of specialized skills in some geographical regions of the interior. However, there is a risk that 50% of small businesses will fail in the first 4 years of operation. This reality has diverse implications for local economic development, in the following aspects [4–6]:

- Small businesses are important because they can generate employment for residents.
- Small businesses often carry out activities in areas of technological innovation or artistic or creative areas that do not require many resources to operate the business.
- The development of small businesses contributes to the creation of local and regional economic capital (specialized knowledge and brands).
- Significant efforts must be made to ensure that the companies created will not fail.
- Because of the risk of small business failure, incubators should not be seen as the cornerstone of an economic development strategy but rather as a contribution of efforts to promote the development of SMEs in a given community.

A brief note to mention is that start-ups usually fit into the reality of a small business.

1.2 Objectives of incubation programs

Start-up incubators support the creation and growth of business through organizational and technical assistance, which at the same time contributes to the reduction of entrepreneurial failure. The three most common objectives of incubation programs are the following [5, 7]:

1. The creation of employment in the community
2. The creation—or acceleration of growth—of a local industry
3. Diversification of the local economy

The incubation can be physical or virtual. Virtual incubation does not consist of a work space, but it is included in a credible address destined to the market for professional contacts, including the holding of work meetings. We can affirm that an incubator is constituted by a common space of which a space (like office) is made available that is used for the beginning of activity of a new business. The price of rents may be lower than the market price due to public subsidies to promote entrepreneurship.

In addition to lower incomes, location sharing, or coworking among start-ups with similar activities, the incubator includes a set of support services to serve the technical and operational needs of start-ups, often owned by inexperienced entrepreneurs. In turn, coworking constitutes a physical space that fits a transversal work model for entrepreneurs with similar activities at the level of operational resources. It is a functional structure that allows entrepreneurs to have an office as reference location and professional contacts, enjoying a series of services shared with other entrepreneurs.

1.3 Physical installations

The physical facilities provided by the incubators may take different forms depending on the sector of activity of the start-ups to be incubated. For example, the service start-up incubator may consist of individual offices with shared common areas (reusing a residential or commercial space), while incubators for high-tech manufacturing start-ups require larger spaces (industrial buildings).

1.4 Benefits offered by incubators

Business incubators offer tangible and intangible benefits to start-ups [7, 8]. Tangible benefits often include the following operational aspects:

- Shared use of equipment such as photocopying machines, telephones, computers, and Internet access

- Shared conference spaces and meeting rooms and informal interactions with other incubators

- Shared services for start-ups, such as secretarial, accounting, marketing, and legal support

- Technical assistance in marketing plan, business plan, financial system, and accounting

- Joint acquisition to suppliers and links between incubated start-ups relative to operating factors upstream and downstream in the value chain

- Assistance in obtaining funding in the start-up phase

The intangible benefits derive from the ability of entrepreneurs to act as a support system among incubated start-ups. Intangible benefits are more likely to occur among start-ups with similar activities. For example, incubated high-tech start-ups can share the development of ideas and innovation. Biotech start-ups can support each other in the development and commercialization of innovative products.

Even in incubators with start-ups operating in distinct sectors of activity, entrepreneurs can share their experience, ideas, and knowledge on certain subjects such as marketing, product development, recruitment, and accounting.

Following the above, we can briefly state that the main objective of incubators is to support the development of start-ups, which leave the incubator when they increase in size or become sufficiently stable to operate without specific benefits offered by the incubator. This makes room for other start-ups to start their incubator operations.

2. Economic development instruments

There are several economic development tools that can be used in conjunction with the incubation of start-ups, which will be addressed in the following subsections.

2.1 Small business financing

For entrepreneurs, money is a resource but not an end in itself. It is true that an innovative idea needs capital to subsist. It is also true that a large number of businesses fail due to lack of adequate funding. However, other resources are equally vital to entrepreneurial success, such as specialized work teams and sales and distribution capabilities. Having financial capacity is not (always) a guarantee that the appropriate resources are put together in the right way and at the right time.

Initial or seed financing programs can take a variety of forms and are often used in combination with the most effective incubators. Small loans from investment funds (made up of grants from the government and/or local government), with below-market interest rates, are provided to support the creation of new businesses [9]. As the loans are paid, the money of the fund is reinvested in subsequent deals. The incubators can also help start-ups incubated to obtain financing, first linking up with business angels and venture capital investors and on the other hand giving technical support in the preparation of documents and presentations.

Business angels invest in small start-ups or entrepreneurs, can have multiple origins (including family or friends of the entrepreneur), and invest in one go to boost the business or make a continuous injection of money to support the company in the early stages more difficult. Venture capital consists of investor financing for start-ups and small businesses that are believed to have long-term growth potential. For companies that do not have access to the capital market, venture capital is an essential source of money. The risk is typically high for investors, but they have intervention in company decisions, which is a disadvantage for the company funded.

Business angels offer advantages compared to venture capital: business angels invest in the early stage of the business, that is, they help start-ups take their first steps in the market, while venture capital investors bet on the viability of the business and can profit from the business by the investment. In this sense, business angels are the opposite of venture capital investors.

Another way for entrepreneurs to get the resources they need or use is through crowdfunding, which is a process directed at individuals to raise funds to finance a specific cause or project in return for a variety of rewards. Thus, we can say that crowdfunding bases its dynamics on raising funds to finance a business or a project: (i) in exchange for share capital; (ii) in exchange for tangible, non-monetary rewards, such as a product finished; or (iii) in exchange for a financial return at a future date.

2.2 Industrial parks

Although not essential to the effective operation of a small business incubator, there are benefits to locating it within municipal industrial parks. The incubator can provide a space with the necessary infrastructure at the lowest cost and close to similar start-ups. The industrial park also wins with the installation of the incubator, as it enhances the local demonstration effect for the creation of other start-ups. Incubators can also be installed in old abandoned facilities (state, military, and industrial) to stimulate local development [10].

2.3 Professional qualification

Employment and skill development programs enhance local qualifications, increasing individuals' willingness to develop innovative start-ups or collaborate on incubated start-ups. The existence of qualified human resources at the level of high technology facilitates the development of start-ups.

2.4 Entrepreneurial training

Programs aimed at the emergence of local entrepreneurs are directly complementary to the start-up incubators. These programs provide the necessary skills and competencies—for example, marketing, financial planning, hiring and human resource management, information systems and strategy—to successfully build and manage start-ups.

2.5 Investment in education

In addition to entrepreneurship training, investing in local education infrastructure is a boon to the development of start-ups. Educational institutions provide the human resource base crucial to economic development. Thus, higher education institutions can create a series of synergies with the community—for example, service delivery and the development of strategic partnerships—increasing the effectiveness of start-up incubators. Universities are sources of new ideas to create start-ups of high technology and with differentiated value for society. The faculty can, on the one hand, provide students with the necessary skills to encourage the creation of start-ups and, on the other hand, provide services to the community, thereby contributing to economic growth.

3. Education in the development of entrepreneurship

Education plays a vital role in the development of entrepreneurship in society. Being the curricular structure of higher education courses—first and second cycles—is a good indicator of the relationship between the training provided (knowledge transmitted) in educational institutions and the technical skills and competences needs verified in society and in business fabric.

Currently, there is a great difficulty in obtaining a job where the knowledge acquired in a higher education course can be applied, through the conclusion of a stable employment contract, and with a remuneration proportional to the education effort carried out as a personal investment. Therefore, it is imperative to adapt the education system to the challenges in the labor market. Therefore, rather than teaching someone to work for entrepreneurs, it will be necessary to pass on knowledge in order to encourage the emergence of new entrepreneurs in the community.

The university as a reference in entrepreneurship education contributes to the preparation of future economic actors through the execution of programs in entrepreneurship. This allows you to impart knowledge and techniques that facilitate the creation of a business and simultaneously encourage students to create new business. In this way it is possible to increase the entrepreneurial potential of the students, but few start new business during and after the conclusion of the studies [1, 11].

In this sense, the entrepreneurial education constitutes a challenge, on the one hand, to the institutions of higher education in what concerns the design and implantation of incubation in articulated network with diverse economic actors and, on the other hand, to the traditional pedagogical methodology of transmission of knowledge and learning in the classroom.

Therefore, entrepreneurship education aims at increasing students' awareness of the various aspects of business creation, emphasizing a philosophy of learning oriented to practice and action in a turbulent environment.

4. Creating business in a turbulent environment

Entrepreneurs are challenging existing competitive assumptions by creating value for consumers through new forms of business. This created value may lead to consumer willingness to (i) pay for a new benefit, (ii) pay more for something perceived as better, or (iii) receive a previously available benefit at a lower cost. Consequently, value translates the willingness of the consumer to purchase a product or a service, at a certain price, for recognizing attributes that contribute to their satisfaction of needs, fulfillment of wishes, or resolution of a problem [12].

The constant value creation imposed by increased competition is changing management practice by redefining operational activity in the fields of production, sales, and distribution of products and services. This competitive reality stems from an unstoppable, complex change in which advances in technology combine with the development of suppliers and customers. We can identify eight major areas of change in the competitive environment:

1. *Technological environment*: accelerated development of new technologies, rapid product obsolescence, and greater difficulty in protecting intellectual property

2. *Economic environment*: unpredictability of prices, operating costs, exchange rates, interest rates, tax incentives, and shorter business life cycle

3. *Competitive environment*: highly innovative competitors, competition from nontraditional strategies, and threat of new competitors who may also be customers or business partners—which sets up a competition between economic actors

4. *Work environment*: shortage of skilled employees, greater mobility and less employee loyalty, increased employee costs, and contractual obligations in labor relations

5. *Resource environment*: increasing scarcity of resources, increasingly specialized resources, limited alternative sources, and rapid obsolescence of resources

6. *Customer environment*: greater demand through varied channels, more complex customers in markets that are more fragmented or atomized (more competitors), more segmented (greater variety of customers) and focused on creating value for the consumer—which stems from an innovation process that establishes or enhances the consumer's assessment of the consumer benefits (value in use) of a product or service

7. *Legal and regulatory environment*: more aggressive regulation, virtually unlimited product liability, increasing regulatory compliance costs, increased emphasis on free and fair trade, and increased environmental regulation and associated compliance costs

8. *Global environment*: real-time communication and production, distribution to anywhere in the world, suppliers as business partners, customers and competitors more sophisticated and located anywhere in the world, and obtaining a competitive advantage, for example, by means of outsourcing and strategic alliances

This change has important implications for business, as many entrepreneurs struggle more to survive than to achieve sustained growth. Stakeholders are constantly changing (customers, suppliers, distributors, alliance partners, and regulators). As the required resources (physical, organizational, technological, and human) have become increasingly specialized and less predictable in terms of the duration of their competitive relevance, entrepreneurs tend to contract in the short term the use of resources subject to greater competitive obsolescence, instead of opting for their acquisition.

Thus, entrepreneurs have, in general, a lack of control over their competitive environment. And the size of business is not an unequivocal condition of success. However, the exploitation of valuable, rare, and inimitable resources generates a sustainable competitive advantage and, consequently, a superior performance in the market [13].

4.1 How to get a sustainable competitive advantage

Turbulence in the competitive environment has caused and forced a transformation in management operations. Traditional bureaucratic models, hierarchical management systems, and a philosophy of controlling the company's operations are not feasible in the contemporary competitive environment. However, it is not clear what gives us assurances of working well, but management must consider that the organizational structure, leadership style, and ways of rewarding and motivating employees can contribute to increases in competitiveness.

There is also a positive side to the competitive environment as it becomes more complex and dynamic, as there are opportunities to serve customers who are dissatisfied. Traditionally, competitive advantage was achieved through a number of strands, namely:

- Lower costs than competitors
- Offer superior product quality
- Addition of new product features
- Providing better customer services

At present, the continuous improvement of these aspects is a minimum criterion for maintaining market competitiveness.

The pursuit of competitive advantage requires entrepreneurs to continually reinvent business and can come from five key capabilities:

1. *Adaptability*: timely adjustment to new technologies, customer needs, regulatory rules, and other changes in competitive conditions without losing the focus of their core business.

2. *Flexibility*: design strategies, processes, and operational approaches that can simultaneously meet the diverse demands of stakeholders (customers, distributors, suppliers, financiers, and regulators).

3. *Speed*: act quickly on emerging opportunities, develop new products and services more swiftly, and make critical operational decisions without lengthy deliberations.

4. *Aggressiveness*: a focused and proactive market approach in order to differentiate itself from competitors, retaining customers and motivating employees.

5. *Innovation*: continuous priority of development and launch of new products, services, and technologies, aiming at market leadership.

The most adaptable, flexible, fast, aggressive, and innovative entrepreneurs are best positioned not only to adjust to a complex, threatening, and dynamic competitive environment but also to create the change in that environment. Entrepreneurs must affirm themselves as agents of change by leading clients instead of following them, creating new markets and defining new competitive rules [14].

Entrepreneurship is the main source of sustainable competitive advantage through the production and/or marketing of products and services that are more advanced than the competition, i.e., unique in the market compared to the value supplied to consumers.

4.2 Change as an opportunity for small businesses

Although competitive instability is most felt in some sectors, none is immune to its challenges. Increasingly, competitive conditions in markets become unpredictable beyond the short term. This economic landscape has implications for entrepreneurs, which can turn in their favor.

A measure generally adopted in the face of aggressive price pressure from competitors is to reduce costs to the lowest possible levels. The goal of this cost reduction effort is often the workforce (the employees), but the need to produce the product or provide the service remains. Hence, suppliers are used to perform the operational tasks eliminated via downsizing, engaging in outsourcing, which has become a business opportunity for small businesses, which include small and microenterprises.

The threats that large companies experience offer small business opportunities. In addition to receiving outsourcing requests, a small business can also compete in another market based on subcontracting services to other companies.

In reality, a small business can establish partnerships (strategic alliances or joint ventures) with a variety of suppliers covering value chain activities and thus can enter into markets it might not otherwise be able to achieve. In practice, we are talking about a virtual company, that is, a company that does not have the (own) resources needed to compete in a particular market segment but has the possibility of forming partnerships with other companies in order to perform the key management functions to the pursuit of the own business [15, 16].

Another change that is happening in the markets is their continued fragmentation (increase in the number of competitors) or the development of niches. Within the markets there are small groups of consumers who value a set of unique attributes in a product, which is a niche market. Many niches do not interest large corporations because they are small in terms of turnover, providing small businesses with business opportunities. To benefit from these opportunities, entrepreneurs must focus on a clearly identified market niche so that they understand and meet the expectations of these consumers.

4.3 Advantages of small businesses

Small businesses have important advantages that enable them to be successful, namely, their sensitivity to market conditions and trends, which derives from their close relationship with customers, enabling them to understand their needs.

The existence of a personal relationship with customers ensures that the entrepreneur is the first to perceive the changes in consumer preferences that will affect the market as well as gives him the possibility to convey the message that interests the customer. This small business communication process encourages market learning by expressing interest in the business of customers.

Another factor that distinguishes successful small business from typical large enterprises is their ability to innovate. The entrepreneurial company has a quick reaction when changes or opportunities arise in the market. While large corporations recognize the need to change quickly, the burdens of bureaucratic procedures slow them down. The ability of small businesses to innovate encompasses product innovation (new relevant features), process innovation (improvement of the production process), and service innovation (offering something new in the service). It should be noted that innovation is related to organizational flexibility, which comes from personal attitude and organizational practices based on the creation of knowledge as the main competitive resource [17, 18].

In addition, small businesses tend to invest less than large companies in rigid production equipment. This enables greater agility in changing.

Together, responsiveness, organizational flexibility, and innovation practices make small businesses more competitive in a rapidly changing environment.

Small businesses can be developed within the family universe, translating into family businesses, or constitute a situation of self-employment.

5. Family businesses and self-employment

A small business is not necessarily a family business. In the family business, ownership and management are concentrated in the family members, predominantly a family-based intraorganizational relationship. Family nature issues are prioritized against other objectives. For example, the company's property control by the family will not be sacrificed to fund the development and growth of the business. Indeed, family property is not diluted to include non-family investors. Therefore, the available financial resources are those generated by the company and those of the family itself. However, credit may be used with banking institutions to finance the growth of the business.

The uniqueness of the family business lies in the integration of family and business in the same context. The collaboration of the family members in the company may be an indication that the admission criteria are not governed by the higher academic and professional qualifications, which are more suitable for the performance of duties [19]. However, instead of prevailing the replacement of generations in the management of the company, the owners can choose to hire professional managers to create wealth but preserving the intra-family relationship in the company. On the other hand, family firms often find it difficult to attract and retain highly skilled managers, partly because of the limitations of career advancement and the absence of personal reward policies, as well as the lack of goal-oriented professional management and continuous improvement.

5.1 Self-employment: advantages and disadvantages

There are immense advantages and disadvantages of self-employment (being your own boss), and the entrepreneur must be aware of both before starting a business. We start by highlighting the three main advantages:

1. *Autonomy*: the need for independence and freedom to make decisions are the main advantages. The feeling of being your own boss is very satisfying to most entrepreneurs.

2. *Challenge of a new company/sense of accomplishment*: for a large number of entrepreneurs, the challenge of a new company is fun. The opportunity to develop a concept and make it a profitable business provides a meaningful sense of accomplishment where the entrepreneur knows that he or she is solely responsible for the success of the idea.

3. *Independence/financial control*: while frequent mention is made of the financial independence of entrepreneurs, it does not necessarily mean that they want to be wealthy but want more control over their financial situation. They do not want to be subject to unexpected announcement dismissal of employees after years of dedicated work to the company.

If self-employment were easy to achieve, there could be a much larger number of self-employed people. In fact, it is one of the most difficult professional careers anyone can choose. Some of the disadvantages of this life option are described below:

1. *Personal sacrifices*: especially in the early years of the business, the entrepreneur often has to work many hours during the 6 or 7 days of the week. This leads almost to lack of time for fun, family life, or personal reflection. Business takes up a lot of time in the lives of entrepreneurs, resulting in stress in family life and a high level of stress. The entrepreneur must wonder about how much he is willing to sacrifice himself in order to make the business successful.

2. *Overload of responsibility*: the entrepreneur has a burden of responsibility distinct from that of the employees of a company. In companies, employees are usually surrounded by other people—of a similar professional or technical level—with the same interests. It is possible to share information while having lunch or after working hours, assuming a sense of cooperation. In turn, the entrepreneur knows that he is alone in the organizational top. While employees in companies specialize in specific areas such as marketing, financial, or commercial, entrepreneurs have to manage all these operational functions until the business is sufficiently profitable to hire employees with the necessary technical knowledge. The need to master several technical areas is a considerable burden on the entrepreneur.

3. *Small margin for error*: large companies often make decisions that prove to be unprofitable, for example, the launch of products that are not well accepted by the market and the opening of points of sale in disadvantageous places. On the other hand, small businesses operate with a narrow financial cushion because the only financial resources available are those of the entrepreneur. Even after years of successful activity, a wrong decision or a weakness in management can result in the end of the business.

In short, small businesses' ability to innovate stems from their learning of the market, recognition of the need for rapid change, and organizational flexibility [20]. These valences are a support to the decision-making in the self-employment before the obtained feedback of the market.

6. Conclusions

Incubation of new businesses contributes to the creation of new businesses and, consequently, to economic and social development.

The installation of incubators is a way of encouraging the creation of small businesses and recognition of their role in local economic dynamism in terms of job creation, the establishment of qualified young people, and the development of areas of sectorial and technological specialization [6].

In this context, complementary instruments can be used to promote economic development (local, regional, and national), such as:

- Professional training to meet the technical needs of the labor market

- Entrepreneurial training leading to the emergence of new start-ups

- Academic training in line with Government's sectoral and regional bets

- Creation of specialized university citadels, by technical-scientific areas, with the provision of all sociocultural, economic, and financial services inherent in business development

- Creation of sectoral industrial parks

- Launching public funding programs in conjunction with (i) technological parks, (ii) sectoral industrial parks, (iii) incubators, and (iv) universities (units/centers/research centers), in order to place academic research at the service of development and economic growth, in particular through its practical application to business and economic realities

In this respect, the following question may be raised:

What is the current added value for the economics emanating from academic papers published in specialty journals—for example, in terms of setting up start-ups, creating business and new products and services in incumbent companies, and penetrating new international markets or expansion in regional markets, increased efficiency, and business productivity?

Therefore, an integrated national structure (incubators, technological parks, sectoral industrial parks, and specialized university centers) will have to be implemented in order to propagate a climate conducive to the emergence of new, tangible ideas, on the one hand, in improving the competitiveness of established companies and, on the other hand, in creating new businesses.

Acknowledgements

This work was partially supported by the Polytechnic Institute of Lisbon through the Projects for Research, Development, Innovation and Artistic Creation (IDI&CA), within the framework of the project IEOMAB—internationalization of companies operating in the Angolan and Brazilian markets, IPL/2019/IEOMAB_ISCAL.

Author details

José Moleiro Martins[1]*, António Abreu[2] and João M.F. Calado[3]

1 Polytechnic Institute of Lisbon, Business Research Unit (BRU-IUL)/ISCTE-IUL, Lisbon, Portugal

2 Mechanical Engineering Department, ISEL—Instituto Superior de Engenharia de Lisboa/CTS—Uninova, Lisbon, Portugal

3 Mechanical Engineering Department, ISEL—Instituto Superior de Engenharia de Lisboa/IDMEC-LAETA-IST-UL, Lisbon, Portugal

*Address all correspondence to: zdmmartins@gmail.com

References

[1] Bruneel J, Ratinho T, Clarysse B, Groen A. The evolution of business incubators: Comparing demand and supply of business incubation services across different incubator generations. Technovation. 2012;**32**:110-121. DOI: 10.1016/j.technovation.2011.11.003

[2] Hackett S, Dilts D. A systematic review of business incubation research. Journal of Technology Transfer. 2004;**29**:55-82. DOI: 10.1023/B:JOTT.0000011181.11952.0f

[3] Sherman H, Chappell D. Methodological challenges in evaluating business incubator outcomes. Economic Development Quarterly. 1998;**12**:313-321. DOI: 10.1177/089124249801200403

[4] Campbell C, Allen D. The small business incubator industry: Micro-level economic development. Economic Development Quarterly. 1987;**1**:178-189. DOI: 10.1177/089124248700100209

[5] Greene P, Butler J. The minority community as a natural business incubator. Journal of Business Research. 1996;**36**:51-58. DOI: 10.1016/0148-2963(95)00162-X

[6] Mian S, Lamine W, Fayolle A.Technology business incubation: An overview of the state of knowledge. Technovation. 2016;**50**:1-12. DOI: 10.1016/j.technovation.2016.02.005

[7] Bøllingtoft A, Ulhøi J. The networked business incubator: Leveraging entrepreneurial agency? Journal of Business Venturing. 2005;**20**:265-290. DOI: 10.1016/j.jbusvent.2003.12.005

[8] Barberom J, Casillas J, Ramos A, Guitar S. Revisiting incubation performance: How incubator typology affects results. Technological Forecasting and Social Change. 2012;**79**:888-902. DOI: 10.1016/j.techfore.2011.12.003Get

[9] Lukeš M, Longo M, Zouhar J. Do business incubators really enhance entrepreneurial growth? Evidence from a large sample of innovative Italian start-ups. Technovation. 2019;**82**:25-34. DOI: 10.1016/j.technovation.2018.07.008

[10] McAdam M, McAdam R. The networked incubator: The role and operation of entrepreneurial networking with the university science park incubator (USI). The International Journal of Entrepreneurship and Innovation. 2006;**7**:87-97. DOI: 10.5367/000000006776928663

[11] Von Graevenitz G, Harhoff D, Weber R. The effects of entrepreneurship education. Journal of Economic Behavior & Organization. 2010;**76**:90-112. DOI: 10.1016/j.jebo.2010.02.015

[12] Priem R. A consumer perspective on value creation. Academy of Management Review. 2007;**32**:219-235. DOI: 10.5465/amr.2007.23464055

[13] Barney J, Wright M, Ketchen D. The resource-based view of the firm: Ten years after 1991. Journal of Management. 2001;**27**:625-641. DOI: 10.1177/014920630102700601

[14] Bull I, Willard G. Towards a theory of entrepreneurship. Journal of Business Venturing. 1993;**8**:183-195. DOI: 10.1016/0883-9026(93)90026-2

[15] Donckels R, Lambrecht J. The network position of small businesses: An explanatory model. Journal of Small Business Management. 1997;**35**:13-25

[16] Walker E, Brown A. What success factors are important to small business owners? International Small Business Journal. 2004;**22**:577-594. DOI: 10.1177/0266242604047411

[17] Ward T. Cognition, creativity, and entrepreneurship. Journal of Business Venturing. 2004;**19**:173-188. DOI: 10.1016/S0883-9026(03)00005-3

[18] Wiklund J, Patzelt H, Shepherd D. Building an integrative model of small business growth. Small Business Economics. 2009;**32**:351-374. DOI: 10.1007/s11187-007-9084-8

[19] Covin T. Profiling preferences for employment in family-owned firms. Family Business Review. 1994;7:287-296. DOI: 10.1111/j.1741-6248.1994.00288.x

[20] Wood M, McKinley W. The production of entrepreneurial opportunity: A construct perspective. Strategic Entrepreneurship Journal. 2010;**4**:66-84. DOI: 10.1002/sej.83